VOLTAIRE

CONTENTS.

CHAPTER I.

PRELIMINARY.

CHAPTER II.

ENGLISH INFLUENCES.

CHAPTER III.

LITERATURE.

CHAPTER IV.

BERLIN.

CHAPTER V.

RELIGION.

(1) *Conditions of the Voltairean attack.*

(2) *His method.*

CHAPTER VI.

HISTORY.

CHAPTER VII.

FERNEY.

CONTENTS. XV

τὰ μὲν γὰρ σωφρόνων ἤθη σφόδρα μὲν εὐλαβῆ καὶ δίκαια καὶ σωτήρια, δριμύτητος δὲ καί ι ινος ἰταμότητος ὀξείας καὶ πρακτικῆς ἐνδεῖται . . . τὰ δ' ἀνδρεῖά γε αὖ πρὸς μὲν τὸ δίκαιον καὶ εὐλαβὲς ἐκείνων ἐπιδεέστερα, τὸ δ' ἐν ταῖς πράξεσι διαφερόντως ἴσχει. πάντα δὲ καλῶς γίγνεσθαι τὰ περὶ τὰς πόλεις, τούτοιν μὴ παραγενομένοιν ἀμφοῖν, ἀδύνατον.—Politicus, 311 A.

πότερον τοὺς ἀνδρείους θαρραλέους λέγεις, ἢ ἄλλο τι; Καὶ ἴτας γε, ἔφη, ἐφ' ἃ οἱ πολλοὶ φοβοῦνται ἰέναι. —Protagoras, 349 E.

CHAPTER I.

PRELIMINARY.

WHEN the right sense of historical proportion is more
fully developed in men's minds, the name of Voltaire
will stand out like the names of the great decisive
movements in the European advance, like the Revival
of Learning, or the Reformation. The existence,
character, and career of this extraordinary person
constituted in themselves a new and prodigious era.
The peculiarities of his individual genius changed the
mind and spiritual conformation of France, and in a
less degree of the whole of the West, with as far-
spreading and invincible an effect as if the work had
been wholly done, as it was actually aided, by the
sweep of deep-lying collective forces. A new type of
belief, and of its shadow, disbelief, was stamped by
the impression of his character and work into the
intelligence and feeling of his own and the following
times. We may think of Voltairism in France somewhat as we think of Catholicism or the Renaissance
or Calvinism. It was one of the cardinal liberations

B

of the growing race, one of the emphatic manifestations of some portion of the minds of men, which an
immediately foregoing system and creed had either
ignored or outraged.

Christianity originally and generically at once
awoke and satisfied a spiritual craving for a higher,
purer, less torn and fragmentary being, than is permitted to sons of men on the troubled and corrupt
earth. It disclosed to them a gracious, benevolent,
and all-powerful being, who would one day redress
all wrongs and recompense all pain, and who asked
no more from them meanwhile than that they should
prove their love of him whom they had not seen, by
love of their brothers whom they had seen. Its great
glory was to have raised the moral dignity and self-
respect of the many to a level which had hitherto
been reached only by a few. Calvin, again, like some
stern and austere step-son of the Christian God, jealous
of the divine benignity and abused open-handedness
of his father's house, with word of merciless power
set free all those souls that were more anxious to
look the tremendous facts of necessity and evil and
punishment full in the face, than to reconcile them
with any theory of the infinite mercy and loving-
kindness of a supreme creator. Men who had been
enervated or helplessly perplexed by a creed that had
sunk into ignoble optimism and self-indulgence, became
conscious of new fibre in their moral structure, when
they realised life as a long wrestling with unseen and
invincible forces of grace, election, and fore-destiny,

the agencies of a being whose ways and dealings, whose contradictory attributes of unjust justice and loving vindictiveness, it was not for man, who is a worm and the son of a worm, to reconcile with the puny logic of human words, or the shallow consistency of human ideas. Catholicism was a movement of mysticism, and so in darker regions was the Calvinism which in so many important societies displaced it. Each did much to raise the measure of worth and purify the spiritual self-respect of mankind, and each also discouraged and depressed the liberal play of intelligence, the cheerful energizing of reason, the bright and many-sided workings of fancy and imagination. Human nature, happily for us, ever presses against this system or that, and forces ways of escape for itself into freedom and light. The scientific reason urgently seeks instruments and a voice ; the creative imagination unconsciously takes form to itself in manifold ways, of all of which the emotions can give good account to the understanding. Hence the glorious suffusion of light which the ardent desire of men brought over the face of Europe in the latter half of the fifteenth century. Before Luther and Calvin in their separate ways brought into splendid prominence their new ideas of moral order, more than two generations of men had almost ceased to care whether there be any moral order or not, and had plunged with the delight of enchantment among ideas of grace and beauty, whose forms were old on the earth, but which were full of seemingly inexhaustible

novelty and freshness to men, who had once begun
to receive and to understand all the ever-living gifts
of Grecian art and architecture and letters. If the
Reformation, the great revival of northern Europe,
was the enfranchisement of the individual from
bondage to a collective religious tradition that had
lost its virtue, the Renaissance, the earlier revival of
southern Europe, was the admission to participate in
the noblest collective tradition of free intellect which
the achievements of the race could then hand down.

Voltairism may stand for the name of the Renaissance of the eighteenth century, for that name
takes in all the serious haltings and shortcomings of
this strange movement, as well as all its terrible fire,
swiftness, sincerity, and strength. The rays from
Voltaire's burning and far-shining spirit no sooner
struck upon the genius of the time, seated dark and
dead like the black stone of Memnon's statue, than
the clang of the breaking chord was heard through
Europe, and men awoke in new day and more spacious
air. The sentimentalist has proclaimed him a mere
mocker. To the critic of the schools, ever ready with
compendious label, he is the revolutionary destructive.
To each alike of the countless orthodox sects his name
is the symbol for the prevailing of the gates of hell.
Erudition figures him as shallow and a trifler ; culture
condemns him for pushing his hatred of spiritual falsehood much too seriously ; Christian charity feels constrained to unmask a demon from the depths of the
pit. The plain men of the earth, who are apt to

measure the merits of a philosopher by the strength
of his sympathy with existing sources of comfort,
would generally approve the saying of Dr. Johnson,
that he would sooner sign a sentence for Rousseau's
transportation than that of any felon who had gone
from the Old Bailey these many years, and that the
difference between him and Voltaire was so slight,
that 'it would be difficult to settle the proportion of
iniquity between them.' Those of all schools and
professions who have the temperament which mistakes
strong expression for strong judgment, and violent
phrase for grounded conviction, have been stimulated
by antipathy against Voltaire to a degree that in any
of them with latent turns for humour must now and
then have even stirred a kind of reacting sympathy.
The rank vocabulary of malice and hate, that noisome
fringe of the history of opinion, has received many
of its most fulminant terms from critics of Voltaire,
along with some from Voltaire himself, who unwisely
did not always refuse to follow an adversary's bad
example.

Yet Voltaire was the very eye of eighteenth-
century illumination. It was he who conveyed to
his generation in a multitude of forms the consciousness at once of the power and the rights of human
intelligence. Another might well have said of him
what he magnanimously said of his famous contemporary, Montesquieu, that humanity had lost its title-
deeds, and he had recovered them. The fourscore
volumes which he wrote are the monument, as they

were in some sort the instrument, of a new renascence
They are the fruit and representation of a spirit of
encyclopædic curiosity and productiveness. Hardly
a page of all these countless leaves is common form.
Hardly a sentence is there which did not come forth
alive from Voltaire's own mind, or which was said
because some one else had said it before. His works
as much as those of any man that ever lived and
thought are truly his own. It is not given, we all
know, even to the most original and daring of leaders
to be without precursors, and Voltaire's march was
prepared for him before he was born, as it is for all
mortals. Yet he impressed on all he said, on good
words and bad alike, a marked autochthonic quality,
as of the self-raised spontaneous products of some
miraculous soil, from which prodigies and portents
spring. Many of his ideas were in the air, and did
not belong to him peculiarly; but so strangely rapid
and perfect was his assimilation of them, so vigorous
and minutely penetrative was the quality of his
understanding, so firm and independent his initiative,
that even these were instantly stamped with the
express image of his personality. In a word, Voltaire's
work from first to last was alert with unquenchable
life. Some of it, much of it, has ceased to be alive
for us now in all that belongs to its deeper significance,
yet we recognise that none of it was ever the dreary
still-birth of a mind of hearsays. There is no
mechanical transmission of untested bits of current
coin. In the realm of mere letters, Voltaire is one of

the little band of great monarchs, and in style he remains of the supreme potentates. But literary variety and perfection, however admirable, like all purely literary qualities, are a fragile and secondary good which the world is very willing to let die, where it has not been truly begotten and engendered of living forces.

Voltaire was a stupendous power, not only because his expression was incomparably lucid, or even because his sight was exquisitely keen and clear, but because he saw many new things, after which the spirits of others were unconsciously groping and dumbly yearning. Nor was this all. Fontenelle was both brilliant and far-sighted, but he was cold, and one of those who love ease and a safe hearth, and carefully shun the din, turmoil, and danger, of the great battle. Voltaire was ever in the front and centre of the fight. His life was not a mere chapter in a history of literature. He never counted truth a treasure to be discreetly hidden in a napkin. He made it a perpetual war-cry and emblazoned it on a banner that was many a time rent, but was never out of the field.

This is the temper which, when the times are auspicious, and the fortunes of the fight do not hurry the combatant to dungeon or stake, raises him into a force instead of leaving him the empty shadow of a literary name. There is something in our nature which leads men to listen coolly to the most eager hints and pregnant innuendoes of scepticism, on the lips of teachers who still in their own persons keep

adroitly away from the fiery darts of the officially
orthodox. The same something, perhaps a moral
relish for veritable proofs of honesty, perhaps a
quality of animal temperament, drives men to grasp
even a crudity with fervour, when they see it wielded
like a battle-axe against spiritual oppression. A man
is always so much more than his words, as we feel
every day of our lives ; what he says has its momentum
indefinitely multiplied, or reduced to nullity, by the
impression that the hearer for good reasons or bad
happens to have formed of the spirit and moral size
of the speaker. There are things enough to be said
of Voltaire's moral size, and no attempt is made in
these pages to dissemble in how much he was condemn-
able. It is at least certain that he hated tyranny,
that he refused to lay up his hatred privily in his
heart, and insisted on giving his abhorrence a voice,
and tempering for his just rage a fine sword, very
fatal to those who laid burdens too hard to be borne
upon the conscience and life of men. Voltaire's contemporaries felt this. They were stirred to the quick
by the sight and sound and thorough directness of
those ringing blows. The strange and sinister method
of assault upon religion which we of a later day watch
with wondering eyes, and which consists in wearing
the shield and device of a faith, and industriously
shouting the cry of a church, the more effectually to
reduce the faith to a vague futility, and its outward
ordering to a piece of ingeniously reticulated pretence ;
this method of attack might make even the champions

of prevailing beliefs long for the shrewd thrusts, the flashing scorn, the relentless fire, the downright grapples, with which the hated Voltaire pushed on his work of 'crushing the Infamous.' If he was bitter, he was still direct. If he was often a mocker in form, he was always serious in meaning and laborious in matter. If he was unflinching against theology, he always paid religion respect enough to treat it as the most important of all subjects. The contest was real, and not our present pantomimic stage-play, in which muffled phantoms of debate are made to gesticulate inexpressible things in portentously significant silence. The battle was demoralized by its virulence. True; but is this worse than to have it demoralized by cowardice of heart and understanding, when each controversial man-at-arms is eager to have it thought that he wears the colours of the other side, when the theologian would fain pass for rationalist, and the free-thinker for a person with his own ortho-doxies if you only knew them, and when philosophic candour and intelligence are supposed to have hit their final climax in the doctrine that everything is both true and false at the same time?

A man like Montaigne, as has been said, could slumber tranquilly on the pillow of doubt, content to live his life, leaving many questions open. Such men's meditations, when composed in the genial literary form proper to them, are naturally the delight of people with whom the world goes fairly well materially, who have sensibility enough to be aware

that there are unseen lands of knowledge and truth
beyond the present, and destinies beyond their own;
but whose sensibility is not intense and ardent enough
to make wholly unendurable to them unscrutinizing
acquiescence in half-thoughts and faint guesses, and
pale unshapen embryos of social sympathy. There
are conjunctures when this mingling of apprehension
and ease, of aspiration and content, of timorous adventure and reflective indolence, is the natural mood of
even high natures. The great tides of circumstance
swell so tardily, that whole generations that might
have produced their share of skilful and intrepid
mariners, wait in vain for the full flood on which the
race is borne to new shores.

Nor assuredly is it well for men that every age
should mark either a revolution, or the slow inward
agitation that prepares the revolution, or that doubters
and destroyers should divide between them all admiration and gratitude and sympathy. The violent
activity of a century of great change may end in a
victory, but it is always a sacrifice. The victory may
more than recompense its cost. The sacrifice may
repay itself a thousand-fold. It does not always
repay itself, as the too neglected list of good causes
lost, and noble effort wasted, so abundantly shows.
Nor in any case is sacrifice ever an end. Faith and
order and steady strong movement are the conditions
which everything wise is directed to perfect and con-
solidate. But for this process of perfection we need
first the meditative, doubting, critical type, and next,

the dogmatic destroyer. 'In counsel it is good to
see dangers,' Bacon said; 'and in execution not to
see them, except they be very great.' There are, as
history instructs us, eras of counsel and eras of execution; the hour when those do best who walk most
warily, feeling with patience and sagacity and painstaking for the new ways, and then the hour of march
and stout-hearted engagement.

Voltaire, if he adroitly or sagely preserved his
buckler, felt that the day was come to throw away
the scabbard; that it was time to trust firmly to the
free understanding of men for guidance in the voyage
after truth, and to the instincts of uncorrupted benevolence in men for the upholding of social justice.
His was one of the robust and incisive constitutions,
to which doubt figures as a sickness, and where
intellectual apprehension is an impossibility. The
old-fashioned nomenclature puts him down among
sceptics, because those who had the official right to
affix these labels could think of no more contemptuous
name, and could not suppose the most audacious soul
capable of advancing even under the leadership of
Satan himself beyond a stray doubt or so. He had
perhaps as little of the sceptic in his constitution as
Bossuet or Butler, and was much less capable of
becoming one than De Maistre or Paley. This was
a prime secret of his power, for the mere critic and
propounder of unanswered doubts never leads more
than a handful of men after him. Voltaire boldly
put the great question, and he boldly answered it.

He asked whether the sacred records were historically true, the Christian doctrine divinely inspired and spiritually exhaustive, and the Christian church a holy and beneficent organization. He answered these questions for himself and for others beyond possibility of misconception. The records were saturated with fable and absurdity, the doctrine imperfect at its best, and a dark and tyrannical superstition at its worst, and the church was the arch-curse and infamy. Say what we will of these answers, they were free from any taint of scepticism. Our lofty new idea of rational freedom as freedom from conviction, and of emancipation of understanding as emancipation from the duty of settling whether important propositions are true or false, had not dawned on Voltaire.

He had just as little part or lot in the complaisant spirit of the man of the world, who from the depths of his mediocrity and ease presumes to promulgate the law of progress, and as dictator to fix its speed. Who does not know this temper of the man of the world, that worst enemy of the world? His inexhaustible patience of abuses that only torment others; his apologetic word for beliefs that may perhaps not be so precisely true as one might wish, and institutions that are not altogether so useful as some might think possible; his cordiality towards progress and improvement in a general way, and his coldness or antipathy to each progressive proposal in particular; his pygmy hope that life will one day become somewhat better, punily shivering by the side of his

gigantic conviction that it might well be infinitely
worse. To Voltaire, far different from this, an
irrational prejudice was not the object of a polite
coldness, but a real evil to be combated and overthrown at every hazard. Cruelty was not to him as
a disagreeable dream of the imagination, from thought
of which he could save himself by arousing to sense
of his own comfort, but a vivid flame burning into
his thoughts and destroying peace. Wrong - doing
and injustice were not simple words on his lips;
they went as knives to the heart; he suffered with
the victim, and consumed with an active rage against
the oppressor.

Nor was the coarse cruelty of the inquisitor or the
politician, who wrought iniquity by aid of the arm
of flesh, the only kind of injury to the world which
stirred his passion. He had imagination enough and
intelligence enough to perceive that they are the
most pestilent of all the enemies of mankind, the
sombre hierarchs of misology, who take away the
keys of knowledge, thrusting truth down to the
second place, and discrowning sovereign reason to be
the serving drudge of superstition or social usage.
The system which threw obstacles into the way of
publishing an exposition of Newton's discoveries and
ideas was as mischievous and hateful to him, as the
darker bigotry which broke Calas on the wheel
because he was a Protestant. To check the energetic
discovery and wide propagation of scientific truth,
he rightly held to be at least as destructive in the

long run to the common weal, as the unjust extermination of human life; for it is the possession of
ever more and more truth that makes life ever better
worth having and better worth preserving. And
must we not admit that he was right, and that no
age nor school of men nor individual has ever been
mortally afraid, as every good man is afraid, of inflicting any wrong on his fellow, and has not also
been afraid of extinguishing a single ray from the
great sun of knowledge?

It is well enough to say that in unscientific ages,
like the twelfth century for instance, the burner of
books and the tormentor of those who wrote them,
did not feel either that he was doing an injustice to
man or a mischief to truth. It is hard to deny that
St. Bernard was a good man, nor is it needful that we
should deny it; for good motives, owing to our great
blindness and slow enlightenment, have made grievous
havoc in the world. But the conception of justice towards heretics did not exist, any more than it existed
in the mind of a low type of white man towards a black
man, or than the conception of pity exists in the mind
of a sportsman towards his prey. These were ages of
social cruelty, as they were ages of intellectual repression. The debt of each to his neighbour was as little
felt, as the debt of all to the common faculties and
intelligence. Men owed nothing to man, but everything to the gods. All the social feeling and intellectual effort and human energizing which had made
the high idea of God possible and real, seemed to have

expended themselves in a creation which instantly
swallowed them up and obliterated their recollection.
The intelligence which by its active straining upwards
to the light had opened the way for the one God,
became itself forthwith identified with the chief of
the devils. He who used his reason was the child of
this demon. Where it is a duty to worship the sun,
it is pretty sure to be a crime to examine the laws of
heat. The times when such was the universal idea
of the rights of the understanding, were also the times
when human life was cheapest, and the tiny bowl of a
man's happiness was spilt upon the ground with least
compunction.

The companionship between these two ideas of disrespect for the rights of man, and disrespect for reason
or the highest distinction of man, has been an inseparable companionship. The converse is unhappily only
true with a modification, for there have been too many
men with an honourable respect for a demonstration
and a proper hospitality towards a probability, who
look on the rights of man, without disrespect indeed,
but also without fervour. To Voltaire reason and
humanity were but a single word, and love of truth
and passion for justice but one emotion. None of the
famous men who have fought that they themselves
might think freely and speak truly, have ever seen
more clearly that the fundamental aim of the contest
was that others might live happily. Who has not
been touched by that admirable word of his, of the
three years in which he laboured without remission

for justice to the widow and descendants of Calas :
'*During that time not a smile escaped me without my
reproaching myself for it, as for a crime.*' Or by his
sincere avowal that of all the words of enthusiasm
and admiration which were so prodigally bestowed
upon him on the occasion of his last famous visit to
Paris in 1778, none went to his heart like that of a
woman of the people, who in reply to one asking the
name of him whom the crowd followed, gave answer,
'*Do you not know that he is the preserver of the Calas ?*'

The same kind of feeling, though manifested in
ways of much less unequivocal nobleness, was at the
bottom of his many efforts to make himself of consequence in important political business. We know
how many contemptuous sarcasms have been inspired
by his anxiety at various times to perform diplomatic
feats of intervention between the French government
and Frederick the Second. In 1742, after his visit
to the Prussian king at Aix-la-Chapelle, he is supposed
to have hinted to Cardinal Fleury that to have written
epic and drama does not disqualify a man for serving
his king and country on the busy fields of affairs.
The following year, after Fleury's death, when French
fortunes in the war of the Austrian succession were
near their lowest, Voltaire's own idea that he might
be useful from his intimacy with Frederick, seems to
have been shared by Amelot, the secretary of state,
and at all events he aspired to do some sort of active,
if radically futile, diplomatic work. In later times
when the tide had turned, and Frederick's star was

clouded over with disaster, we again find Voltaire the
eager intermediary with Choiseul, pleasantly compar
ing himself to the mouse of the fable, busily striving
to free the lion from the meshes of the hunter's
net.

The man of letters, usually unable to conceive
loftier services to mankind or more attractive aims to
persons of capacity than the composition of books,
has treated these pretensions of Voltaire with a
supercilious kind of censure, which teaches us nothing
about Voltaire, while it implies a particularly shallow
idea alike of the position of the mere literary life in
the scale of things, and of the conditions under which
the best literary work is done. To have really contributed in the humblest degree, for instance, to a
peace between Prussia and her enemies in 1759,
would have been an immeasurably greater performance for mankind than any given book which Voltaire
could have written. And, what is still better worth
observing, Voltaire's books would not have been the
powers they were, but for this constant desire of his
to come into the closest contact with the practical
affairs of the world. He who has never left the life
of a recluse, drawing an income from the funds and
living in a remote garden, constructing past, present,
and future, out of his own consciousness, is not
qualified either to lead mankind safely, or to think
on the course of human affairs correctly. Every page
of Voltaire has the bracing air of the life of the
world in it, and the instinct which led him to seek

the society of the conspicuous actors on the great scene was essentially a right one. The book-writer takes good advantage of his opportunity to assure men expressly or by implication that he is their true king, and that the sacred bard is a mightier man than his hero. Voltaire knew better. Though himself perhaps the most puissant man of letters that ever lived, he rated literature as it ought to be rated below action, not because written speech is less of a force, but because the speculation and criticism of the literature that substantially influences the world, make far less demand than the actual conduct of great affairs on qualities which are not rare in detail, but are amazingly rare in combination,—on temper, foresight, solidity, daring,—on strength, in a word, strength of intelligence and strength of character. Gibbon rightly amended his phrase, when he described Boethius not as stooping, but rather as rising, from his life of placid meditation to an active share in the imperial business. That he held this sound opinion is quite as plausible an explanation of Voltaire's anxiety to know persons of station and importance, as the current theory that he was of sycophantic nature. Why, he asks, are the ancient historians so full of light? 'It is because the writer had to do with public business; it is because he could be magistrate, priest, soldier; and because if he could not rise to the highest functions of the state, he had at least to make himself worthy of them. I admit,' he concludes, 'that we must not expect such an

advantage with us, for our own constitution happens
to be against it;' but he was deeply sensible what an
advantage it was that they thus lost.[1]

In short, on all sides, whatever men do and think
was real and alive to Voltaire. Whatever had the
quality of interesting any imaginable temperament,
had the quality of interesting him. There was no
subject which any set of men have ever cared about,
which, if he once had mention of it, Voltaire did not
care about likewise. And it was just because he was
so thoroughly alive himself, that he filled the whole
era with life. The more closely one studies the
various movements of that time, the more clear it
becomes that, if he was not the original centre and
first fountain of them all, at any rate he made many
channels ready and gave the sign. He was the initial
principle of fermentation throughout that vast commotion. We may deplore, if we think fit, as Erasmus
deplored in the case of Luther, that the great change
was not allowed to work itself out slowly, calmly, and
without violence and disruption. These graceful
regrets are powerless, and on the whole they are
very enervating. Let us make our account with the
actual, rather than seek excuses for self-indulgence in
pensive preference of something that might have been.
Practically in these great circles of affairs, what only
might have been is as though it could not be; and
to know this may well suffice for us. It is not in
human power to choose the kind of men who rise from

[1] *Œuvres*, xxxv. p. 214.

time to time to the supreme control of momentous changes. The force which decides this immensely important matter is as though it were chance. We cannot decisively pronounce any circumstance whatever an accident, yet history abounds with circumstances which in our present ignorance of the causes of things are as if they were accidents.

In this respect history is neither better nor worse than the latest explanation of the origin and order of the world of organised matter. Here too we are landed in the final resort at what is neither more nor less than an accident. Natural selection, or the survival of the fittest in the universal struggle for existence, is now held by the most competent inquirers to be the principal method to which we owe the extinction, preservation, and distribution of organic forms on the earth. But the appearance both of the forms that conquer and of those that perish still remains a secret, and to science an accident and a secret are virtually and provisionally the same thing. In a word, there is an unknown element at the bottom of the varieties of creation, whether we agree to call that element a volition of a supernatural being, or an undiscovered set of facts in embryology. So in history the Roman or Italo-Hellenic empire, rising when it did, was the salvation of the West, and yet the appearance at the moment when anarchy threatened rapidly to dissolve the Roman state, of a man with the power of conceiving the best design for the new structure, seems to partake as much of the nature of chance, as the non-appearance of men with similar vision and power in equally momentous crises, earlier and later. The rise of a great constructive chief like Charlemagne in the eighth century can hardly be enough to persuade us that the occasion invariably brings the leader whom its conditions require, when we remember that as concerns their demands the conditions of the end of the eighth century were not radically different from those of the beginning of the sixth, yet that in the earlier epoch there arose no successor to continue the work of Theodoric. We have only to examine the origin and fundamental circumstances of the types of civilisation which rule western communities and guide their advance, to discern in those original circumstances a something inscrutable, a certain element of what is as though it were fortuitous. No science can as yet tell us how such a variation from previously existing creatures as man had its origin; nor, any more than this, can history explain the law by which the most striking variations in intellectual and spiritual quality within the human order have had their origin. The appearance of the one as of the other is a fact which cannot be further resolved. It is hard to think in imagination of the globe as unpeopled by man, or peopled, as it may at some remote day come to be, by beings of capacity superior enough to extinguish man. It is hard also to think of the scene which western Europe and all the vast space which the light of western Europe irradiates, might have offered at this moment, if nature or the unknown forces had not produced a Luther, a Calvin, or a Voltaire.

It was one of the happy chances of circumstance that there arose in France on the death of Lewis XIV. a man with all Voltaire's peculiar gifts of intelligence, who added to them an incessant activity in their use, and who besides this enjoyed such length of days as to make his intellectual powers effective to the very fullest extent possible. This combination of physical and mental conditions so amazingly favourable to the spread of the Voltairean ideas, was a circumstance independent of the state of the surrounding atmosphere, and was what in the phraseology of præscientific times might well have been called providential. If Voltaire had seen all that he saw, and yet been indolent; or if he had been as clear-sighted and as active as he was, and yet had only lived fifty years, instead of eighty-four, Voltairism would never have struck root.[1] As it was, with his genius, his industry, his longevity, and the conditions of the time being what they were, that far-spreading movement of destruction was inevitable.

Once more, we cannot choose. Those whom temperament or culture has made the partisans of calm order, cannot attune progress to the stately and harmonious march which would best please them, and which they are perhaps right in thinking would lead with most security to the goal.

Such a liberation of the human mind as Voltairism

[1] See Comte's *Philosophie Positive*, v 520.

can only be effected by the movement of many spirits,
and they are only the few who are moved by moder
ate, reflective, and scientific trains of argument. The
many need an extreme type. They are struck by
what is flashing and colossal, for they follow imagination and sympathy, and not the exactly disciplined
intelligence. They know their own wants, and have
dumb feeling of their own better aspirations. Their
thoughts move in the obscurity of things quick but
unborn, and by instinct they push upwards in whatever direction the darkness seems breaking. They are
not critics nor analysts, but when the time is ripening
they never fail to know the word of freedom and of
truth, with whatever imperfections it may chance to
be spoken. No prophet all false has ever yet caught
the ear of a series of generations. No prophet all
false has succeeded in separating a nation into two
clear divisions. Voltaire has in effect for a century
so divided the most emancipated of western nations.
This is beyond the power of the mere mocker, who
perishes like the flash of lightning ; he does not
abide as a centre of solar heat.

There are more kinds of Voltaireans than one, but
no one who has marched ever so short a way out of
the great camp of old ideas is directly or indirectly
out of the debt and out of the hand of the first
liberator, however little willing he may be to recognise one or the other. Attention has been called by
every writer on Voltaire to the immense number of
the editions of his works, a number probably un-

paralleled in the case of any author within the same
limits of time. Besides being one of the most volu-
minous book-writers, he is one of the cheapest. We
can buy one of Voltaire's books for a few halfpence, and
the keepers of the cheap stalls in the cheap quarters
of London and Paris will tell you that this is not from
lack of demand, but the contrary. So clearly does
that light burn for many even now, which scientifically speaking ought to be extinct, and for many indeed
is long ago extinct and superseded. The reasons for
this vitality are that Voltaire was himself thoroughly
alive when he did his work, and that the movement
which that work began is still unexhausted.

How shall we attempt to characterise this movement? The historian of the Christian church usually
opens his narrative with an account of the depravation
of human nature and the corruption of society which
preceded the new religion. The Reformation in like
manner is only to be understood after we have
perceived the enormous mass of superstition, injustice,
and wilful ignorance, by which the theological idea
had become so incrusted as to be wholly incompetent
to guide society, because it was equally repugnant to
the intellectual perceptions and the moral sense, the
knowledge and the feelings, of the best and most
active-minded persons of the time. The same sort
of consideration explains and vindicates the enormous
power of Voltaire. France had outgrown the system
that had brought her through the middle ages. The
further development of her national life was fatally

hindered by the tight bonds of an old order, which clung with the hardy tenacity of a thriving parasite, diverting from the roots all their sustenance, eating into the tissue, and feeding on the juices of the living tree. The picture has often been painted, and we need not try to paint it once more in detail here. The whole power and ordering of the nation were with the sworn and chartered foes of light, who had every interest that a desire to cling to authority and wealth can give, in keeping the understanding subject.

And, what was more important, there had been no sign made in the nation itself of a consciousness of the immense realms of knowledge that lay immediately in front of it, and still less of any desire or intention to win lasting possession of them. That intellectual curiosity which was so soon to produce such amazing fruits was as yet unstirred. An era of extraordinary activity had just come to a close, and the creative and artistic genius of France had risen to the highest mark it attained until the opening of our own century. The grand age of Lewis XIV. had been an age of magnificent literature and unsurpassed eloquence. But, in spite of the potent seed which Descartes had sown, it had been the age of authority, protection, and patronage. Consequently all those subjects for which there was no patronage, that is to say the subjects which could add nothing to the splendour and dignity of the church and the pageantry of the court, were virtually repressed. This ought not to blind us to the real loftiness and magnanimity

of the best or earlier part of the age of Lewis XIV.
It has been said that the best title of Lewis XIV. to
the recollection of posterity is the protection he
extended to Molière; and one reason why this was
so meritorious is that Molière's work had a markedly
critical character, in reference both to the devout
and to the courtier. The fact of this, undoubtedly
the most durable work of that time, containing critical
quality, is not of importance in reference to the
generally fixed or positive aspect of the age. For
Molière is only critical by accident. There is nothing
organically negative about him, and his plays are the
pure dramatic presentation of a peculiar civilisation.
He is no more a destructive agency because he drew
hypocrites and coxcombs, than Bossuet was destructive
or critical because he inveighed against sin and the
excess of human vainglory. The epoch was one of
entire loyalty to itself and its ideas. Voltaire himself
perceived and admired these traits to the full. The
greatest of all overthrowers, he always understood
that it is towards such ages as these, the too short
ages of conviction and self-sufficience, that our endeavour works. We fight that others may enjoy; and
many generations struggle and debate, that one
generation may hold something for proven.

The glories of the age of Lewis XIV. were the
climax of a set of ideas that instantly afterwards lost
alike their grace, their usefulness, and the firmness of
their hold on the intelligence of men. A dignified
and venerable hierarchy, an august and powerful

monarch, a court of gay and luxurious nobles, all lost
their grace, because the eyes of men were suddenly
caught and appalled by the awful phantom, which
was yet so real, of a perishing nation. Turn from
Bossuet's orations to Boisguillebert's *Détail de la
France;* from the pulpit rhetorician's courtly re-
minders that even majesty must die, to Vauban's pity
for the misery of the common people ;[1] from Corneille
and Racine to La Bruyère's picture of 'certain wild
animals, male and female, scattered over the fields,
black, livid, all burnt by the sun, bound to the earth
that they dig and work with unconquerable pertinacity ; they have a sort of articulate voice, and when
they rise on their feet, they show a human face, and,
in fact, are men.' The contrast had existed for
generations. The material misery caused by the wars
of the great Lewis deepened the dark side, and the
lustre of genius consecrated to the glorification of
traditional authority and the order of the hour height-
ened the brightness of the bright side, until the old
contrast was suddenly seen by a few startled eyes,
and the new and deepest problem, destined to strain
our civilisation to a degree that not many have even
now conceived, came slowly into pale outline.

There is no reason to think that Voltaire ever saw
this gaunt and tremendous spectacle. Rousseau was
its first voice. Since him the reorganisation of the

---

[1] Vauban and Boisguillebert are both to be found in *Les
Economistes Financiers du XVIIIième Siècle,* published by
Guillaumin, 1851.

relations of men has never faded from the sight either
of statesmen or philosophers, with vision keen enough
to admit to their eyes even what they dreaded and
execrated in their hearts. Voltaire's task was different and preparatory. It was to make popular the
genius and authority of reason. The foundations of
the social fabric were in such a condition that the
touch of reason was fatal to the whole structure,
which instantly began to crumble. Authority and
use oppose a steadfast and invincible resistance to
reason, so long as the institutions which they protect
are of fair practicable service to a society. But after
the death of Lewis xiv., not only the grace and
pomp, but also the social utility of spiritual and
political absolutism passed obviously away. Spiritual
absolutism was unable to maintain even a decent
semblance of unity and theological order. Political
absolutism by its material costliness, its augmenting
tendency to repress the application of individual
energy and thought to public concerns, and its pursuit of a policy in Europe which was futile and
essentially meaningless as to its ends, and disastrous
and incapable in its choice of means, was rapidly
exhausting the resources of national well-being and
viciously severing the very tap-root of national life.
To bring reason into an atmosphere so charged, was,
as the old figure goes, to admit air to the chamber of
the mummy. And reason was exactly what Voltaire
brought; too narrow, if we will, too contentious, too
derisive, too unmitigatedly reasonable, but still reason.

And who shall measure the consequence of this difference in the history of two great nations; that in France absolutism in church and state fell before the sinewy genius of stark reason, while in England it fell before a respect for social convenience, protesting against monopolies, benevolences, ship-money? That in France speculation had penetrated over the whole field of social inquiry, before a single step had been taken towards application, while in England social principles were applied, before they received any kind of speculative vindication? That in France the first effective enemy of the principles of despotism was Voltaire, poet, philosopher, historian, critic; in England, a band of homely squires?

Traditional authority, it is true, had been partially and fatally undermined in France before the time of Voltaire, by one of the most daring of thinkers, and one of the most acute and sceptical of scholars, as well as by writers so acutely careless as Montaigne, and apologists so dangerously rational as Pascal, who gave a rank and consistency to doubt even in showing that its seas were black and shoreless. Descartes's Discourse on Method had been published in 1637, and Bayle's Thoughts on the Comet, first of the series of critical onslaughts on prejudice and authority in matters of belief, had been published in 1682. The metaphysician and the critic had each pressed forward on the path of examination, and had each insisted on finding grounds for belief, or else showing the absence of such grounds with a fatal distinctness that made belief impossible. Descartes was constructive, and was bent on reconciling the acceptance of a certain set of ideas as to the relations between man and the universe, and as to the mode and composition of the universe, with the logical reason. Bayle, whose antecedents and environment were Protestant, was careless to replace, but careful to have evidence for whatever was allowed to remain. No parallel nor hint of equality is here intended between the rare genius of Descartes and the relatively lower quality of Bayle. The one, however high a place we may give to the regeneration of thought effected by Bacon in England, or to that wrought by the brilliant group of physical experimentalists in Italy, still marks a new epoch in the development of the human mind, for he had decisively separated knowledge from theology, and systematically constituted science. The other has a place only in the history of criticism. But, although in widely different ways, and with vast difference in intellectual stature, they both had touched the prevailing notions of French society with a fatal breath.

The blast that finally dispersed and destroyed them came not from Descartes and Bayle, but directly from Voltaire and indirectly from England. In the seventeenth century the surrounding conditions were not ripe. Social needs had not begun to press. The organs of authority were still too vigorous, and performed their functions with something more than the mechanical half-heartedness of the next century.

Long familiarity with sceptical ideas as enemies must
go before their reception as friends and deliverers.
They have perhaps never gained an effective hold in
any community, until they have found allies in the
hostile camp of official orthodoxy, and so long as that
orthodoxy was able to afford them a vigorous social
resistance. Voltaire's universal talents made one of
the most powerful instruments for conveying these
bold and inquisitive notions among many sorts and
conditions of men, including both the multitude of
common readers and playgoers in the towns, and the
narrower multitude of nobles and sovereigns. More
than this, the brilliance and variety of his gifts
attracted, stimulated, and directed the majority of
the men of letters of his time, and imparted to them
a measure of his own singular skill in conveying the
principles of rationalistic thought.

The effect of all this was to turn a vast number of
personages who were officially inimical to free criticism,
to be at heart abettors and fellow-conspirators in the
great plot. That fact, combined with the independent
causes of the incompetency of the holders of authority
to deal with the crying social necessities of the time,
left the walls of the citadel undermined and un-
defended, and a few of the sacred birds that were
still found faithful cackled to no purpose. It has
often been said that in the early times of Christianity
its influence gave all that was truest and brightest in
colour to the compositions of those who were least or
not at all affected by its dogma. It is more certain

that Voltaire by the extraordinary force of his personality gave a peculiar tone and life even to those who
adhered most staunchly to the ancient ordering.   The
champions of authority were driven to defend their
cause by the unusual weapons of rationality ; and if
Voltaire had never written, authority would never,
for instance, have found such a soldier on her side as
that most able and eminent of reactionaries, Joseph
de Maistre.   In reply to the favourite assertion of
the apologists of Catholicism, that whatever good side
its assailants may present is the product of the very
teaching which they repudiate, one can only say that
there would be at least as much justice in maintaining
that the marked improvement which took place in
the character and aims of the priesthood between the
Regency and the Revolution,[1] was an obligation
unconsciously incurred to those just and liberal ideas
which Voltaire had helped so powerfully to spread.
De Maistre compares Reason putting away Revelation
to a child who should beat its nurse.   The same
figure would serve just as well to describe the thank-
lessness of Belief to the Disbelief which has purged
and exalted it.

[1] 'Je ne sais si, à tout prendre, et malgré les vices éclatants
de quelques uns de ses membres, il y eut jamais dans le monde
un clergé plus remarquable que le clergé catholique de France
au moment où la Révolution l'a surpris, plus éclairé, plus
national, moins retranché dans les seules vertus privées, mieux
pourvu de vertus publiques et en même temps de plus de foi :
la persécution l'a bien montré.'—De Tocqueville, *Ancien
Régime.* liv. ii. c. 11.

One of the most striking features of the revolution wrought by Voltaire is that it was the one great revolt in history which contained no element of asceticism, and achieved all its victories without resort to an instrument so potent, inflexible, and easy, but so gravely dangerous. Such revolts are always reactions against surrounding corruption and darkness. They are the energetic protests of the purer capacities and aspirations of human nature ; and as is the inevitable consequence of vehement action of this sort, they seem for a while to insist on nothing less than the extirpation of those antagonistic parts which are seen to have brought life into such debasement. With this stern anger and resolve in their hearts, men have no mind to refine, explain, or moderate, and they are forced by one of the strangest instincts of our constitution into some system of mortification, which may seem to clear the soul of the taint of surrounding grossness. In such exalted mood, there is no refuge but in withdrawal from the common life into recesses of private conscience, and in severest purification of all desires. There are not many types of good men even in the least ascetic or least reactionary epochs, to whom this mood, and its passion for simplicity, self-applied rigour, minute discipline, firm regulation, and veritable continence of life, do not now and again recur, in the midst of days that march normally on a more spacious and expansive theory.

There was, however, no tinge of ascetic principle in Voltairism. Pascal had remarked that relaxed

D

opinions are naturally so pleasing to men, that it is
wonderful they should ever be displeasing. To which
Voltaire had thus retorted: 'On the contrary, does
not experience prove that influence over men's minds
is only gained by offering them the difficult, nay the
impossible, to perform or believe? Offer only things
that are reasonable, and all the world will answer,
We knew as much as that. But enjoin things that
are hard, impracticable; paint the deity as ever
armed with the thunder; make blood run before the
altars; and you will win the multitude's ear, and
everybody will say of you, He must be right, or he
would not so boldly proclaim things so marvellous.' [1]
Voltaire's ascendency sprung from no appeal to those
parts of human nature in which ascetic practice has
its foundation. On the contrary, full exercise and
play for every part was the key of all his teaching,
direct and indirect. He had not Greek serenity and
composure of spirit, but he had Greek exultation in
every known form of intellectual activity, and this
audacious curiosity he made general.

Let us remember that Voltairism was primarily
and directly altogether an intellectual movement, for
this reason, that it was primarily and directly a
reaction against the subordination of the intellectual
to the moral side of men, carried to an excess that
was at length fraught with fatal mischief. Are our
opinions true, provably answering to the facts of
the case, consistent with one another; is our intelli-

[1] Rem. sur les Pensées de M. Pascal. *Œuvres*, xliii. p. 68.

gence radiant with genuine light and knowledge;
and are we bent more than all else on testing and
improving and diffusing this knowledge and the
instruments for acquiring it? The system to which
this was the powerful counter-formula, even in its
least dark shapes, always reserved a large class of
most important facts from the searching glare of that
scrutiny which Voltairism taught men to direct upon
every proposition that was presented to them.

For many centuries truth had been conceived as
of the nature of a Real Universal, of which men had
full possession by the revelation of a supreme divinity.
All truth was organically one; and the relations of
men to something supernatural, their relations to one
another, the relations of outward matter, were all
comprehended in a single synthesis, within which,
and subject to which, all intellectual movement proceeded. An advancing spirit of inquiry dissolved
this synthesis; and the philosophers, as distinguished
from the steadfast and single students of science,
ceasing to take it for granted as an indisputable
starting-point that truth was an assured possession,
went off on two different lines. Men of one cast of
mind fell into doubt whether truth was a reality after
all, and the discovery of it accessible to mankind.
Thinkers of a different cast accepted this doctrine of
the impotence of the human understanding to discover knowledge and prove truth, but they proceeded
to the retrograde inference that therefore the ancient
tradition of knowledge actually contains that approved

truth, which had just been pronounced unattainable.
This oblique mode of regaining a position of which
they had been by their own act dispossessed, was
impossible for so keen and direct a spirit as Voltaire's. However filled his mind may have been
with the false notions of the Tribe, of the Market,
and above all of the Cave, at all events it was more
free than most, certainly than most of those subalterns
of the schools, from the Idols of the Theatre, and
from either kind of that twofold excess, ' one sort of
which too hastily constitutes sciences positive and
hierarchic, while the other presents scepticism and
the pursuit of a vague inquiry that has no limit.' [1]

The consequence of this peculiarity, call it a
destructive and blind narrowness, or call it a wise
and justly-measured openness of mind, as we may
choose, has been that Voltaire has been condemned
with unsparing severity by three of the most influential schools of modern opinion. Every one who has
a system to defend is the enemy of the famous man
who destroyed the reigning system of his day, with
engines that seem to point with uncomfortable directness against all other systems. Every one who
thinks that we have turned over the last leaf of the
book of knowledge, whatever the inscription that he
may find written upon it, naturally detests the whole
spirit and impulse of one who felt all his life that
he and his generation were the first band of men
who had shaken off their chains, and ascended to the

[1] *Novum Organum*, § 67.

light of the sun and the contemplation of some portion of an inexhaustible universe of realities.   Hence,
the partisans of the Christian religion, in any of its
forms, have dealt unrelenting contempt and hatred to
the foe who did more than any one else to reduce
their churches, once so majestically triumphant, to
their present level, where they are forced under
various guises and with much obsolete pretension to
plead for the tolerance of rational men, on the comparatively modest ground of social fitness.   Their
hostility, we may agree, is not very astonishing, when
we reflect on the provocation.

Many of those, however, who have least hope of any
future revival of the ancient creed, and who least regret its fall, are even less hostile to the Jesuits than
they are to Voltaire.   Comte, for example, who elaborated a doctrine with a corresponding system of life
deduced from it, and the central principle of whose
method of social action and movement is to destroy
by replacing, has adjudged an emphatically secondary
place to Voltaire's claims on our good-will.[1]   Nor

[1] Some fault has been found with this passage by one or two
private critics, as being not entirely just to the eminent thinker
to whom it refers, and to whom my own obligations, direct and
indirect, are so numerous, notwithstanding my final inability
to follow him in his ideas of social reconstruction, that the idea
of adding to the sum of misrepresentation of which Comte and
his doctrines have been the victims, is particularly disagreeable
to me.   Here, therefore, is one passage in which Comte seems
to speak rather more warmly of Voltaire than the words in the
text imply : ' Toutefois, l'indispensable nécessité mentale et
sociale d'une telle élaboration provisoire laissera toujours, dans

ought this seriously to surprise us, when we consider
that Voltaire trusted to the individual to replace for
himself, by the motion of his own faculties, the old
collective tradition of action and belief; and that he
showed himself too keenly alive to the curses of that
empire of prejudice, authority, social fixity, which he
devoted his life to overthrowing, to lend any help to
the restoration of a similar reign with changed watch-
words.   He is perhaps the one great Frenchman who
has known how to abide in patient contentment with
an all but purely critical reserve, leaving reconstruction, its form, its modes, its epoch, for the fulness of
time and maturity of effort to disclose.   It has been
the fatal quality of the genius of his countrymen,
from Descartes down to Comte, to decline to rest on
an uncompleted interpretation of experience, and to
insist on a hasty supplement of unconcluded analysis
by what is virtually an à priori synthesis.   Voltaire
deserves no special praise for this abstention from a

l'ensemble de l'histoire humaine, une place importante à ses
principaux coopérateurs, et surtout à leur type le plus éminent,
auquel la postérité la plus lointaine assurera une position
vraiment unique ; parceque jamais un pareil office n'avait pu
jusqu'alors échoir, et pourra désormais encore moins appartenir
à un esprit de cette nature, chez lequel la plus admirable com-
binaison qui ait existé jusqu'ici entre les diverses qualités
secondaires de l'intelligence présentait si souvent la séduisante
apparence de la force et du génie ' (*Phil. Pos.* v. 518).   Against
this we have to place the highly significant fact that Voltaire
only appears in the calendar as a dramatic poet, as well as the
whole tenour and spirit of Comte's teaching, namely, as he puts
it in one place, that ' *une pure critique ne peut jamais mériter
beaucoup d'estime*' (*Politique Positive,* iii. 547).

PRELIMINARY. 39

premature reconstruction ; for it probably was not so much the result of deliberate persuasion that we must wait on the time, as of an inability to conceive of need for a cultus and a firm ordering of our knowledge, as prime demands of human nature and essential conditions of stable progress. Whatever value we may set on this sage reserve, the fact that Voltaire had no scheme for replacing the scheme which he destroyed, accounts very amply for the disparagement of him by those who think almost any fabric of common and ordered belief better for men, than the seeming chaos of intricate and multitudinous growths which now overspread the field of European opinion. And does it not involve us in a defective conception of the way in which human progress accomplishes itself, to place in our calendar of benefactors, supposing us to compose a calendar, only those who have built up truth, to the exclusion of those who have with pain and labour helped to demolish impudent error? Has Jericho always fallen without the blasts from the seven trumpets? Is it sufficiently demonstrated from history that false opinions vanish spontaneously, without a direct blow struck; that a system of belief, corroborated in the breasts of the multitude by all the authority of a long tradition, sanctified to the powerful few by dignity or emolument, entrenched with a strength that seems inexpugnable among the ordinances and institutions and unwritten uses of a great community, will straigntway succumb from inherent want of life and courage?

There is a third kind of opinion, that is as little merciful in its own way as either of the two others, and this is the scientific or cultured opinion. Objections from this region express themselves in many forms, some of them calm and suggestive, others a little empty and a little brutal. They all seem to come to something of this kind : that Voltaire's assault on religion, being conducted without any smallest spark of the religious spirit, was therefore necessarily unjust to the object of his attack, and did the further mischief of engendering in all on whom his influence was poured out a bitterness and moral temerity which is the worst blight that can fall upon the character either of a man or a generation : that while truth is relative and conditional, and while belief is only to be understood by those who have calmly done justice to the history of its origin and growth, Voltaire carelessly, unphilosophically, and maliciously, handled what had once possessed a relative truth, as if it had always been absolutely false, and what had sprung from the views and aspirations of the best men, as if it had had its root in the base artifices of the worst : that what ought to have gone on, and would have gone on, as a process of soft autumnal dissolution, was converted by the infection of Voltaire into a stained scene of passion and battle : that assuming to possess and to furnish men with a broad criticism of life, he left out of life its deepest, holiest, and most exalting elements, as well as narrowed and depraved criticism, from its right rank as the high art of stating and collating ideas, down to an acrid trick of debate, a thing of proofs, arguments, and rancorous polemic.

It is certain that there is much truth in this particular strain of objection to Voltaire's power and his use of it, or else it would not have found mouthpieces, as it has done, among some of the finest spirits of the modern time. But it is the natural tendency of the hour rather to exaggerate what weight there really is in such criticism, which, though claiming to be the criticism of temperance and moderation and relativity, does not as a matter of fact escape the fatal law of excess and absoluteness even in its very moderation and relativity. In estimating an innovator's method, all depends on the time and the enemy; and it may sometimes happen that the time is so out of joint and the enemy so strong, so unscrupulous, so imminently pernicious, as to leave no alternative between finally succumbing, and waging a war of deliverance for which coming generations have to bear the burdens in feuds and bitterness; between abridging somewhat of the richness and fulness of life, and allowing it all to be gradually choked up by dust and enwrapped in night. For let us not forget that what Catholicism was accomplishing in France in the first half of the eighteenth century, was really not anything less momentous than the slow strangling of French civilisation. Though Voltaire's spirit may be little edifying to us, who after all partake of the freedom which he did so much to win, yet it is only just to remember what was the spirit of his foe, and that in so pestilent a presence a

man of direct vision may well be eager to use such
weapons as he finds to his hand.   Let the scientific
spirit move people to speak as it lists about Voltaire's
want of respect for things held sacred, for the good
deeds of holy men, for the sentiment and faith of
thousands of the most worthy among his fellows.
Still there are times when it may be very questionable
whether, in the region of belief, one with power and
with fervid honesty ought to spare the abominable
city of the plain, just because it happens to shelter
five righteous.   There are times when the inhumanity
of a system stands out so red and foul, when the
burden of its iniquity weighs so heavy, and the con-
tagion of its hypocrisy is so laden with mortal plague,
that no awe of dilettante condemnation nor minute
scruple as to the historic or the relative can stay the
hand of the man whose direct sight and moral energy
have pierced the veil of use, and revealed the shrine
of the infamous thing.   The most noble of the holy
men said long ago that 'the servant of the Lord must
not strive, but be gentle unto all men, apt to teach,
patient, in meekness instructing those that oppose
themselves.'   The history of the churches is in one
of its most conspicuous aspects the history of a prolonged outrage upon these words by arrogant and
blasphemous persons, pretending to draw a sacred
spirit from the very saint who uttered them.   We
may well deplore that Voltaire's attack, and every
other attack of the same sort, did not take the fair
shape prescribed by the apostle to the servant of the

Lord, of gentleness, patience, and the instruction of a
sweet and firm example.   But the partisans of the
creed in whose name more human blood has been
violently shed than in any other cause whatever,
these, I say, can hardly find much ground of serious
reproach in a few score epigrams.   Voltaire had no
calm breadth of wisdom.   It may be so.   There are
moments which need not this calm breadth of wisdom,
but a two-edged sword, and when the deliverers of
mankind are they who 'come to send fire on the
earth.'

CHAPTER II.

ENGLISH INFLUENCES.

VOLTAIRISM may be said to have begun from the flight of its founder from Paris to London. This, to borrow a name from the most memorable instance of outward change marking inward revolution, was the decisive hegira, from which the philosophy of destruction in a formal shape may be held seriously to date. Voltaire landed in England in the middle of May, 1726. He was in the thirty-third year of his age, that earlier climacteric, when the men with vision first feel conscious of a past, and reflectively mark its shadow. It is then that they either press forward eagerly with new impulse in the way of their high calling, knowing the limitations of circumstance and hour, or else fainting draw back their hand from the plough, and ignobly leave to another or to none the accomplishment of the work. The narrowness of the cribbed deck that we are doomed to tread, amid the vast space of an eternal sea with fair shores dimly seen and never neared, oppresses the soul with a burden that sorely tries its strength, when the fixed limits first define themselves before it. Those are the strongest who do not tremble beneath this gray ghostly light, but make it the precursor of an industrious day.

The past on which Voltaire had to look back was full of turmoil, contention, impatience, and restless production. François Marie Arouet was born in 1694, so feeble in constitution that, as in the case of Fontenelle, whose hundred years surpassed even Voltaire's lengthy span, his life was long despaired of His father was a notary of good repute for integrity and skill, and was entrusted with the management of their affairs by several of the highest families in France. His mother is supposed to have had some of the intellectual alertness which penetrated the character of her son, but she died when he was seven years old, and he remained alone with his father until 1704, when he was sent to school. His instructors at the Collége Louis-le-Grand were the Jesuits, whose wise devotion to intellectual education in the broadest sense that was then possible, is a partial set-off against their mischievous influence on morals and politics. The hardihood of the young Arouet's temper broke out even from the first, and we need not inquire minutely what were the precise subjects of education of a child, whom his tutor took an early opportunity of pointing out as the future coryphæus of deism in France. He used to say in after life that he had learnt nothing worth learning. A lad who could launch infidel epigrams at 'his Jansenist of a brother,' and declaim a poem in which so important a hero as

Moses figures as an impostor,[1] was of that originality of mental turn on whose freedom the inevitably mechanical instruction of the school cannot be expected to make any deep or decisive impression. The young of this independent humour begin their education where those of less energetic nerve hardly leave off, with character ready made.

Between a youth of bold, vivacious, imaginative disposition, and a father of the temperament proper to a notary with many responsibilities, there could be no sympathy, and the two were not long in coming to open quarrel without terms. The son was taken out by his godfather, the abbé Châteauneuf, into that gay world which presently became the infamous world of the regency, where extraordinary sprightliness and facility in verse gained him welcome and patronage. We need waste no words on the corruption and intellectual trifling of the society into which Voltaire was thus launched. For shallowness and levity, concealed by literary artifice and play of frivolous wit which only makes the scene more dreary or detestable, it has never been surpassed. There was brightness in it, compared with the heavy brutality and things obscene of the court of Lewis xv., but after all we seem to see over the brightness a sort of foul glare, like the iridescence of putrefaction. Ninon de l'Enclos, a friend of his mother's, was perhaps the one free and honest soul with whom the young Arouet had to do. Now extremely old,

[1] J. B. Rousseau's *Moïsade.*

she still preserved both her wit and her fine probity of intellect. She had always kept her heart free of cant, from the time when she had ridiculed, as the Jansenists of love, the pedantical women and platonic gallants of the Hôtel Rambouillet, down to her rejection of Madame de Maintenon's offer of an invitation to the court, on condition of her joining the band of the devout. The veteran Aspasia, now over eighty, was struck by the brilliance and dazzling promise of the young versifier, and left him a legacy for the purchase of books.

The rest of the society into which Voltaire was taken was saturated with a spirit of reaction against the austere bigotry of the court, and bad and miserable as such austerity is, the rebellion against it is always worse and more miserable still. The licence seems not to have been of the most joyous sort, as indeed licence protesting and defiant is not apt to be. The abbé Chaulieu, a versifier of sprightly fancy, grace, and natural ease, was the dissolute Anacreon of the people of quality who during the best part of the reign of Lewis XIV. had failed to sympathise with its nobility and stateliness, and during the worst part revolted against its gloom. Voltaire at twenty was his intimate and his professed disciple.[1] To this intimacy we may perhaps trace that remarkable continuity of tradition between Voltaire and the grand age, which distinguishes him from the school of famous men who were called Voltaireans, and of

[1] *Œuvres*, lxii. p. 45.

whom the special mark was that they had absolutely
broken with the whole past of French history and
literature. Princes, dukes, and marquises were of
Chaulieu's band. The despair and fury of the elder
Arouet at such companions and such follies reproduce
once more a very old story in the records of youthful
genius. Genius and fine friends reconcile no prudent
notary to a son's hatred for law and the desk. Orgies
with the Duke of Sully, and rhyming bouts with
Chaulieu, have sunk into small size for us, who know
that they were but the mischievous and unbecoming
prologue of a life of incessant and generous labour,
but we may well believe that such enormities bulked
big in the vision of the father, as portents of degradation and ruin. We have a glimpse of the son's temper
towards the profession to which his father had tried
so hard to bind him, in the ironical definition, thrown
out long afterwards, of an *avocat* as a man who, not
having money enough to buy one of those brilliant
offices on which the universe has its eyes fixed, studies
for three years the laws of Theodosius and Justinian
so as to know the custom of Paris, and who at length
having got matriculated has the right of pleading for
money, if he has a loud voice.[1] The young Arouet
did actually himself get matriculated and acquire this
right, but his voice proved so loud that his pleadings
were destined to fill wider courts than those of Paris.

Arouet the elder persuaded Châteauneuf's brother,
who was a diplomatist, to take into his company the

[1] Dictionnaire Philosophique, *s.v.* *Œuvres*, lii. p. 378.

law-student who had made verse instead of studying
the laws of Theodosius. So the youth went to the
Hague. Here he straightway fell into new misad-
venture by conceiving an undying passion, that lasted
several weeks, for a young countrywoman whom he
found in Holland. Stolen interviews, letters, tears,
and the other accustomed circumstances of a juvenile
passion on which the gods frown, were all discovered.
The ambassador sent the refractory boy back to his
father, with full details and documents, with results
on the relations of the pair that need not be described.

In the autumn of 1715 Lewis XIV. died, and
the Regent D'Orleans reigned in his stead. There
presently appeared some pungent lines, entitled *Les
j'ai vu*, in which the writer recounted a number of
evil things which he had seen in the state—a thousand
prisons crowded with brave citizens and faithful
subjects, the people groaning under rigorous bondage,
the magistrates harassing every town with ruinous
taxes and unrighteous edicts; *j'ai vu, c'est dire tout, le
Jésuite adoré.* The last line ran that all these ills
the writer had seen, yet was but twenty years old.[1]
Voltaire was twenty-two, but the authorities knew
him for a verse-writer of biting turn, so they treated
the discrepancy of age as a piece of mere prosopopœia,
and laid him up in the Bastille (1716). As a matter
of fact, he had no hand in the offence. Even amid
these sombre shades, where he was kept for nearly a
year, his spirit was blithe and its fire unquenchable.

[1] *Œuvres*, i. 513.

E

The custom of Paris and the Codes were as little
handled as ever; and he divided his time between
the study of the two great epics of Greece and Rome,
and the preparation of what he designed to be the
great epic of France. He also gave the finishing
strokes to his tragedy of Œdipe, which was represented
in the course of the following year with definite
success, and was the opening of a brilliant dramatic
career, that perhaps to a mortal of more ordinary
mould might alone have sufficed for the glory of a
life.

The next six years he divided between a lively
society, mostly of the great, the assiduous composition of new plays, and the completion of the Henriade.
His fibre was gradually strengthening. By the end
of this period, the recklessness of the boyish disciple
of Chaulieu had wholly spent itself; and although
Voltaire's manner of life was assuredly not regular
nor decorously ordered, now nor for many years to
come, if measured by the rigid standard on which an
improved society properly insists, yet it was always
a life of vigorous industry and clear purposes. For
a brief time his passion for the Maréchale de Villars
broke the tenacity of his diligence, and he always
looked back on this interruption of his work with the
kind of remorse that might afflict a saint for a grave
spiritual backsliding. He was often at the country
seats of Sully, Villars, and elsewhere, throwing off
thousands of trifling verses, arranging theatricals,
enlivening festivals, and always corresponding inde-

fatigably ; for now and throughout his life his good sense and good will, his business-like quality and his liking for his friends, both united to raise him above the idle pretences and self-indulgence of those who neglect the chief instrument of social intercourse and friendly continuity.   He preferred the country to the town.   ' I was born,' he says to one, ' to be a faun or creature of the woods ; I am not made to live in a town.'   To another, ' I fancy myself in hell, when I am in the accursed city of Paris.'[1]   The only recommendation of the accursed city was that a solitude was attainable in it, as in other crowded spots, which enabled him to work better there than in the small and exacting throng of country - houses.   ' I fear Fontainebleau, Villars, and Sully, both for my health and for Henry IV. ; I should do no work, I should over-eat, and I should lose in pleasures and in complaisance to others an amount of precious time that I ought to be using for a necessary and creditable task.'[2]

Yet there was even at this period much of that marvellous hurrying to and fro in France and out ot it, which continued to mark the longer portion of Voltaire's life, and fills it with such a busy air of turmoil and confusion, explaining many things, when we think of the stability of life and permanence ol outward place of the next bright spirit that shone upon Europe.   Goethe never saw London, Paris, nor Vienna, and made no journey save the famous visit to

[1] *Œuvres*, lxii. pp. 86 and 89.   [2] *Ib*. lxii. p. 107.

Italy, and the march at Valmy. Voltaire moved
hither and thither over the face of Europe like the
wind, and it is not until he has passed through half
of his life that we can begin to think of his home.
Every association that belongs to his name recalls
tumult and haste and shrill contention with men
and circumstance. We have, however, to remember
that these constant movements were the price which
Voltaire paid for the vigour and freedom of his speech,
in days when the party of superstition possessed the
ear of the temporal power, and resorted without
sparing to the most violent means of obliterating
every hardy word and crushing every independent
writer. The greater number of Voltaire's ceaseless
changes of place were flights from injustice, and the
recollection of this may well soothe the disturbance
of spirit of the most fastidious zealot for calm and
orderly living. They were for the most part retreats
before packs of wolves.

In 1722 the elder Arouet died, to the last relent-
lessly set against a son, not any less stubborn than
himself, and unfortunately a great deal more poetical.
About the same time the name of Arouet falls away,
and the poet is known henceforth by that ever famous
symbol for so much, Voltaire ; a name for which
various explanations, none of them satisfactory, have
been offered, the latest and perhaps the least improbable resolving it into a fanciful anagram.[1]

Industrious as he was, and eager as he was for

---

[1] A. R. O. V. E. T., L(e). I(eune).

rural delights and laborious solitude, Voltaire was
still pre-eminently social.   His letters disclose in him,
who really possessed all arts, the art of one who knew
how to be graciously respectful to the social superiors
who took him for a companion, without forgetting
what was due to his own respect for himself.   We
are all princes or poets, he exclaimed jubilantly on
the occasion of one of those nights and suppers of the
gods.   Such gay-hearted freedom was not always well
taken, and in time Voltaire's eyes were opened to
the terms on which he really stood.   *Who is the
young man who talks so loud ?*' called out some Chevalier
Rohan, at one of these sprightly gatherings at the
house of the Duke of Sully.[1]   *My lord,*' the young
man replied promptly, *he is one who does not carry
about a great name, but wins respect for the name he has.*'
A few days afterwards the high-spirited patrician
magnanimously took an opportunity of having a
caning inflicted by the hands of his lackeys on the
poet who had thrown away this lesson upon him.
Voltaire, who had at all events that substitute for true
physical courage which springs up in an intensely irrit-
able and susceptive temperament, forthwith applied
himself to practise with the small-sword.   He did his
best to sting his enemy to fight, but the chevalier
either feared the swordsman, or else despised an
antagonist of the middle class ; and by the influence
of the Rohan family the poet once more found him-

[1] Chevalier appears to have been a title given by courtesy to
the cadets of certain great families.

self in the Bastille, then the house of correction at the disposal and for the use of the nobles, the court, and the clergy. Here for six months Voltaire, then only representing a very humble and unknown quantity in men's minds, chafed and fretted. The pacific Fleury, as is the wont of the pacific when in power, cared less to punish the wrong-doer than to avoid disturbance, knowing that disturbance was most effectually avoided by not meddling with the person most able to resent. The multitude, however, when the day of reckoning came, remembered all these things, and the first act of their passion was to raze to the ground the fortress into which nearly every distinguished champion of the freedom of human intelligence among them had at one time or another been tyrannically thrown.

On his release Voltaire was ordered to leave Paris. A clandestine visit to the city showed him that there was no hope of redress from authority, which was in the hands of men whose pride of rank prevented them from so much as even perceiving, much more from repairing, such grievance as a mere bourgeois could have : as if, to borrow Condorcet's bitter phrase, a descendant of the conquering Franks, like De Rohan, could have lost the ancient right of life and death over a descendant of the Gauls.[1] And this was no ironic taunt ; for while Voltaire was in the Bastille, that astounding book of the Count of Boulainvilliers was in the press, in which it was shown that the feudal

[1] *Œuvres,* iv. 18.

system is the master-work of the human mind, and
that the advance of the royal authority and the increase of the liberties of the people were equally unjust
usurpations of the rights of the conquering Franks.[1]

Voltaire was no patient victim of the practice which
corresponded to this trim historic theory. In a tumult
of just indignation he quitted France, and sought
refuge with that stout and free people, who had by
the execution of one king, the deposition of another,
and the definite subjugation of the hierarchy, won a
full liberty of thought and speech and person. A
modern historian has drawn up a list of the men of
mark who made the same invigorating pilgrimage.
'During the two generations which elapsed between
the death of Lewis XIV. and the outbreak of the
Revolution, there was hardly a Frenchman of eminence
who did not either visit England or learn English ;
while many of them did both.'[2] Among those who
actually came to England and mixed in its society
besides Voltaire, were Buffon, Brissot, Helvétius,
Gournay, Jussieu, Lafayette, Montesquieu, Maupertuis, Morellet, Mirabeau, Roland and Madame Roland,
Rousseau. We who live after Wordsworth, Shelley,
Byron, Scott, have begun to forget the brilliant group
of the Queen Anne men. They belong to a self-complacent time, and we to a time of doubt and unsatisfied
aspiration, and the two spirits are unsympathetic.
Yet they were assuredly a band, from Newton and

[1] *Histoire de l'ancien Gouvernement de la France* (1727).
[2] Buckle's *Hist. of Civilisation*, i. 657-664.

Locke down to Pope, of whom, taking them for all
the qualities which they united, in science, correct
judgment, love of letters, and taste, England has as
good reason to be proud as of any set of contemporary
writers in her history.

— Up to this moment Voltaire had been a poet, and
his mind had not moved beyond the region of poetic
creation. He had beaten every one once and for all
on the ground of light and graceful lyric verse, 'a
kind of poetry,' says a French critic whose word in
such a matter we can hardly refuse to take, 'in which
Voltaire is at once with us the only master and the
only writer supportable, for he is the only one whom
we can read.'[1] He had produced three tragedies.
His epic was completed, though undergoing ceaseless
labour of the file. Two lines in his first play had
served to mark him for no friend to the hierophants:

> Nos prêtres ne sont point ce qu'un vain peuple pense ;
> Notre crédulité fait toute leur science.[2]

And the words of Araspe in the same play had
breathed the full spirit of the future liberator:

> Ne nous fions qu'à nous ; voyons tout par nos yeux :
> Ce sont là nos trépieds, nos oracles, nos dieux.[3]

Such expressions, however, were no more than the
vague and casual word of the *esprit fort*, the friend of
Chaulieu, and the rhymer of a dissolute circle, where
religion only became tinged with doubt, because

---

[1] Sainte-Beuve, *Causeries*, v. 111.   [2] *Œdipe*, iv. sc. 1.
[3] *Ib.* ii. v.

conduct had already become penetrated with licence. More important than such stray words was the Epistle to Uranie (1722), that truly masculine and terse protest against the popular creed, its mean and fatuous and contradictory idea of an omnipotent God, who gave us guilty hearts so as to have the right of punishing us, and planted in us a love of pleasure so as to torment us the more effectually by appalling ills that an eternal miracle prevents from ever ending; who drowned the fathers in the deluge and then died for the children; who exacts an account of their ignorance from a hundred peoples whom he has himself plunged helplessly into this ignorance :

> Je ne reconnais point à cette indigne image
>   Le dieu que je dois adorer ;
>   Je croirais le déshonorer
> Par une telle insulte et par un tel hommage.[1]

Though called The For and Against, the poet hardly tries to maintain any proportion between the two sides of the argument. The verses were addressed to a lady in a state of uncertainty as to belief, of whom there were probably more among Voltaire's friends of quality than he can have cared to cure or convert. Scepticism was at this time not much more than an interesting fashion.

The dilettante believer is indeed not a strong spirit, but the weakest, and the facts of life were by this time far too serious for Voltaire, for that truth

---

[1] Le Pour et le Contre, ou Epître à Uranie. *Œuvres*, xv. pp. 399, 403.

to have missed his keen-seeing eye. It is not hard
to suppose that impatient weariness of the poor life
that was lived around him, had as large a share as
resentment of an injustice, in driving him to a land
where men did not merely mouth idle words of making reason their oracle, their tripod, their god, but
where they had actually systematised the rejection of
Christianity, and had thrown themselves with grave
faith on the disciplined intelligence and its lessons.
Voltaire left a country where freedom of thinking was
only an empty watchword, the name for a dissipated
fashion. It was considered free-thinking if a man
allowed himself to regard the existence of the Five
Propositions in Jansenius's book as a thing indifferent
to the happiness of the human race.[1] He found in
England that it was a far-spreading reality, moulding
not only the theological ideas, but the literature,
manners, politics, and philosophy, of a great society.
Voltaire left France a poet, he returned to it a sage.
Before his flight, though we do not know to what
extent he may have read such history as was then
accessible, he had been actively productive only in
the sphere of the imaginative faculties, and in criticism of the form and regulation proper to be imposed
upon them. When he returned, while his poetic
power had ripened, he had tasted of the fruit of the
tree of scientific reason, and, what was not any less
important, he had become alive to the central truth
of the social destination of all art and all knowledge.

[1] Condorcet, *Vie de Voltaire.* *Œuvres,* iv. 20.

In a word, he was transformed from the penman into the captain and man-at-arms. 'The example of England,' says Condorcet, 'showed him that truth is not made to remain a secret in the hands of a few philosophers, and a limited number of men of the world, instructed, or rather indoctrinated, by the philosophers; smiling with them at the errors of which the people are the victims, but at the same time making themselves the champions of these very errors, when their rank or position gives them a real or chimerical interest in them, and quite ready to permit the proscription, or even persecution, of their teachers, if they venture to say what in secret they themselves actually think. From the moment of his return, Voltaire felt himself called to destroy the prejudices of every kind, of which his country was the slave.'[1]

It is not difficult to perceive the sorts of fact which would most strike the exile's attention, though it would be rash to suppose that things struck him in exact proportion to their real weight and the depth of their importance, or that he detected the connection subsisting among them at their roots. Perhaps the first circumstance to press its unfamiliarity upon him was the social and political consequence of the men of letters in England, and the recognition given to the power of the pen. The patronage of men of genius in the reign of Anne and part of the reign of the first George had been profuse and splendid. The

[1] Condorcet, *Vie de Voltaire. Œuvres*, iv. 20.

poet who had been thrown into prison for resenting a
whipping from a nobleman's lackeys, found himself in
a land where Newton and Locke were rewarded with
lucrative posts in the administration of the country,
where Prior and Gay acted in important embassies,
and where Addison was a Secretary of State. The
author of Œdipe and the Henriade had to hang
ignobly about in the crowd at Versailles at the
marriage of Lewis xv. to gain a paltry pittance from
the queen's privy purse,[1] while in England Hughes
and Rowe and Ambrose Philips and Congreve were
all enjoying amply endowed sinecures. The familiar
intercourse between the ministers and the brilliant
literary group of that age has been often painted.
At the time of Voltaire's exile it had just come to an
end with the accession to supreme power of Walpole,
who neither knew anything nor cared anything about
the literature of his own time. But the usage was
still new, and the men who had profited and given
profit by it were alive, and were the central figures
in the circles among which Voltaire was introduced
by Bolingbroke. Newton died in 1727, and Voltaire
saw his death mourned as a public calamity, and surrounded with a pomp and circumstance in the eye of
the country that could not have been surpassed if he
had been, not a geometer, but a king who was the
benefactor of his people.[2] The author of Gulliver's

[1] Correspondence, 1725. Œuvres, lxii. pp. 140-49.
[2] Lettres sur les Anglais, xv. Œuvres, xxxv. p. 114. Cf.
also Letter xxiv. (pp. 197-202).

Travels was still a dignitary in the state church, and there was still a large association of outward power and dignity with literary merit.

In so far as we consider literature to be one of the purely decorative arts, there can be no harm in this patronage of its most successful, that is its most pleasing, professors by the political minister; but the more closely literature approaches to being an organ of serious things, a truly spiritual power, the more danger there is likely to be in making it a path to temporal station or emolument. The practical instinct, which on some of its sides seems like a miraculously implanted substitute for scientific intelligence in English politics, has led us almost too far in preserving this important separation of the new church from the functions and rewards of the state. The misfortunes of France since the Revolution have been due to no one circumstance so markedly as to the predominance which the man of letters has acquired in that country; and this fatal predominance was first founded, though assuredly not of set design, by Voltaire.

Not less amazing than the high honour paid to intellectual eminence was the refugee from the city of the Bastille likely to find the freedom with which public events and public personages were handled by any one who could pay a printer. The licence of this time in press and theatre has only been once or twice equalled since, and it has never been surpassed. From Bolingbroke and Swift down to the author of

The Golden Rump,[1] every writer who chose to consider himself in opposition treated the minister with
a violence and ferocity, which neither irritated nor
daunted that sage head, but which would in France
have crowded the lowest dungeons of the Bastille
with victims of Fleury's anger and fright. Such
license was as natural in a country that had within
ninety years gone through a violent civil war, a
revolutionary change of government and line, and a
half-suppressed dispute of succession, as it would have
been astonishing in France, where the continuity of
outward order had never been more than superficially
ruffled, even in the most turbulent times of the factious
wars of the League and the Fronde. No new idea
of the relations between ruler and subject had ever
penetrated into France, as it had done so deeply in
the neighbouring country. No serious popular issues
had been so much as stated. As Voltaire wrote, in
the detestable times of Charles IX. and Henry III.
it was only a question whether the people should be
the slave of the Guises, while as for the last war, it
deserved only hisses and contempt; for what was De
Retz but a rebel without a purpose and a stirrer of
sedition without a name, and what was the parliament
but a body which knew neither what it meant nor
what it did not mean?[2] The apologies of Jesuit
writers for the assassination of tyrants deserve an
important place in the history of the doctrine of

[1] Lord Stanhope's *Hist. of England*, ii. 231 (ed. 1858).
[2] Lettres sur les Anglais, ix. *Œuvres*, xxxv. p. 73.

divine right; but they were theoretical essays in casuistry for the initiated few, and certainly conveyed no general principles of popular right to the many.

Protestantism, on the other hand, loosened the conception of authority and of the respect proper for authority, to a degree which has never been realised in the most anarchic movements in France, whose anarchy has ever sprung less from a disrespect for authority as such, than from a passionate and uncompromising resolve in this or that group that the authority shall be in one set of hands and not another. Voltairism has proved itself as little capable as Catholicism of inspiring any piece that may match with Milton's Areopagitica, the noblest defence that was ever made of the noblest of causes. We know not whether Voltaire ever thought much as to the history and foundation of that freedom of speech, which even in its abuse struck him as so wonderful a circumstance in a country that still preserved a stable and orderly society. He was probably content to admire the phenomenon of a liberty so marvellous, without searching very far for its antecedents. The mere spectacle of such free, vigorous, many-sided, and truly social and public activity of intellect as was visible in England at this time, was in itself enough to fix the gaze of one who was so intensely conscious of his own energy of intellect, and so bitterly rebellious against the system which fastened a gag between his lips.

If we would realise the impression of this scene of

free speech on Voltaire's ardent spirit, we need only
remember that, when in time he returned to his own
country, he had to wait long and use many arts and
suffer harassing persecution, before he could publish
what he had to say on Newton and Locke, and in
other less important respects had to suppress much
of what he had most at heart to say. 'One must
disguise at Paris,' he wrote long after his return,
'what I could not say too strongly at London;' and
he vaunts his hardihood in upholding Newton against
René Descartes, while he confesses that an unfortunate
but necessary circumspection forced him to try to
make Locke obscure.[1] Judge the light which would
come into such a mind as his, when he first saw the
discussion and propagation of truth freed from these
vile and demoralising affronts.   The very conception
of truth was a new one, as a goddess not to be
shielded behind the shades of hierophantic mystery,
but rather to be sought in the free tumult and joyous
strife of many voices, there vindicating her own
majesty and marking her own children.

Penetrating deeper, Voltaire found not only a new
idea of truth as a something rude, robust, and self-
sufficient, but also what was to him a new order of
truths, the triumphs of slow-footed induction and the
positive reason. France was the hotbed of systems
of the physical universe. The provisional and
suspensive attitude was intolerable to her impetuous
genius, and the gaps which scientific investigation

[1] Correspondence, 1732. *Œuvres*, lxii. p. 253.

was unable to fill, were straightway hidden behind an artificial screen of metaphysical phantasies. The Aristotelian system died harder in France than anywhere else, for so late as 1693, while Oxford and Cambridge and London were actually embracing the Newtonian principles, even the Cartesian system was forbidden to be taught by decrees of the Sorbonne and of the Council of the King.[1] When the Cartesian physics once got a foothold, they kept it as firmly as the system which they had found so much difficulty in displacing. It is easy to believe that Voltaire's positive intelligence would hold aloof by a certain instinct from physical explanations which were unverified and incapable of being verified, and which were imbrangled with theology and metaphysics.

We can readily conceive, again, the sensation of freshness and delight with which a mind so essentially real, and so fundamentally serious, paradoxical as this may sound in connection with the name of the greatest mocker that has ever lived, would exchange the poetised astronomy of Fontenelle, excellently constituted as Fontenelle was in a great many ways, for the sure and scientific discoveries of a Newton. Voltaire, in whatever subject, never failed to see through rhetoric, and for rhetoric as the substitute for clear reasoning he always had an aversion as deep as it was wholesome. Nobody ever loved grace and form in style more sincerely than Voltaire, but he has shown in a great many ways that nobody ever

[1] Martin's *Hist. de France*, vol xiv. 265-67.

valued grace and form more truly at their worth, compared with correctness of argument and precision and solidity of conclusion.

Descartes, Fontenelle had said, 'essaying a bold flight, insisted on placing himself at the source of all, on making himself master of the first principles of things by a certain number of clear and fundamental ideas, having thus only to descend to the phenomena of nature as necessary consequences; Newton, more timid or more modest, began his advance by resting on phenomena in order to ascend to the unknown principles, resolved to admit them, however the combination of the results might present them. The one starts from what he understands clearly to discover the cause of what he sees : the other starts from what he sees, to discover its cause, whether clear or obscure.' Caution and reserve and sound method had achieved a generalisation more vast and amazing than the boldest flight, or most resolute reasoning downwards from a clearly held conception to phenomena, could possibly have achieved. This splendid and unrivalled discovery was probably expounded to Voltaire by Dr. Samuel Clarke, with whom he tells us that he had several conferences in 1726,[1] and who was one of the ablest of the Newtonians. He had no doubt learnt the theory of vortices from the Jesuits, and clear exposition was the only thing needed to convert him to the new theory, which shines by its own light, and must, in an unbiassed intelligence with the

---

[1] Philosophie de Newton, Pt. i. c. i. *Œuvres*, xli. p. 46.

humblest scientific quality, have extinguished every
artificial explanation.   One of the truest signs of
the soundness of Voltaire's intellectual activity was
that his glad reception of the Newtonian doctrine of
attraction did not blind him to the signal service and
splendid genius of Descartes.   That loud-shouting yet
feeble-footed enthusiasm, which can only make sure of
itself by disparaging the object of a counter-enthusiasm,
had no place in an intellect so emphatically sincere
and self-penetrative.   He prefaces his account of the
system of attraction by a hearty and loyal appreciation
of the propounder of the system of vortices.[1]

The acquisition of the special theory of attraction
was in itself less important for Voltaire, than the
irresistible impulse which it would give to the innate
rationality or positivity of his own mind.   It fitted
him to encounter with proper freedom not only vortices, but that tremendous apparatus of monads,
sufficient reason, and pre-established harmony, with
which Leibnitz then overawed European philosophy.
' O Metaphysics ! ' he cried, ' we have, then, got as
far as they had in the time of the earliest Druids !'[2]

Locke's essay impelled him further in the same path
of patient and cautious interrogation of experience ;
for the same method which established gravitation
presided over the birth of the experiential psychology.
Newton instead of elaborating a system of vortices,
or another, out of his own consciousness, industriously

[1] Lettres sur les Anglais, xv.   Œuvres, xxxv. pp. 115-20.
[2] Philos. de Newton Pt. i. c. ix.   Œuvres, xli. p. 108.

and patiently waited on the phenomena. Locke, too, instead of inventing a romance of the soul, to use Voltaire's phrase, sagaciously set himself to watch the phenomena of thought, and 'reduced metaphysics to being the experimental physics of the soul.'[1] Malebranche, then the reigning philosopher in France, 'astonished the reason of those whom he delighted by his style. People trusted him in what they did not understand, because he began by being right in what they did understand; he seduced people by being delightful, as Descartes seduced them by being daring, while Locke was nothing more than sage.'[2] 'After all,' Voltaire once wrote, 'we must admit that anybody who has read Locke, or rather who is his own Locke, must find the Platos mere fine talkers, and nothing more. In point of philosophy, a chapter of Locke or Clarke is, compared with the babble of antiquity, what Newton's optics are compared with those of Descartes.'[3] It is curious to observe that De Maistre, who thought more meanly of Plato than Voltaire did, and hardly less meanly than he thought of Voltaire himself, cried out that in the study of philosophy contempt for Locke is the beginning of knowledge.[4] Voltaire, on the other hand, is enchanted to hear that his niece reads the great English philosopher, like a good father who sheds tears of joy that

---

[1] D'Alembert.
[2] Dictionnaire Philosophique, s.v. Locke. *Œuvres*, lvi. p. 447
[3] Corr. 1736. *Œuvres*, lxiii. p. 29.
[4] *Soirées de St. Pétersbourg, 6ième Fentretien*, i. 403.

his children are turning out well.[1] Augustus published
an edict *de coercendo intra fines imperio*, and like him,
Locke has fixed the empire of knowledge in order to
strengthen it.[2] Locke, he says elsewhere, traced the
development of the human reason, as a good anatomist
explains the machinery of the human body : instead
of defining all at once what we do not understand, he
examines by degrees what we want to understand :
he sometimes has the courage to speak positively, but
sometimes also he has the courage to doubt.[3] This
is a perfectly appreciative account. Locke perceived
the hopelessness of defining things as they are in
themselves, and the necessity before all else of understanding the reach of the human intelligence ; the
impossibility of attaining knowledge absolute and
transcendent ; and the limitations of our thinking
and knowing faculties within the bounds of an experience that must always be relative. The doubt
which Voltaire praised in Locke had nothing to do
with that shivering mood which receives overmuch
poetic praise in our day, as the honest doubt that has
more faith than half your creeds. There was no
question of the sentimental juvenilities of children
crying for light. It was by no means religious doubt,
but philosophic ; and it affected only the possibilities
of ontological knowledge, leaving the grounds of faith
on the one hand, and practical conduct on the other,

[1] Corr. 1737 ; lxiii. p. 154.
[2] *Ib.* p. 248.   Cf. also lxii. p. 276.
[3] Lettres sur les Anglais, xiv.   *Œuvres*, xxxv. pp. 102-5.

exactly where they were. His intense feeling for
actualities would draw Voltaire irresistibly to the
writer who, in his judgment, closed the gates of the
dreamland of metaphysics, and banished the vaulting
ambition of à priori certainties, which led nowhere
and assured nothing. Voltaire's keen practical instinct
may well have revealed to him that men were most
likely to attribute to the great social problem of the
improvement of mankind its right supremacy, when
they had ceased to concentrate intellectual effort on
the insoluble; and Locke went a long way towards
showing how insoluble those questions were, on which,
as it chanced, the most strenuous efforts of the intellect
of Europe since the decline of theology had been
concentrated.

That he should have acquired more scientific views
either upon the origin of ideas, or the question whether
the soul always thinks, or upon the reason why an
apple falls to the ground, or why the planets remain
in their orbits, was on the whole very much less
important for Voltaire, than a profound and very
vital sentiment which was raised to supreme prominence in his mind, by the spectacle of these vast
continents of knowledge newly discovered by the
adventurous yet sure explorers of English thought.
This sentiment was a noble faith, none the less firm
because it was so passionate, in the ability of the
relative and practical understanding to reach truth;
a deep-rooted reverence for it, as a majestic power
bearing munificent and unnumbered gifts to mankind.

Hence the vivacity of the annotations which about
this time (1728) Voltaire affixed to Pascal's famous
Thoughts, and which were regarded at that time as
the audacious carpings of a shallow poet against a
profound philosopher. They were in truth the protest of a lively common sense against a strained,
morbid, and often sophistical, misrepresentation of
human nature and human circumstance. Voltaire
shot a penetrative ray through the clouds of doubt,
out of which Pascal had made an apology for mysticism. Even if there were no direct allusions to
Locke, as there are, we should know from whom the
writer had learnt the art of insisting on the relativity
of propositions, reducing them to definable terms,[1]
and being very careful against those slippery unob-
served transitions from metaphor to reality, and from
a term used in its common sense to the same term in
a transcendental sense, by which Pascal brought the
seeming contradictions of life, and its supposed petti-
ness, into a light as oppressively glaring as it was
artificial. 'These pretended oppositions that you call
contradictions are necessary ingredients in the composition of man, who is, like the rest of nature, what
he is bound to be.'[2] And where is the wise man
who would be full of despair because he cannot find
out the exact constitution of his thought, because
he only knows a few attributes of matter, because
God has not disclosed to him all his secrets? He
might as well despair because he has not got four feet

[1] *Œuvres*, vol. xliii. p. 77.   [2] *Ib.* p. 20.

and two wings.[1] This sage strain was the restoration
to men of their self-respect, the revival of that intelligence which Pascal had so humiliated and thrust
under foot. It was what he had seen in England of
the positive feats which reason had achieved, that
filled Voltaire with exultation in its power, and confidence in the prospects of the race which possessed
such an instrument. 'What strange rage possesses
some people, to insist on our all being miserable!
They are like a quack, who would fain have us
believe we are ill, in order to sell us his pills. Keep
thy drugs, my friend, and leave me my health.'[2]

From this there flowed that other vehement
current in his soul, of energetic hatred toward the
black clouds of prejudice, of mean self-love, of sinister
preference of class or order, of indolence, obstinacy,
wanton fancy, and all the other unhappy leanings of
human nature, and vexed and fatal conjunctures of
circumstance, which interpose between humanity and
the beneficent sunbeams of its own intelligence, that
central light of the universe. Hence, again, by a
sufficiently visible chain of thought, his marked dis-
esteem for far-sounding names of brutal conquerors,
and his cold regard for those outward and material
circumstances in the state of nations, which strike the
sense, but do not touch the inward reason. 'Not
long ago,' he writes once, 'a distinguished company
were discussing the trite and frivolous question, who
was the greatest man, Cæsar, Alexander, Tamerlane,

[1] *Œuvres*, vol. xliii. p. 26.   [2] Corr. 1737. *Œuvres*, lxiii. p. 248.

or Cromwell. Somebody answered that it was undoubtedly Isaac Newton. This person was right; for
if true greatness consists in having received from
heaven a powerful understanding and in using it to
enlighten oneself and all others, then such an one as
Newton, who is hardly to be met with once in ten
centuries, is in truth the great man. . . . It is to
him who masters our minds by the force of truth, not
to those who enslave men by violence; it is to him
who understands the universe, not to those who disfigure it, that we owe our reverence.'[1] This may
seem trite to us, as the question which suggested it
seemed to Voltaire, but we need only reflect, first,
how new this was, even as an idea, in the France
which Voltaire had quitted, and, second, how in spite
of the nominal acceptance of the idea, in the England
of our own time there is, with an immense majority
not only of the general vulgar but of the special
vulgar who presume to teach in press and pulpit, no
name of slight at once so disdainful and so sure of
transfixing as the name of thinker.

The discovery of the New World did not fire the
imagination and stir the thought of Europe more
intensely, than the vision of these new worlds of
knowledge kindled the ardour of the receptive spirit
which had just come into contact with them. But
besides the speculative aspects of what he saw in
England, Voltaire was deeply penetrated by the social
differences between a country that had been effec-

[1] Lettres sur les Anglais, xiii. *Œuvres*, xxxv. p. 95.

tively, if only partially, transformed from feudalism, and his own, where feudalism had only been transformed into a system more repressive than itself, and more unfit to conduct a nation to the free and industrious developments of new civilisation. It is a remarkable thing that though Voltaire's habitual companions or patrons had belonged to the privileged class, he had been sufficiently struck by the evils incident to the privileged system to notice the absence of such evils in England, and to make a clear attempt, though an insufficient one, to understand the secret of the English immunity from them. One of the worst curses of France was the taille or capitation-tax, and the way in which it was levied and assessed. In England, Voltaire noticed, the peasant has not his feet bruised in wooden shoes, he eats white bread, is decently clad, is not terrified to increase the number of his stock, or to roof his dwelling with tiles, lest his tax should be raised next year. Again, he placed his finger on one of the circumstances that did most to spoil the growth of a compact and well-knit society in France, when he pointed to the large number of farmers in England with five or six hundred pounds sterling a year, who do not think it beneath them to cultivate the earth which has made them rich, and on which they live in active freedom.[1] The profoundest modern investigator of the conditions of French society in the eighteenth century has indicated the eagerness of every man who got a little

[1] Lettres, etc. x.   Œuvres, xxxv. p. 81.

capital to quit the country and buy a place in a town, as doing more harm to the progress of the agriculture and commerce of France than even the taille itself and the trade corporations.[1]

Voltaire perceived the astonishing fact that in this country a man because he is a noble or a priest was not exempt from paying certain taxes, and that the Commons who regulated the taxes, though second to the Lords in rank, were above them in legislative influence.[2] His acute sight also revealed to him the importance of the mixture of ranks and classes in common pursuits, and he records with admiration instances of the younger sons of peers of the realm following trade. 'Whoever arrives in Paris from the depths of a remote province with money to spend and a name in *ac* or *ille*, can talk about 'a man like me, a man of my quality,'[3] and hold a merchant in sovereign contempt. The merchant again so constantly hears his business spoken of with disdain that he is fool enough to blush for it; yet I am not sure which is the more useful to a state, a thickly-bepowdered lord who knows exactly what time the king rises and what time he goes to bed, and gives himself mighty airs of greatness while he plays the part of a slave in a minister's ante-room; or the merchant who enriches his country, gives orders

---

[1] De Tocqueville's *Ancien Régime*, liv. ii. c. 9, p. 137 (ed. 1866).   [2] *Œuvres*, xxxv. p. 80.

[3] The reader of *Zadig* will remember the '*homme comme moi*,' and his ill luck at Babylon. *Œuvres*, lix. pp. 153-59.

from his counting-house at Surat or Cairo, and con-
tributes to the happiness of the globe.'[1] It is easy
to conceive the fury which these contrasts drawn
from English observation would excite among the
personages in France who happened to get the worst
side in them, and there was assuredly nothing surprising in the decree of the Parliament of Paris
(1734), which condemned the Letters on the English
to be publicly burnt, as scandalous and contrary
alike to good manners and the respect due to princi-
palities and powers.

The English reader of the Letters is naturally
struck by the absence of any adequate account of our
political liberties and free constitutional forms. There
is a good chapter on Bacon, one on inoculation, and
several on the Quakers, but on the civil constitution
hardly a word of large appreciativeness. Not only
this, but there is no sign that Voltaire either set any
due or special value on the popular forms of the
Hanoverian time, or clearly understood that the
liberty, which was so amazing and so precious to him
in the region of speculative and literary activity, was
the direct fruit of that general spirit of freedom,
which is naturally engendered in a people accustomed
to take an active part in the conduct of its own affairs.
Liberty in spirituals was adorable to him, but for
liberty in temporals he never seems to have had more
than a very distant and verbal kind of respect; just
because, with all his unmatched keenness of sight, he

---

[1] Lettres sur les Anglais, xi. Œuvres, xxxv. p. 85.

failed to discover that the English sturdiness in the
matter of civil rights was the very root and cause,
not only of that material prosperity which struck him
so much, and of the slightness and movableness of
the line which divided the aristocracy from the commercial classes, but also of the fact that a Newton
and a Locke were inwardly emboldened to give free
play to their intelligence without fear of being
punished for their conclusions, and of the only less
important fact that whatever conclusions speculative
genius might establish would be given to the world
without interposition from any court or university or
official tribunal. Voltaire undoubtedly admired the
English for their parliament, because the material
and superficial advantages that delighted him were
evidently due to the system, which happened to be
parliamentary. What we miss is any consciousness
that these advantages would not have been what they
were, if they had been conferred by an absolute sovereign ; any recognition that political activity throughout a nation works in a thousand indirect but most
potent ways, and is not more to be prized for this,
than for its direct and most palpable consequences.
In one place, indeed, he mentions that the honour
paid to men of letters is due to the form of government, but his language betrays a wholly inadequate
and incorrect notion of the true operation of the form
of government.   'There are in London,' he says,
'about eight hundred people with the right of speaking in public, and maintaining the interests of the

nation. Some five or six thousand pretend to the same honour in their turn. All the rest set themselves up to judge these, and everybody can print what he thinks. So all the nation is bound to instruct itself. All talk is about the governments of Athens and Rome, and it becomes necessary to read the authors who have discussed them. That naturally leads to love of polite learning.'[1] This is to confound a very trivial accident of popular governments with their essence. If culture thrives under them—a very doubtful position—it is not because voters wish to understand the historical allusions of candidates, but because the general stir and life of public activity tends to commove the whole system. Political freedom does not produce men of genius, but its atmosphere is more favourable than any other to their making the best of their genius in the service of mankind.

Voltaire, in this as in too much besides, was content with a keen and rapid glance at the surface. The reader may remember his story of meeting a boatman one day on the Thames, who seeing that he was a Frenchman, with a too characteristic kind of courtesy, took the opportunity of bawling out, with the added emphasis of a round oath, that he would rather be a boatman on the Thames than an archbishop in France. The next day Voltaire saw his man in prison with irons on and praying an alms from the passers-by, and so asked him whether he

[1] Lett. Ang. xxi. ; xxxv. pp. 172, etc.

still thought as scurvily of an archbishop in France. 'Ah, sir,' cried the man, 'what an abominable government! I have been carried off by force to go and serve in one of the king's ships in Norway. They take me from my wife and my children, and lay me up in prison with irons on my legs until the time for going on board, for fear I should run away.' A countryman of Voltaire's confessed that he felt a splenetic joy that a people who were constantly taunting the French with their servitude, were in sooth just as much slaves themselves; but for my own part, says Voltaire, I felt a humaner sentiment, I was afflicted at there being no liberty on the earth.[1]

This is well enough as a comment on the abomination of impressment; yet we feel that there is behind it, and not here only but generally in Voltaire, a sort of confusion between two very distinct conceptions, that both in his day and ever since have been equally designated by the common name of civil liberty. The first of these ideas is a mere privative, undoubtedly of sovereign importance, but still a privative, and implies absence, more or less complete, of arbitrary control from without, of interference with individual action by authority, of any pretension on the part of any organised body to hinder any member of the society from doing or abstaining from doing what may seem right in his own eyes, provided he pays a corresponding respect to the freedom of his fellows. Freedom in this sense Voltaire fully understood, and

[1] Lettres sur les Anglais, i. ; xxxv. p. 31.

valued as profoundly as it deserves to be valued.
Political liberty, however, has not only a meaning of
abstention, but a meaning of participation. If in one
sense it is a sheer negative, and a doctrine of rights,
in another sense it is thoroughly positive, and a gospel
of duties. The liberty which has really made England
what it so delighted and stimulated and inflamed Voltaire to find her, has been quite as much of the second
kind as of the first; that liberty which consists in a
national habit of independent and watchful interest in
the transaction of the national affairs by the persons
most concerned in them; in a general consciousness
of the duty of having some opinion on the business of
the state; in a recognition on the part of the government that the balance of this opinion is necessary as a
sanction to any policy, to which the effective force of
the state is applied. It is true that this public participation in public concerns has sometimes been very
dark and blind, as it has often been in the highest
degree enlightened, but for good or for evil it has
been the root of the matter.

The great Frenchmen, who have been most char-
acteristically French, while valuing all and envying
many of the best products of our liberty, may be said
generally to have failed entirely to detect that the
salt of English character, in days when it had more
robustness than we can see just now, sprung from the
double circumstance of every man being at liberty
to have, and being inclined to take the trouble to
have, an opinion about the method and doings of his

government; and of so many men being called upon in high capacity or low, in an important function or an obscure one, to take an independent and free share in controlling or initiating the doings of their government. Take Montesquieu, for example. He came to England just when Voltaire quitted it, and studied carefully those political facts which his countryman had so neglected. Yet he saw no deeper into the spirit of our institutions than to fix on the constitutional balance of powers as the great secret of our freedom and order. And Montesquieu, in spite of this, was wiser than most of his contemporaries, for he at least saw the worth of constitutional freedom, if he failed to see other ingredients of still more importance. French statesmen and publicists have been systematically blind to the great truth that there is no royal road to national well-being, and that nations will deliberately put away happiness from themselves, unless such happiness comes to them in a given way. The Physiocrats, who were with all their shortcomings the most nearly scientific social thinkers France possessed, could rise to no higher conception of a national life than the supreme authority of a wise and benevolent monarch, giving good gifts to his subjects. Turgot, with all the breadth and sagacity of his genius, when five-and-forty years after our present date he came into power, austerely clung to the same disastrous idea of passing reasoned laws, in the shape of the beneficial edicts of an absolute power. Voltaire, in the same way, never rose above the simple political conception of an eastern tale, a good-tempered despot with a sage vizier.   In politics, then, he failed to carry away from England the very essence and principle of our institutions, with which it was so much more important that his countrymen should be familiarised than that they should follow inoculation.

It may at first sight be astonishing to find that, while Voltaire was impressed only in a vague and general way with the free variety of theological opinion which Protestantism had secured for England, the sect which made a sort of mark on his mind was that which conceived the idea that Christianity has after all something to do with the type and example of Christ.   We know how laughable and monstrous the Quaker scheme has appeared to people who have been steeped from their youth upwards in elaborate systems of abstruse metaphysical dogma, mystic ceremonies, hierarchic ordering, and profuse condemnation of rival creeds.   Voltaire's imagination was struck by a sect who professed to regard the religion of Christ as a simple and austere discipline of life, who repudiated ritual, and held war for the worst of anti-christian practices.   The forms and doctrines of the established church of the country he would be likely to take merely for so much of the common form of the national institutions.   He would simply regard it as the English way of narrowing the mind and consolidating the social order.   Gibbon's famous sentence was not yet written, which described all religions as equally true in the eyes of the people.

equally false in the eyes of the philosopher, and equally useful in the eyes of the magistrate. But the idea was the idea of the century, and Voltaire would justly look upon the Anglican profession as a temporarily useful and statesmanlike settlement. He praised its clergy for the superior regularity of their manners. 'That indefinable being, who is neither ecclesiastic nor secular, in a word, who is called *abbé*, is an unknown species in England; the clergy here are all prigs, and nearly all pedants. When they learn that in France young men notorious for their debauchery, and raised to preferment by the intrigues of women, pursue their amours publicly, amuse themselves by the composition of gallant verses, give everyday prolonged and luxurious suppers, and rise from them to implore the enlightenment of the holy spirit, boldly calling themselves the successors of the apostles—why, then our English thank God that they are Protestants.'[1]

If, however, in face of a young and lively French graduate, bawling theology in the schools in the morning and in the evening singing tender songs with the ladies, an Anglican divine is a very Cato, this Cato is a downright gallant before a Scotch presbyterian, who assumes a grave step and a sour mien, preaches from the nose, and gives the name of harlot of Babylon to all churches in which some of the ecclesiastics are so fortunate as to receive an income of fifty thousand livres a year. However, each man takes whatever road to heaven he pleases.

[1] Lett. Ang. vi. ; xxxv. p. 62.

If there were one religion in England, they would
have to fear its despotism; if there were only two,
they would cut one another's throats; but there are
thirty; so they live peaceably and happily together.[1]

In the Quakers Voltaire saw something quite
different from the purely political pretensions and
internecine quarrels of doctrine of the ordinary worldly
sects. It is impossible to say how much of the kind-
liness with which he speaks of them is due to real
admiration of their simple, dignified, and pacific life,
and how much to a mischievous desire to make their
praise a handle for the dispraise of overweening com-
petitors. On the whole there is a sincerity and
heartiness of interest in his long account of this sect,
which persuades one that he was moved by a genuine
sympathy with a religion that could enjoin the humane
and peaceful and spiritual precepts of Christ, while
putting away baptism, ceremonial communion, and
hierophantic orders. The nobility of the social
theories of the Society of Friends would naturally
stir Voltaire even more deeply than their abstention
from practices that were in his eyes degrading superstitions. He felt that the repugnance to lower the
majesty of their deity, by taking his name upon their
lips as solemn ratification of their words, had the
effect of elevating the dignity of man, by making his
bare word fully credible without this solemn ratification. Their refusal to comply with the deferential
usages of social intercourse, though nominally based

[1] Lett. Ang. vii. pp. 62-65.

on the sinfulness of signs of homage to any mere mortal, insinuated a consciousness of equality and self-respect in that mere mortal who was careful to make no bows and to keep his hat on in every presence. Above all, Voltaire, who was nowhere more veritably modern or better entitled to our veneration than by reason of his steadfast hatred of war, revered a sect so far removed from the brutality of the military régime as to hold peace for a first principle of the Christian faith and religious practice. The reason why we do not go to war, his Quaker says, is not that we are afraid of death, but because we are not wolves, nor tigers, nor dogs, but Christian men. 'Our God, who has bidden us love our enemies and suffer evil without complaint, assuredly has no mind that we should cross the sea to go and cut the throats of our brothers, because murderers in red clothes and hats two feet high enlist citizens, making a noise with two little sticks on an ass's skin tightly stretched. And when, after victories won, all London blazes with illuminations, the sky is aflame with rockets, and the air resounds with the din of bells, organs, cannon, we mourn in silence over the slaughter that causes all the public joy.'[1]

Voltaire, let us add, was no dilettante traveller constructing views and deducing theories of national life out of his own uninstructed consciousness. No German could have worked more diligently at the facts, and we may say here, once for all, that if it is

[1] Lett. Ang. ii. ; xxxv. p. 42.

often necessary to condemn him for superficiality, this lack of depth seldom at any time proceeds from want of painstaking. His unrivalled brilliance of expression blinds us to the extreme and conscientious industry that provided matter. The most illustrious exile that our free land has received from France in our own times, and assuredly far more of a giant in the order of imagination than Voltaire, never had intellectual curiosity enough to learn the language of the country that had given him twenty years of shelter. Voltaire, in the few months of his exile here acquired such an astonishing mastery over English as to be able to read and relish an esoteric book like Hudibras, and to compass the enormously difficult feat of rendering portions of it into good French verse.[1] He composed an essay on epic poetry in the English tongue, and he wrote one act of Brutus in English.

He read Shakespeare, and made an elaborate study of his method. He declares that Milton does as much honour to England as the great Newton, and he took especial pains not only to master and appreciate the secret of Milton's poetic power, but even to ascertain the minutest circumstances of his life.[2] He studied Dryden, 'an author who would have a glory without blemish, if he had only written the tenth part of his works.'[3] He found Addison the first

[1] *Œuvres*, xxxv. p. 185.
[2] Ess. sur la Poésie Epique. *Œuvres*, xiii. p. 445, and pp. 513-26.   [3] *Œuvres*, xxxv. p. 155.

Englishman who had written a reasonable tragedy, and Addison's character of Cato one of the finest creations of any stage.[1] Wycherley, Vanbrugh, and Congreve he esteemed more highly than most of their countrymen do now. An act of a play of Lillo's was the base of the fourth act of Mahomet. Rochester, Waller, Prior, and Pope, he read carefully and admired as heartily as they deserved. Long after he had left England behind, he places Pope and Addison on a level for variety of genius with Machiavel and Leibnitz and Fontenelle;[2] and Pope he evidently for a long while kept habitually by his elbow. Swift he placed before Rabelais, calling him Rabelais in his senses, and, as usual, giving good reasons for his preference; for Swift, he says justly, has not the gaiety of Rabelais, but he has all the finesse, the sense, the variety, the fine taste, in which the priest of Meudon was wanting.[3] In philosophy, besides Locke, there is evidence that he read something of Hobbes, and something of Berkeley, and something of Cudworth.[4] Always, however, 'harassed, wearied, ashamed of having sought so many truths and found so many chimeras, I returned to Locke; like a prodigal son returning to his father, I threw myself into the arms of that modest man, who never pretends to know what he

---

[1] *Œuvres*, xxxv. p. 159.

[2] Corr. 1736. *Œuvres*, lxiii. p. 4. *Ib.* 60.

[3] *Œuvres*, xxxv. pp. 189, 190.

[4] For Berkeley, see Corr. 1736 (*Œuv.* lxiii. pp. 130, 164, etc.), and for the other two, see Le Philosophe Ignorant (*Œuvres*, xliv. p. 69 and p. 47).

does not know, who in truth has no enormous possessions, but whose substance is well assured.'[1]

Nor did Voltaire limit himself to the study of science, philosophy, and poetry. He plunged into the field of theology, and mastered that famous deistical controversy, of which the seed had been sown in the first half of the seventeenth century by Lord Herbert of Cherbury, the correspondent of Descartes and the earliest of the English metaphysical thinkers.[2] Lord Herbert's object was to disengage from revelation both our conceptions of the one supreme power, and the sanctions of good and bad conduct. Toland, whom we know also that Voltaire read, aimed at disengaging Christianity from mystery, and discrediting the canon of the New Testament. In 1724 Collins published his Discourse on the Grounds and Reasons of the Christian Religion, of which we are told that few books ever made a greater noise than this did at its first publication. The press teemed with vindications, replies, and rejoinders to Collins's arguments during the whole of Voltaire's residence in England.[3] His position was one which no modern freethinker would dream of making a central point of attack, and which hardly any modern apologist would take the pains to reply to. He maintained that Jesus Christ and the apostles trusted to the prophecies of the Old Testament for their credentials, and then he showed,

[1] *Œuv.*, xliv. p. 47.   [2] The *De Veritate* was published in 1624.
[3] See the list from 1725 to 1728 in Leland's *View of the Deistical Writers*, i. 132-144.

or tried to show, in various ways, that these prophecies would not bear the weight which was thus laid upon them. We may be sure that Voltaire's alert curiosity would interest him profoundly in the lively polemical ferment which this notable contention of Collins's stirred up.

Woolston's discourses, written to prove that the miracles of the New Testament are as mythical and allegorical as the prophecies of the old, appeared at the same time, and had an enormous sale. Voltaire was much struck by this writer's coarse and hardy way of dealing with the miraculous legends, and the article on Miracles in the Philosophical Dictionary shows how carefully he had read Woolston's book.[1] We find references to Shaftesbury and Chubb in Voltaire's letters and elsewhere, though they are not the references of an admirer,[2] and Bolingbroke was one of the most influential and intimate of his friends. It is not too much to say that Bolingbroke was the direct progenitor of Voltaire's opinions in religion, and that nearly every one of the positive articles in Voltaire's rather moderately sized creed was held and inculcated by that brilliant and disordered genius. He did not always accept Bolingbroke's optimism, but even as late in the century as 1767 Voltaire thought it worth while to borrow his name for a volume of compendious attack on the popular religion.[3] Boling-

---

[1] Œuvres, lvii. pp. 107-114.
[2] Corr. 1736-37. Œuv. lxiii. p. 60, p. 86, and p. 112.
[3] Examen Important de Milord Bolingbrocke. Œuv. xliv. p. 89

broke's tone was peculiarly light and peculiarly well-
bred. His infidelity was strictly infidelity for the
upper classes;[1] ingenious, full of literature, and
elegantly supercilious. He made no pretence to
theological criticism in any sense that can be gravely
admitted, but looked at the claims of revelation with
the eye of a polished man of the world, and met its
arguments with those general considerations of airy
probability which go so far with men who insist on
having plausible opinions on all subjects, while they
will not take pains to work to the bottom of any.

Villemain's observation that there is not one of
Voltaire's writings that does not bear the mark of his
sojourn in England, is specially true of what he wrote
against theology. It was the English onslaught which
sowed in him the seed of the idea, and eventually
supplied him with the argumentative instruments, of
a systematic and reasoned attack upon that mass of
doctrinal superstition and social abuse, which it had
hitherto been the fashion for even the strongest spirits
in his own country to do no more than touch with a
cool sneer or a flippant insinuation, directed to the
private ear of a sympathiser. Who, born within the
last forty years, cried Burke, has read one word of
Collins, and Toland, and Chubb, and Morgan, and
that whole race who called themselves Freethinkers?
Who now reads Bolingbroke? Who ever read him
through?[2] This was very well, but hundreds of

---

[1] See Lechler's *Geschichte des Englischen Deismus*, p. 396.
[2] *Reflections. Works*, i. 419 (ed. 1842).

thousands of persons born within those last forty years had read Voltaire, and Voltaire had drawn from the armoury of these dead and unread Freethinkers the weapons which he made sharp with the mockery of his own spirit. He stood on the platform which they had constructed, to stretch forth his hand against the shrine and the image before which so many credulous generations had bowed down. It was in this most transformed shape among others that at length, late and changed, but directly of descent, the free and protesting genius of the Reformation made its decisive entry into France.

It is easy to cite proofs of the repudiation by Protestant bodies of the Protestant principle, to multiply instances of the narrow rigidity of their dogma, and the intolerance of their discipline. This method supplies an excellent answer as against Protestants who tax Catholics with the crime of persecution, or the crime of opposing intellectual independence. It cannot, however, touch the fact that Protestantism was indirectly the means of creating and dispersing an atmosphere of rationalism, in which there speedily sprang up philosophical, theological, and political influences, all of them entirely antagonistic to the old order of thought and institution. The whole intellectual temperature underwent a permanent change, that was silently mortal to the most flourishing tenets of all sorts. It is futile to ask for a precise logical chain of relations between the beginning of a movement and its end; and there is no more direct and

logical connection between the right of private judgment and an experiential doctrine of psychology, than
there is between experiential psychology and deism.
Nobody now thinks that the effect is homogeneous
with its cause, or that there is any objective resem-
blance between a blade of wheat and the moisture and
warmth which fill and expand it. All we can see is
that the proclamation of the rights of free judgment
would tend to substitute reason for authority, and
evidence for tradition, as the arbiters of opinion; and
that the political expression of this change in the civil
wars of the middle of the seventeenth century would
naturally deepen the influence of the new principle,
and produce the Lockian rationalism of the end of
that century, which almost instantaneously extended
from the region of metaphysics into the region of
theology.

The historian of every kind of opinion, and the
student of the great chiefs of intellectual movements,
habitually do violence to actual circumstances, by
imparting too systematic a connection to the various
parts of belief, and by assuming an unreal degree of
conscious logical continuity among the notions of
individual thinkers. Critics fill in the frame with a
completeness and exactitude that had no counterpart
in the man's own judgments, and they identify him
with a multitude of deductions from his premisses,
which may be fairly drawn, but which never at all
entered into his mind, and formed no part of his
character. The philosophy of the majority of men

is nothing more shaped and incorporate than a little group of potential and partially incoherent tendencies. To stiffen these into a system of definite formulas is the most deceptive, as it is the most common, of critical processes. A few persons, with an exceptional turn for philosophy, consciously embody their metaphysical principles with a certain detail in all the rest of their thinking. With most people, however, even people of superior capacity, the relation between their ground-system, such as a critic might supply them with, and their manifestations of intellectual activity, is of an extremely indirect and general kind.

Hence the untrustworthiness of those critical schemata, so attractive for their compact order, which first make Voltaire a Lockian sensationalist, and then trace his deism to his sensationalism. We have already seen that he was a deist before he came to England, just as Lord Herbert of Cherbury was a deist, who wrote before Locke was born. It was not the metaphysical revolution of Locke which led to deism, but the sort of way in which he thought about metaphysics, a way which was immediately applied to theology by other people, whether assailants or defenders of the current opinions. Locke's was 'common-sense thinking,' and the fashion spread. The air was thick with common-sense objections to Christianity, as it was with common-sense ideas as to the way in which we come to have ideas. There was no temperament to which such an atmosphere could be so congenial as Voltaire's, of whom we cannot too

often repeat, considering the vulgar reputation he has
for violence and excess, that he was in thought the
very genius of good sense, whether or no we fully
admit M. Cousin's qualification of it as superficial good
sense. It has been said that he always speaks of
Descartes, Leibnitz, and Spinoza, like a man to whom
nature has refused the metaphysical sense.[1] At any
rate he could never agree with them, and he never
tried to find truth by the roads which they had made.
It is true, however, that he shows no sign of special
fitness for metaphysics, any more than he did for
physical science. The metaphysics of Locke lay un-
developed in his mind, just as the theory of evolution
lies in so many minds at the present time. There is
a faint informal reference of other theories to this
central and half-seen standard. When metaphysical
subjects came before him, he felt that he had this
for a sheet-anchor, and he did not greatly care to
keep proving it again and again by continued criticism
or examination. The upshot of his acquaintance with
Locke was a systematic adherence to common-sense
modes of thinking; and he always betrayed the faults
and shortcomings to which such modes inevitably lead,
when they are brought, to the exclusion of comple-
mentary ideas, to the practical subjects that comprehend more than prudence, self-interest, and sobriety.
The subject that does beyond any other comprehend

[1] *Encyclopédie Nouvelle* de Jean Reynaud et Pierre Leroux,
s.v. Voltaire, p. 736. De Maistre audaciously denies that
Voltaire ever did more than dip into Locke. *Soirées*, vi.

more than these elements is religion, and the substantial vices of Voltaire's objections to religion
first arose from his familiarity with the English
form of deism, and his instinctive feeling for its
method.

The deism of Leibnitz was a positive belief, and
made the existence of a supreme power an actual and
living object of conviction. The mark of this belief
has remained on German speculation throughout its
course, down to our own day. English deism, on the
contrary, was only a particular way of repudiating
Christianity. There was as little of God in it as
could well be. Its theory was that God had given
each man the light of reason in his own breast ; that
by this reason every scheme of belief must be tried,
and accepted or rejected ; and that the Christian
scheme being so tried was in various ways found
wanting. The formula of some book of the eighteenth
century, that God created nature and nature created
the world, must be allowed to have reduced theistic
conception to something like the shadow of smoke.
The English eighteenth-century formula was, theistic-
ally, nearly as void. The Being who set the reason
of each individual on a kind of judicial bench
within the forum of his own conscience, and left
him and it together to settle belief and conduct
between them, was a tolerably remote and unreal
sort of personage. His spiritual force, according to
such a doctrine, became very much as if it had no
existence.

It was not to be expected that a sovereign dwelling in such amazingly remote lands as this would continue long with undisputed authority, when all the negative forces of the time had reached their full momentum. In England the reaction against this strange absentee government of the universe took the form which might have been anticipated from the deep hold that Protestantism had won, and the spirituality which had been engendered by Protestant reference to the relations between the individual conscience and the mystic operations of faith. Deism became a reality with a God in it in the great Evangelical revival, terrible and inevitable, which has so deeply coloured religious feeling and warped intellectual growth in England ever since. In France, thought took a very different and much simpler turn. Or perhaps it would be more correct to say that it took no turn at all, but carried the godless deism of the English school to its fair conclusion, and dismissed a deity who only reigned and did not govern. The whole movement had a single origin. There is not one of the argu ments of the French philosophers in the eighteenth century, says a very competent authority, which cannot be found in the English school of the beginning of the century.[1] Voltaire, who carried the English way of thinking about the supernatural power into

---

[1] Villemain's *Cours de Lit. Française*, i. p. 111. See also De Maistre, *Soirées de St. Pétersbourg*, vi. p. 424. On the other hand, see Lanfrey's *L'Eglise et les Philosophes du 18ième Siècle*, pp. 99, 108, etc.

France, lived to see a band of trenchant and energetic disciples develop principles which he had planted, into a system of dogmatic atheism.   The time came when he was spoken of contemptuously as retrograde and superstitious: '*Voltaire est bigot, il est déiste.*'

CHAPTER III.

LITERATURE.

ON the whole, the critic's task is perhaps less to classify a type of character as good or bad, as worthy of so much praise or so much censure, than to mark the material out of which a man has his life to make, and the kind of use and form to which he puts his material. To begin with, the bald division of men into sheep and goats is in one sense so easy as not to be worth performing, and in another sense it is so hard as only to be possible for some being with supernatural insight. And even were the qualities employed in the task of a rarer kind than they are, the utility of the performance is always extremely slight, compared with that other kind of criticism which dwells less on the final balance of good or evil, than on the first innate conditions of temperament, the fixed limitations of opportunity, and the complex interplay of the two with that character, which is first their creature and then their master. It is less the concern of criticism to pronounce its man absolutely rich or absolutely poor, than to count up his talents and the usury of his own which he added to them. Assuredly there

ought to be little condonation of the foibles, and
none at all of the moral obliquities, of the dead,
because this would mean the demoralisation of the
living. But it is seriously to overrate the power of
bald words and written opinion, to suppose that a
critic's censure of conduct which a thousand other
agents, from the child's hornbook up to the obvious
and pressing dictates of social convenience, are daily
and hourly prescribing, can be other than a work of
supererogation, which fixes the mind on platitudes,
instead of leading it on in search of special and dis-
tinctive traits.

It would be easy to pour overflowing vials of condemnation on many sides of Voltaire's character and
career. No man possessed of so much good sense ever
fell so constantly into the kinds of error against which
good sense particularly warns men. There is no more
wearisome or pitiful leaf in the biographies of the
great, than the tale of Voltaire's quarrels with ignoble
creatures; with a wrecked soul, like J. B. Rousseau
(whom the reader will not confound with Jean
Jacques); with a thievish bookseller, like Jore; with
a calumnious journalist, like Desfontaines; with a
rapacious knave like Hirschel; and all the other
tormentors in the Voltairean history, whose names
recall vulgar, dishonest, and indignant pertinacity on
the one side, and wasteful, undignified fury on the
other. That lesson in the art of life which concerns
a man's dealings with those who have shown patent
moral inferiority, was never mastered by Voltaire.

Instead of the silence, composure, and austere oblivion, which it is of the essence of strength to oppose
to unworthy natures, he habitually confronted the
dusty creeping things that beset his march, as if they
stood valiant and erect; and the more unworthy they
were, the more vehement and strenuous and shrill
was his contention with them. The ignominy of such
strife is clear. One thing only may perhaps be said.
His intense susceptibility to vulgar calumny flowed
from the same quality in his nature which made
unbearable to him the presence of superstition and
injustice, those mightier calumnies on humanity. The
irritated protests against the small foes of his person
were as the dregs of potent wine, and were the lower
part of that passionate sensibility which made him
the assailant of the giant oppressors of the human
mind. This reflection does not make any less tedious
to us the damnable iteration of petty quarrel and
fretting complaint which fills such a space in his
correspondence and in his biographies, nor does it
lessen our regret at the havoc which this fatal defect
of his qualities made with his contentedness. We
think of his consolation to a person as susceptible as
himself: 'There have always been Frérons in literature; but they say there must be caterpillars for
nightingales to eat, that they may sing the better:'
and we wish that our nightingale had devoured its
portion with something less of tumult. But it may
do something to prevent us from giving a prominence,
that is both unfair and extremely misleading, to mere

shadow, as if that had been the whole substance. Alas, why after all should men, from Moses downwards, be so cheerfully ready to contemplate the hinder parts of their divinities?

The period of twenty years between Voltaire's departure from England and his departure for Berlin, although often pronounced the happiest time of his life, is very thickly set with these humiliating incidents. To us, however, they are dead, because though vivid enough to Voltaire—and it is strange how constantly it happens that the minor circumstance of life is more real and ever-present to a man than his essential and abiding work in it—they were but transitory and accidental. Just as it does little good to the understanding to spend much time over tenth-rate literature, so it is little edifying to the character to rake among the private obscurities of even first-rate men, and it is surely a good rule to keep ourselves as much as we can in contact with what is great.

The chief personal fact of this time was the connection which Voltaire formed with the Marquise du Châtelet, and which lasted from 1733 to 1749. She was to him that important and peculiar influence which, in one shape or another, some woman seems to have been to nearly every foremost man. In Voltaire's case this influence was not the rich and tender inspiration with which women have so many a time sweetened the lives and glorified the thought of illustrious workers, nor was he bound to her by those bonds of passion which have often the effect of exalting the strength and widening the range of the whole of the nature that is susceptive of passion. Their inner relations hardly depended on anything more extraordinary or more delicate than the sentiment of a masculine friendship. Voltaire found in the divine Emily a strong and active head, a keen and generous admiration for his own genius, and an eagerness to surround him with the external conditions most favourable to that steady industry which was always a thing so near his own heart. They are two great men, one of whom wears petticoats, said Voltaire of her and of Frederick. It is impossible to tell what share vanity had in the beginning of a connection, which probably owed its long continuance more to use and habit than to any deep-rooted sentiment. Vanity was one of the most strongly marked of Voltaire's traits, and to this side of him relations with a woman of quality who adored his genius were no doubt extremely gratifying. Yet one ought to do him the justice to say that his vanity was only skin-deep. It had nothing in common with the greedy egotism which reduces the whole broad universe to a mere microcosm of pygmy self. The vanity which discloses a real flaw in character is a loud and tyrannical claim for acknowledgment of literary supremacy, and with it the mean vices of envy, jealousy, and detraction are usually in company. Voltaire's vanity was something very different from this truculent kind of self-assertion. It had a source

in his intensely sympathetic quality, and was a gay
and eager asking of assurance from others that his
work gave them pleasure. Let us be very careful to
remember that it never stood in the way of self-
knowledge,—the great test of the difference between
the vanity that is harmless, and the vanity that is
fatuous and destructive.

It has been rather the fashion to laugh at the
Marquise du Châtelet, for no better reasons perhaps
than that she, being a woman, studied Newton, and
had relations called tender with a man so little associated in common opinion with tenderness as Voltaire.
The first reason is disgraceful, and the second is perhaps childish. Everything goes to show that Madame
du Châtelet possessed a hardy originality of character,
of which society is so little likely to have an excess
that we can hardly ever be thankful enough for it.
There is probably nothing which would lead to so
rapid and marked an improvement in the world, as a
large increase of the number of women in it with the
will and the capacity to master Newton as thoroughly
as she did. And her long and sedulous affection for
a man of genius of Voltaire's exceptional quality,
entitles her to the not too common praise of recognis-
ing and revering intellectual greatness as it deserves.
Her friendship for him was not the semi-servile and
feebly intelligent solicitude which superior men have
too often the wretched weakness to seek in their
female companions, but an imperial sympathy. She
was unamiable, it is true, and possessed neither the

delicacy which a more fastidious age requires in a woman, nor the sense of honour which we now demand in a man. These defects, however, were not genuinely personal, but lay in the manners of the time. It was not so with all her faults. To the weak and dependent she was overbearing, harsh, mean, and even cruel. A fatuous caprice would often destroy the domestic peace and pleasure of a week. But nothing was suffered to impede the labour of a day. The industry of the house was incessant.

It is said, and it was said first by one who lived with them for some time, and has left a graphic account of the interior of Cirey, that she made Voltaire's life a little hard to him.[1] There were many occasional storms and short sullen fits even in these high regions of science and the finer tastes. Yet such stormful scenes, with great actors as with small, are perhaps more painful in description than they were in reality; and Voltaire was less discomposed by the lively impetuosity of a companion like Madame du Châtelet, than he would have been by the orderly calm of a more precise and perfectly well-regulated person. A man follows the conditions of his temperament, and Voltaire's unresting animation and fire might make him feel a certain joy of life and freedom in the occasional contentiousness of a slightly shrewish temper. We cannot think of him as ever

[1] Madame de Grafigny. Cf. Desnoiresterres, *Voltaire au Château de Cirey*, p. 246, etc.

shrinking, ever craving for repose, as some men do as for a very necessity of existence. The health of your friend, wrote Madame du Châtelet to D'Argental in 1739, is in so deplorable a state that the only hope I have left of restoring it is in the turmoil of a journey.[1] A tolerably frequent agitation was a condition of even such health as he had, to one of Voltaire's nervous and feverish habit.

Let it be said that his restlessness never took a form which involved a sacrifice of the happiness of other people. It was never tyrannical and exigent. There are many, too many, instances of his angry impatience with persons against whom he thought he had cause of offence. There is not a single instance in which any shadow of implacableness lurked for an enemy who had repented or fallen into misfortune; and if his resentment was constantly aflame against the ignoble, it instantly expired and changed into warm-hearted pity, when the ignoble became either penitent or miserable. There are many tales of the readiness with which his anger was appeased. Any one will suffice as a type. On some occasion when Voltaire was harassed by a storm of libels, and happened to be on good terms with the police, a distributor of the libels was arrested. The father, an old man of eighty, hastened to Voltaire to pray for pardon. All Voltaire's fury instantly vanished at the first appeal; he wept with the old man, embraced him, consoled him, and straightway ran to procure

[1] Desnoiresterres, p. 257.

the liberation of the offender.[1] An eye-witness related to Grimm how he happened to be present at Ferney when Voltaire received Rousseau's Lettres de la Montagne, and read the apostrophe relating to himself. His face seemed to take fire, his eyes sparkled with fury, his whole frame trembled, and he cried in terrible tones—'The miscreant! the monster! I must have him cudgelled—yes, I will have him cudgelled in his mountains at the knees of his nurse.' 'Pray, calm yourself,' said the bystander, 'for I know that Rousseau means to pay you a visit, and will very shortly be at Ferney.' 'Ah, only let him come,' replied Voltaire. 'But how will you receive him?' 'Receive him . . . I will give him supper, put him in my own bed, and say, There is a good supper; this is the best bed in the house; do me the pleasure to accept one and the other, and to make yourself happy here.'[2] One does not understand the terrible man, without remembering always how much of the hot generosity of the child he kept in his nature to the last. When the very Jesuits were suppressed with circumstances of extreme harshness, he pitied even them, and took one of their number permanently into his household.[3]

The most important part of a man's private conduct after that which concerns his relations with

[1] Condorcet, *Vie de Voltaire*, p. 61. A graceful and dignified letter in this kind is that to Formey, May 12, 1752. *Œuv.* lxv p. 64.

[2] Grimm, *Correspondance Littéraire*, v. p. 5.

[3] *Œuv.* lxv. p. 395.

women and his family, is generally that which concerns his way of dealing with money, because money in its acquisition and its dispersion is the outward and visible sign of the absence or of the presence of so many inward and spiritual graces. As has often been said, it is the measure of some of the most important of a man's virtues, his honesty, his industry, his generosity, his self-denial, and most of the other elements in keeping the difficult balance between his care for himself and his care for other people. Voltaire perceived very early in life that to be needy was to be dependent; that the rich and poor are as hammer and anvil; that the chronicles of genius demonstrate that it is not by genius that men either make a fortune or live happy lives. He made up his mind from the beginning that the author of the French epic would not share the poverty and straitened lives of Tasso and Milton, and that he for his part would at any rate be hammer and not anvil.[1] I was so wearied, he wrote in 1752, of the humiliations that dishonour letters, that to stay my disgust I resolved to make what scoundrels call a great fortune.[2] He used to give his books away to the printers. He had a small fortune from his father; he is said to have made two thousand pounds by the English subscriptions to the Henriade; and he did not hide his talent in the ground, but resorted skilfully to all sorts of

[1] Correspondence. Also, Essai sur la Poésie Epique, c. vi. Œuvres, xiii. p. 481.
[2] Œuvres, lxv. p. 91.

speculations in stocks, army contracts, and other
authorised means of converting one livre into two
while you sleep. He lent large sums of money,
presumably at handsome interest, to the Duke of
Richelieu and others, and though the interest may
have been handsome, the trouble of procuring it was
often desperate.[1] Yet after much experience Voltaire
came to the conclusion that though he had sometimes
lost money by bankers, by the devout, by the people
of the Old Testament, who would have had many
scruples about a larded capon, who would rather die
than not be idle on the sabbath, and not be thieving
on the Sunday, yet he had lost nothing by the great
except his time.[2]

It is easy to point a sneer at a high priest of
humanity jobbing in the funds. Only let us remember that Voltaire never made any pretence of being
a high priest of humanity; that his transactions were
substantially very like those of any banker or merchant
of to-day; and that for a man who was preaching new
opinions it was extremely prudent to place himself
out of the necessity of pleasing booksellers or the pit
of the theatre on the one hand, and on the other to
supply himself with ready means of frequent flight
from the ceaseless persecutions of authority. Envious
scribes in his lifetime taunted him with avarice, and
the evil association still clings to his memory now that

---

[1] Corr. with the Abbé Moussinot, 1737, and afterwards.
Œuvres, lxiii. pp. 122, 160, 176, etc.

[2] Corr. 1752. Œuvres, lxv. p. 115.

he is dead. One can only say that good and high-minded men, who never shrank from withstanding him when in fault, men like Condorcet for example, heard such talk with disdain, and set it down to the disgraceful readiness of men to credit anything that relieves them from having to admire.[1] The people who dislike prudence in matters of money in those whose distinction is intellectual or spiritual, resemble a sentimental lover who should lose his illusions at sight of his mistress eating a hearty meal. Is their lot, then, cast in the ethereal fluid of the interstellar spaces?

At all events Voltaire had two important gifts which do not commonly belong to the avaricious; he was a generous helper alike of those who had, and those who had not, a claim upon him, and he knew how to bear serious losses with unbroken composure. Michel, the receiver-general, became bankrupt, and Voltaire lost a considerable sum of money in consequence. His fluency of invective and complaint, which was simply boundless when any obscure scribbler earned a guinea by a calumny upon him, went no farther on the occasion of this very substantial injury than a single splenetic phrase, and a harmless quatrain :

> Michel au nom de l'Eternel,
> Mit jadis le diable en déroute ;
> Mais, après cette banqueroute,
> Que le diable emporte Michel !

It has been fairly asked whether a genuine miser

[1] *Vie de Voltaire*, p. 37.

would content himself with a stanza upon the man
who had robbed him.[1] His correspondence with the
Duchess of Saxe-Gotha shows him declining to accept
the thousand louis, which she had sent as a fee for
the composition of the Annales de l'Empire.

Much has been made of the bargaining which he
carried on with Frederick, as to the terms on which
he would consent to go to Berlin. But then the
Prussian king was not one with whom it was wise
to be too nice in such affairs. He was the thriftiest
of men, and as a king is a person who lives on other
people's money, such thrift was in his case the most
princely of virtues. Haggling is not graceful, but it
need not imply avarice in either of the parties to it.
The truth is that there was in Voltaire a curious
admixture of splendid generosity with virulent tenacity
about half-pence. The famous quarrel with the
President de Brosses about the fourteen cords of fire-
wood is a worse affair. Voltaire, who leased Tourney
from him, insisted that De Brosses had made him a
present of the fourteen cords. De Brosses, no doubt
truly, declared that he had only ordered the wood to
be delivered on Voltaire's account. On this despicable
matter a long correspondence was carried on, in which
Voltaire is seen at his very worst; insolent, undignified,
low-minded, and untruthful.[2] The case happily stands
alone in his biography. As a rule, he is a steady

[1] Desnoiresterres, p. 323.
[2] Foisset's *Correspond. de Voltaire avec De Brosses*, etc.,
published in 1836.

practitioner of the Aristotelian μεγαλοπρέπεια, or virtue of magnificent expenditure.

The truly important feature of the life which Voltaire led at Cirey was its unremitting diligence. Like a Homeric goddess, the divine Emily poured a cloud round her hero. There is a sort of moral climate in a household, an impalpable, unseizable, indefinable set of influences, which predispose the inmates to industry and self-control, or else relax fibre and slacken purpose. At Cirey there was an almost monastic rule. Madame Grafigny says that though Voltaire felt himself bound by politeness to pay her a visit from time to time in her apartment, he usually avoided sitting down, apologetically protesting how frightful a thing is the quantity of time people waste in talking, and that waste of time is the most fatal kind of extravagance of which one can be guilty.[1] He seems to have usually passed the whole day at his desk, or in making physical experiments in his chamber. The only occasion on which people met was at the supper at nine in the evening. Until then the privacy of the chamber alike of the hostess, who was analysing Leibnitz or translating Newton, and of the unofficial host, who was compiling material for the Siècle de Louis XIV., or polishing and repolishing Mahomet, or investigating the circumstances of the propagation of fire, was sacredly inviolable.

The rigour of the rule did not forbid theatrical performances, when any company, even a company

[1] Quoted in Desnoiresterres, p. 239.

of marionettes, came into the neighbourhood of the desolate Champagne château. Sometimes after supper Voltaire would exhibit a magic lantern, with explanatory comments after the showman's manner, in which he would convulse his friends at the expense of his enemies.[1] But after the evening's amusement was over, the Marquise would retire to work in her chamber until the morning, and, when morning came, a couple of hours' sleep was the only division between the tasks of the night and the tasks of the day. Two splenetic women have left us a couple of spiteful pictures of Madame du Châtelet, but neither of her detractors could rise to any higher conception of intellectual effort than the fine turn of phrase, the ingenious image, the keen thrust of cruel satire, with which the polished idle of that day whiled away dreary and worthless years. The translator of Newton's Principia was not of this company, and she was wholly indifferent to the raillery, sarcasm, and hate of women whom she justly held her inferiors. It is much the fashion to admire the women of this time, because they contrive to hide behind a veil of witty words the coldness and hollowness of lives which had neither the sweetness of the old industrious domesticity of women, nor the noble largeness of some of those in whom the Revolution kindled a pure fire of patriotism in after days. Madame du Châtelet, with all her faults, was a far loftier character than the malicious gossips who laughed at her. 'Every-

[1] Desnoiresterres, p. 242.

thing that occupies society was within her power, *except slander.* She was never heard to hold up anybody to laughter. When she was informed that certain people were bent on not doing her justice, she would reply that she wished to ignore it.' This was surely better than a talent for barbing epigrams, and she led a worthier life at Cirey than in that Paris which Voltaire described so bitterly.

> Là, tous les soirs, la troupe vagabonde,
> D'un peuple oisif, appelé le beau monde,
> Va promener de réduit en réduit
> L'inquiétude et l'ennui qui la suit.
> Là sont en foule antiques mijaurées,
> Jeunes oisons et bégueules titrées,
> Disant des riens d'un ton de perroquet,
> Lorgnant des sots, et trichant au piquet.
> Blondins y sont, beaucoup plus femmes qu'elles.
> Profondément remplis de bagatelles,
> D'un air hautain, d'une bruyante voix,
> Chantant, dansant, minaudant à la fois.
> Si par hasard quelque personne honnête,
> D'un sens plus droit et d'un goût plus heureux
> Des bons écrits ayant meublé sa tête,
> Leur fait l'affront de penser à leurs yeux ;
> Tout aussitôt leur brillante cohue,
> D'étonnement et de colère émue,
> Bruyant essaim de frélons envieux,
> Pique et poursuit cette abeille charmante.[1]

It was not the fault of Madame du Châtelet that the life of Cirey was not the undisturbed type of Voltaire's existence during the fifteen years of their

[1] Epître à Mdme. la Marquise du Châtelet, sur la Calomnie. *Œuvres,* xvii. p. 85.

I

companionship. Many pages might be filled with a mere list of the movements from place to place to which Voltaire resorted, partly from reasonable fear of the grip of a jealous and watchful government, partly from eagerness to bring the hand of the government upon his enemies, and most of all from the uncontrollable restlessness of his own nature. Amsterdam, the Hague, Brussels, Berlin, the little court of Lunéville, and the great world of Paris, too frequently withdrew him from the solitary castle at Cirey, though he never failed to declare on his return, and with perfect sincerity, that he was never so happy anywhere else. If it was true that the Marquise made her poet's life a little hard to him, it is impossible to read her correspondence without perceiving that he, too, though for no lack of sensibility and good feeling, often made life extremely hard for her. Besides their moral difference, there was a marked discrepancy in intellectual temperament, which did not fail to lead to outward manifestations. Voltaire was sometimes a little weary of Newton and exact science, while the Marquise was naturally of the rather narrow turn for arid truths which too often distinguishes clever women inadequately disciplined by contact with affairs. She and Voltaire both competed for a prize offered by the Academy for essays on the propagation of fire (1737). Neither of them was successful, for the famous Euler was a competitor. The second and third prizes were given to two obscurer persons, because their essays were Cartesian, that is to say, they were scientifically orthodox. The two philosophers of Cirey also took part, and on different sides, in the obstinate physico-mathematical controversy which Leibnitz had first raised towards the close of the seventeenth century, as to the measure of moving forces.[1] The Marquise, under circumstances of equivocal glory and with much angry buzzing, with which one has now no concern,[2] published her analysis of Leibnitz in 1740, and sided with him against Newton and Descartes. In the notice which Voltaire wrote of his friend's book he gave a marvellously simple and intelligible account of the issue of the special controversy of *vis viva*,[3] but he remained Newtonian, and in 1741 presented a paper to the Academy of Sciences, disputing the Leibnitzian view.[4]

Voltaire was not merely one of those 'paper philosophers,' whose intrusion into the fields of physical science its professional followers are justly wont to resent. He was an active experimenter, and more than one letter remains, containing instructions to his agent in Paris to forward him retorts, air-pumps, and other instruments, with the wise hint in one place, a hint by no means of a miser, 'In the matter of buying things, my friend, you should always prefer the good and sound even if a little dear, to what is only middling but cheaper.'[5] His correspondence

---

[1] See Whewell's *Hist. Induc. Sci.* bk. vi. c. v.

[2] Desnoiresterres, pp. 313-21.

[3] Exposition du Livre des Institutions Physiques. *Œuvres*, xlii. pp. 196-206.

[4] *Œuvres*, xlii. p. 207, etc.

[5] Corr. 1737. *Œuvres*, lxiii. p. 182.

for some years proves the diligence and sincerity of
his interest in science.   Yet it is tolerably clear that
the man who did so much to familiarise France with
the most illustrious of physicists, was himself devoid
of true scientific aptitude.   After long and persevering
labour in this region, Voltaire consulted Clairaut on
the progress he had made.   The latter, with a loyal
frankness which Voltaire knew how to appreciate,
answered that even with the most stubborn labour he
was not likely to attain to anything beyond mediocrity
in science, and that he would be only throwing away
time which he owed to poetry and philosophy.[1]   The
advice was taken; for, as we have already said,
Voltaire's self-love was never fatuous, and the independent search of physical truth was given up.   There
is plainly no reason to regret the pains which Voltaire
took in this kind of inquiry, not because the study of
the sciences extends the range of poetic study and
enriches verse with fresh images, but because the
number of sorts of knowledge in which a man feels
at home and is intelligently cognisant of their scope
and issues, even if he be wholly incompetent to assist
in the progress of discovery, increases that intellectual
confidence and self-respect of understanding, which so
fortifies and stimulates him in his own special order
of work.   We cannot precisely contend that this
encyclopædic quality is an indispensable condition of
such self-respect in every kind of temper.   It certainly
was so with Voltaire.   'After all, my dear friend,'

[1] Condorcet *Vie de Voltaire,* p. 43.

he wrote to Cideville, 'it is right to give every possible form to our soul. It is a flame that God has
intrusted to us, we are bound to feed it with all that
we find most precious. We should introduce into
our existence all imaginable modes, and open every
door of the soul to all sorts of knowledge and all sorts
of feelings. So long as it does not all go in pell-mell,
there is plenty of room for everything.'[1]

To us, who can be wise after the event, it is clear
that if ever man was called not to science, nor to
poetry, nor to theology, nor to metaphysics, but to
literature, the art, so hard to define, of showing the
ideas of all subjects in the double light of the practical
and the spiritual reason, that man was Voltaire. He
has himself dwelt on the vagueness of this much-
abused term, without contributing anything more
satisfactory towards a better account of it than a crude
hint that literature, not being a special art, may be
considered a kind of larger grammar of knowledge.[2]
Although, however, it is true that literature is not a
particular art, it is not the less true that there is a
mental constitution particularly fitted for its successful practice. Literature is essentially an art of form,
as distinguished from those exercises of intellectual
energy which bring new stores of matter to the stock
of acquired knowledge, and give new forces to emotion
and original and definite articulation to passion. It
is a misleading classification to call the work of

[1] Corr. 1737. Œuvres, lvi. p. 428.
[2] Dict. Phil. s.v. Œuvres, lvi. p. 428.

Shakespeare and Molière, Shelley and Hugo, literary, just as it would be an equally inaccurate, though more glaring piece of classification, to count the work of Newton or Locke literature. To take another case from Voltaire, it would not be enough to describe Bayle's Dictionary as a literary compilation; it would not even be enough to describe it as a work of immense learning, because the distinguishing and superior mark of this book is a profound dialectic. It forms men of letters and is above them.[1]

What is it then that literature brings to us, that earns its title to high place, though far from a highest place, among the great humanizing arts? Is it not that this is the master organon for giving men the two precious qualities of breadth of interest and balance of judgment; multiplicity of sympathies and steadiness of sight? Unhappily, literature has too often been identified with the smirks and affectations of mere elegant dispersiveness, with the hollow niceties of the virtuoso, a thing of madrigals. It is not in any sense of this sort that we can think of Voltaire as specially the born minister of literature. What we mean is that while he had not the loftier endowments of the highest poetic conception, subtle speculative penetration, or triumphant scientific power, he possessed a superb combination of wide and sincere curiosity, an intelligence of vigorous and exact receptivity, a native inclination to candour and justice, and a pre-eminent mastery over a wide range in the art

---

[1] Dict. Phil. s.v. *Œuvres*, lvi. p. 430.

of expression. Literature being concerned to impose
form, to diffuse the light by which common men are
able to see the great host of ideas and facts that do
not shine in the brightness of their own atmosphere,
it is clear what striking gifts Voltaire had in this
way. He had a great deal of knowledge, and he was
ever on the alert both to increase and broaden his
stock, and, what was still better, to impart of it to
everybody else. He did not think it beneath him to
write on Hemistichs for the Encyclopædia. 'Tis not
a very brilliant task, he said, but perhaps the article
will be useful to men of letters and amateurs; 'one
should disdain nothing, and I will do the word Comma,
if you choose.'[1] He was very catholic in taste, being
able to love Racine without ignoring the lofty stature
of Shakespeare. And he was free from the weakness
which so often attends on catholicity, when it is not
supported by true strength and independence of
understanding; he did not shut his eyes to the shortcomings of the great. While loving Molière, he was
aware of the incompleteness of his dramatic construction, as well as of the egregious farce to which that
famous writer too often descends.[2] His respect for
the sublimity and pathos of Corneille did not hinder
him from noting both his violence and his frigid
argumentation.[3] Does the reader remember that
admirable saying of his to Vauvenargues; '*It is the*

---

[1] Corr. 1758. *Œuvres*, lxxv. p. 50.
[2] Temple du Goût. *Œuvres*, xv. p. 99.
[3] Corr. 1743. *Œuvres*, lxiv. p. 119.

*part of a man like you to have preferences, but no
exclusions?'* [1]   To this fine principle Voltaire was
usually thoroughly true, as every great mind, if
only endowed with adequate culture, must necessarily be.

> Nul auteur avec lui n'a tort,
> Quand il a trouvé l'art de plaire;
> Il le critique sans colère,
> Il l'applaudit avec transport. [2]

Thirdly, that circumfusion of bright light which is
the highest aim of speech, was easy to Voltaire, in
whatever order of subject he happened to treat.   His
style is like a translucent stream of purest mountain
water, moving with swift and animated flow under
flashing sunbeams.   'Voltaire,' said an enemy, 'is
the very first man in the world at writing down what
other people have thought.'   What was meant for a
spiteful censure, was in fact a truly honourable distinction.

The secret is incommunicable.   No spectrum
analysis can decompose for us that enchanting ray.
It is rather, after all, the piercing metallic light of
electricity than a glowing beam of the sun.   We can
detect some of the external qualities of this striking
style.   We seize its dazzling simplicity, its almost
primitive closeness to the letter, its sharpness and
precision, above all, its admirable brevity.   We see
that no writer ever used so few words to produce

---

[1] *Œuvres de Vauvenargues*, ii. 252.
[2] Temple du Goût.   *Œuvres*, xv. p. 100.

such pregnant effects.[1] Those whom brevity only
makes thin and slight, may look with despair on pages
where the nimbleness of the sentence is in proportion
to the firmness of the thought. We find no bastard
attempts to reproduce in words deep and complex
effects, which can only be adequately presented in
colour or in the combinations of musical sound. Nobody has ever known better the true limitations of
the material in which he worked, or the scope and
possibilities of his art. Voltaire's alexandrines, his
witty stories, his mock-heroic, his exposition of
Newton, his histories, his dialectic, all bear the same
mark, the same natural, precise, and condensed mode
of expression, the same absolutely faultless knowledge
of what is proper and permitted in every given kind
of written work. At first there seems something
paradoxical in dwelling on the brevity of an author
whose works are to be counted by scores of volumes.
But this is no real objection. A writer may be in-
sufferably prolix in the limits of a single volume, and
Voltaire was quite right in saying that there are four
times too many words in the one volume of D'Holbach's System of Nature. He maintains too that
Rabelais might advantageously be reduced to one-
eighth, and Bayle to a quarter, and there is hardly a

---

[1] In some readings given before popular audiences in Paris
in 1850, it was found that Voltaire was only partially effective.
'Trop d'artifice,' says Ste. Beuve, 'trop d'art nuit auprès des
esprits neufs ; trop de simplicité nuit aussi ; ils ne s'en étonnent
pas, et ils ont jusqu'à un certain point besoin d'être étonnés.'
(*Causeries*, i. 289.)

book that is not curtailed in the perfecting hands of the divine muses.[1] So conversely an author may not waste a word in a hundred volumes. Style is independent of quantity, and the world suffers so grievously from the mass of books that have been written, not because they are many, but because such vast proportion of their pages say nothing while they purport to say so much.

No study, however, of this outward ease and swift compendiousness of speech will teach us the secret that was beneath it in Voltaire, an eye and a hand that never erred in hitting the exact mark of appropriateness in every order of prose and verse. Perhaps no such vision for the befitting in expression has ever existed. He is the most trenchant writer in the world, yet there is not a sentence of strained emphasis or overwrought antithesis; he is the wittiest, yet there is not a line of bad buffoonery. And this intense sense of the appropriate was by nature and cultivation become so entirely a fixed condition of Voltaire's mind that it shows spontaneous and without an effort in his work. Nobody is more free from the ostentatious correctness of the literary precisian, and nobody preserves so much purity and so much dignity of language with so little formality of demeanour. It is interesting to notice the absence from his writings of that intensely elaborated kind of simplicity in which some of the best authors of a later time express the final outcome of many thoughts.

[1] Temple du Goût. *Œuvres*, xv. p. 95.

The strain that society has undergone since Voltaire's day has taught men to qualify their propositions. It has forced them to follow truth slowly along paths steep and devious. New notes have been struck in human feeling, and all thought has now been touched by complexities that were then unseen. Hence, as all good writers aim at simplicity and directness, we have seen the growth of a new style, in which the rays of many side-lights are concentrated in some single phrase. That Voltaire does not use these focalising words and turns of composition only means that to him thought was less complex than it is to a more subjective generation. Though the literature which possesses Milton and Burke need not fear comparison with the graver masters of French speech, we have no one to place exactly by the side of Voltaire. But, then, no more has France. There are many pages of Swift which are more like one side of Voltaire than anything else that we have, and Voltaire probably drew the idea of his famous stories from the creator of Gulliver, just as Swift got the idea of the Tale of a Tub from Fontenelle's History of Mero and Enegu (that is, of Rome and Geneva). Swift has correctness, invention, irony, and a trick of being effectively literal and serious in absurd situations, just as Voltaire has; but then Swift is often truculent and often brutally gross, both in thought and in phrase. Voltaire is never either brutal or truculent. Even amid the licence of the Pucelle and of his romances, he never forgets what is due to the French

tongue. What always charmed him in Racine and
Boileau, he tells us, was that they said what they
intended to say, and that their thoughts have never
cost anything to the harmony or the purity of the
language.[1] Voltaire ranged over far wider ground
than the two poets ever attempted to do, and trod in
many slippery places, yet he is entitled to the same
praise as that which he gave to them.

Unhappily, one of the many evil effects which have
alloyed the revolution that Voltaire did so much to
set in motion, has been both in his country and ours
that purity and harmony of language, in spite of the
examples of the great masters who have lived since,
have on the whole declined. In both countries
familiarity and slang have actually asserted a place
in literature on some pretence that they are real; an
assumed vulgarity tries to pass for native homeliness,
and, as though a giant were more impressive for having a humped back, some men of true genius seem
only to make sure of fame by straining themselves
into grotesques. In a word, the reaction against a
spurious dignity of style has carried men too far,
because the reaction against the dignified elements in
the old order went too far. Style, after all, as one
has always to remember, can never be anything but
the reflex of ideas and habits of mind, and when respect for one's own personal dignity as a ruling and
unique element in character gave way to sentimental
love of the human race, often real, and often a pre-

[1] Corr. 1732. *Œuvres*, lxii. p. 218.

tence, old self-respecting modes of expression went
out of fashion.   And all this has been defended by
a sort of argument that might just as appropriately
have been used by Diogenes, vindicating the filthiness
of his tub against a doctrine of clean linen.

To follow letters, it is important to observe, meant
then, or at least after Voltaire's influence rose to its
height, it meant distinctly to enter the ranks of the
Opposition.   In our own time the profession of letters
is placed with other polite avocations, and those who
follow it for the most part accept the traditional social
ideas of the time, just as clergymen, lawyers, and
physicians accept them.   The modern man of letters
corresponds to the ancient sophist, whose office it was
to confirm, adorn, and propagate the current prejudice.   To be a man of letters in France in the
middle of the eighteenth century was to be the official
enemy of the current prejudices and their sophistical
defenders in the church and the parliaments.   Parents
heard of a son's design to go to Paris and write books,
or to mix with those who wrote books, with the same
dismay with which a respectable Athenian heard of
a son following Socrates.   The hyper-hellenistic col-
legian need not accuse us of instituting a general
parallel between Socrates and Voltaire.   The only
point on which we are insisting is that each was the
leader of the assault against the sophists of his day,
though their tactics and implements of war were
sufficiently unlike.   To the later assailant the conditions of the time made the pen the most effective

instrument. The clergy had the pulpit and the con-
fessional, and their enemies had the press.

It was during the period of his connection with
Madame du Châtelet, that is in the active literary
years between his return from England and his re-
moval to Berlin, that Voltaire's dramatic talent was
most productive.[1] He is usually considered to hold
the same place relatively to Corneille and Racine
that Euripides held relatively to Æschylus and
Sophocles. It is not easy to see what is the exact
point of analogy on which the critics agree, beyond
the corresponding place in the order of chronological
succession, and such parallels are not really very full
of instruction. If we are to draw any parallel at all,
it must be between the Greek and Racine. The
differences between Euripides and his predecessors
are not those between Voltaire and his predecessors.
There may be one common peculiarity. Each made
the drama an instrument for the expression not merely
of passion, but of speculative and philosophical matter,
and this in each case of a sceptical kind in reference
to the accepted traditions of the time. But apart
from the vast superiority of the Greek in depth and
passion and dramatic invention, in Voltaire this philo-
sophising is very much more indirect, insinuatory,
and furtive, than in the marked sententiousness of

---

[1] The dates of the most famous of his tragedies are these :
Œdipe, 1718 ; *Brutus*, 1730 ; *Zaïre*, 1732 ; *Mort de César*, 1735 ;
Alzire, 1736 ; *Mahomet*, 1741 ; *Mérope*, 1743 ; *Sémiramis*, 1748 ;
Tancrède, 1760.

Euripides. There are critics, indeed, who insist that all Voltaire's poetic work is a series of pamphlets in disguise, and that he ought to be classified, in that jargon which makes an uncouth compound pass muster for a new critical nicety, as a tendency-poet.[1] To accept this would simply be to leave out of account the very best of Voltaire's plays, including Mérope, Sémiramis, Tancrède, in which the most ingenious of men and critics would be at a loss to find any tendency of the pamphleteering kind. Voltaire's ever-present sense of congruity prevented him from putting the harangue of the pulpit or the discourse of the academic doctor upon the tragic stage. If the clergy found in 'Mahomet,' for instance, a covert attack on their own religion, it was much more because the poet was suspected of unbelief, than because the poem contained infidel doctrine. Indeed, nothing shows so clearly as the strange affright at this and some other pieces of Voltaire's, that the purport and effect of poetry must depend nearly as much upon the mind of the audience as upon the lines themselves. His plays may be said to have led to scepticism, only because there was sceptical predisposition in the mind which his public brought to them; and under other circumstances, if for instance it had been produced in the time of Lewis XIV., the exposure of Mahomet would have been counted a glorification of the rival creed. Indeed, Pope Benedict XIV. did by and by

---

[1] Hettnerr, for instance : *Literaturgeschichte des* 18*ten Jahrhunderts*, ii. 227.

accept Voltaire's dedication of the play, whether in
good faith or no we cannot tell, on the express ground
that it was an indirect homage to Christianity. Men
with a sense of artistic propriety far inferior to
Voltaire's, are yet fully alive to the monstrosity of
disguising a pamphleteer's polemic in the form of a
pretended drama.

In choice of subject Voltaire, we may believe, was
secretly guided by his wish to relax the oppressive
hold of religious prejudice. Religion, we cannot too
fully realise, was the absorbing burden of the time.
There was no sort of knowledge, from geometry
onwards, on which it did not weigh.   Whatever work
Voltaire set himself to, he was confronted in it by the
Infamous. Thus in accordance with the narrow theory
of his time, he held Mahomet to be a deliberate and
conscious impostor, and in presenting the founder of
one great religion in this odious shape, he was doubtless suggesting that the same account might be true
of the founder of another.   But the suggestion was
entirely outside of the play itself, and we who have
fully settled these questions for ourselves, may read
'Mahomet' without suspecting the shade of a reference from Mecca to Jerusalem, though hardly without
contemning the feebleness of view which could see
nothing but sensuality, ambition, and crime, in the
career of the fierce eastern reformer.   The sentiments
of exalted deism which are put into the mouth of the
noble Zopire were perhaps meant to teach people that
the greatest devotion of character may go with the

most unflinching rejection of a pretended revelation
from the gods. This again is a gloss from without,
and by no means involves Voltaire in the offence of
art with a moral purpose.

Zaïre was the first play in which French characters
appeared upon the tragic stage. The heroine, the
daughter of Lusignan, has been brought up, unconscious of her descent, in the Mahometan faith and
usage. Consider the philosophy of these lines which
are given to her:

La coutume, la loi plia mes premiers ans
A la religion des heureux musulmans.
Je le vois trop ; les soins qu'on prend de notre enfance
Forment nos sentimens, nos mœurs, notre croyance.
J'eusse été près du Gange esclave des faux dieux,
Chrétienne dans Paris, musulmane en ces lieux.
L'instruction fait tout ; et la main de nos pères
Grave en nos faibles cœurs ces premiers caractères,
Que l'exemple et le temps nous viennent retracer,
Et que peut-être en nous Dieu seul peut effacer.[1]

This of course implied the doctrine of Pope's Universal Prayer, and contains an idea that was always
the favourite weapon for smiting the over-confident
votaries of a single supernatural revelation. Locke
had asked whether 'the current opinions and licensed
guides of every country are sufficient evidence and
security to every man to venture his great concern-
ments on? Or, can these be the certain and infallible oracle and standards of truth which teach one
thing in Christendom, and another in Turkey? Or

[1] *Zaïre*, act i. sc. 1.

K

shall a poor countryman be eternally happy for having
the chance to be born in Italy ? Or a day-labourer
be unavoidably lost because he had the ill-luck to be
born in England ? ' [1] This was exactly the kind of
reasoning to which Zaïre's lines pointed ; and Voltaire
was never weary of arguing that the divine lay outside of the multitudinous variety of creeds that were .
never more than local accidents.   Neither, however,
in Zaïre nor anywhere else is the law of perfect
dramatic fitness violated for the sake of a lesson in
heterodoxy.   With Voltaire tragedy is, as all art
ought to be, a manner of disinterested presentation.
This is not the noblest energy of the human intelligence, but it is truly art, and Voltaire did not forget it.

It would be entirely unprofitable to enter into
any comparison of the relative merits of Voltaire's
tragedies, and those either of the modern romantic
school in his own country, or of the master dramatists
of our own.   Every form of composition must be
judged in its own order, and the order in which
Voltaire chose to work was the French classic, with
its appointed conditions and fixed laws, its three
unities, its stately alexandrines, and all the other
essentials of that special dramatic form.   Here is one
of the many points at which we feel that Voltaire is
trying to prolong in literature, if not in thought, the
impressive tradition of the grand age.   At the same
moment, strangely enough, he was giving that stir to
the opinion of his time, which was the prime agent in

---

[1] *Essay on Hum. Und.* iv. 19, § 3.

definitely breaking the hold of that tradition. It is
no infidelity to the glorious and incomparable genius
of Shakespeare, nor does it involve any blindness to
the fine creation, fresh fancy, and noble thought and
imagery of our less superb men, yet to admit that
there is in these limits of construction a concentration
and regularity, and in these too contemned alexandrines a just and swelling cadence, that confer a
high degree of pleasure of the highest kind, and that
demand intellectual quality only less rare than that
other priceless and unattainable quality of having the
lips touched with divine fire. It is said, however,
that such quality does not produce acting plays, but
only dramatic poems : this is really laughable if we
remember first, that the finest actors in the world have
been trained in the recitation of these alexandrines,
and second, that as large and as delighted an audience
used until within some twenty years ago to crowd to a
tragedy of Corneille or Racine, seen repeatedly before,
as to a bran-new vaudeville, never to be seen again.

'We insist,' said Voltaire, 'that the rhyme shall
cost nothing to the ideas; that it shall neither be
trivial nor too far-fetched; we exact rigorously in a
verse the same purity, the same precision, as in prose.
We do not permit the smallest licence; we require
an author to carry without a break all these chains,
and yet that he should appear ever free.'[1] He
admitted that sometimes they failed in reaching the

---

[1] Discours sur la Tragédie, à Milord Bolingbrocke. *Œuvres*,
ii. p. 337. See also the preface to Œdipe. *Ib.* p. 73.

tragic, through excessive fear of passing its limits.
He does justice, if something less than English justice,
to the singular merits of our stage in the way of
action.[1] Shakespeare, he says, 'had a genius full of
force and fertility, of all that is natural and all that
is sublime.' It is even the merit of Shakespeare—
'those grand and terrible pieces that abound in his
most monstrous farces'—that has been the undoing
of the English stage.[2]

Even the famous criticism on Hamlet has been a
good deal misrepresented. Voltaire is vindicating the
employment of the machinery of ghosts, and he dwells
on the fitness and fine dramatic effect of the ghost in
Shakespeare's play. 'I am very far,' he goes on to
say, 'from justifying the tragedy of Hamlet in everything : it is a rude and barbarous piece. . . . Hamlet
goes mad in the second act, and his mistress goes
mad in the third; the prince slays the father of his
mistress, pretending to kill a rat, and the heroine
throws herself into the river. They dig her grave on
the stage; the gravediggers jest in a way worthy of
them, with skulls in their hands; Hamlet answers
their odious grossnesses by extravagances no less disgusting. Meanwhile one of the characters conquers
Poland. Hamlet, his mother, and his stepfather
drink together on the stage; they sing at table, they
wrangle, they fight, they kill; one might suppose such
a work to be the fruit of the imagination of a drunken

[1] *Œuvres*, ii. p. 339.
[2] Lett. sur les Anglais, xix. *Œuvres*, xxxv. p. 151.

savage. But in the midst of all these rude irregu-
larities, which to this day make the English theatre
so absurd and so barbarous, there are to be found in
Hamlet by a yet greater incongruity sublime strokes
worthy of the loftiest geniuses. It seems as if nature
had taken a delight in collecting within the brain of
Shakespeare all that we can imagine of what is greatest
and most powerful, with all that rudeness without wit
can contain of what is lowest and most detestable.'[1]

If one were to retort upon this that anybody with
a true sense of poetry would sacrifice all the plays that
Voltaire ever wrote, his eight-and-twenty tragedies,
and half-score of comedies, for the soliloquy in Hamlet,
or King Henry at Towton Fight, or ' Roses, their sharp
spines being gone,' there would be truth in such a
retort, but it would be that brutal truth, which is
always very near being the most subtle kind of lie.
Nature wrought a miracle for us by producing Shakespeare, as she did afterwards in an extremely different
way for France by producing Voltaire. Miracles, however, have necessarily a very demoralising effect. A
prodigy of loaves and fishes, by slackening the motives
to honest industry, must in the end multiply paupers.
The prodigy of such amazing results from such glorious
carelessness as Shakespeare's, has plunged hundreds
of men of talent into a carelessness most inglorious,
and made our acting stage a mock. It is quite true

[1] Introduction to Sémiramis. *Œuvres*, v. p. 194. See also
Du Théâtre Anglais (1761). *Ib.* x. p. 88. Lettre à l'Acad.
Franç. (1778), iv. p. 186.

that the academic rule is better fitted for mediocrity than for genius; but we may perhaps trust genius to make a way for itself. It is mediocrity that needs laws and prescriptions for its most effective fertilisation, and the enormous majority even of those who can do good work are still mediocre. We have preferred the methods of lawless genius, and are left with rampant lawlessness and no genius. The very essence of the old French tragedy was painstaking, and painstaking has had its unfailing and exceeding great reward. When people whose taste has been trained in the traditions of romantic and naturalistic art, or even not trained at all except in indolence and presumption, yawn over the French alexandrines, let them remember that Goethe at any rate thought it worth while to translate Mahomet and Tancrède.

An eminent German writer on Voltaire has recently declared the secret of the French classic dramaturgy to be that the drama was a diversion of the court. 'The personages have to speak not as befits their true feelings, their character, and the situation, but as is seemly in the presence of a king and a court; not truth, nature, and beauty, but etiquette, is the highest law of the dramatic art.'[1] This may partially explain how it was that a return to some features of the classic form, its dignity, elevation, and severity, came to take place in France, but no explanation can

---

[1] *Voltaire: sechs Vorträge.* Von D. F. Strauss; p. 74. The same idea is found in a speech of Wilhelm Meister, bk. iii. ch. 8.

be at all satisfactory which reduces so distinct and genuine a manner of dramatic expression to a mere outside accident. Corneille, Racine, Voltaire, treated their tragic subjects as they did, with rigorous concentration of action, stately consistency of motive, and in a solemn and balanced measure, because these conditions answered to intellectual qualities of their own, an affinity in themselves for elegance, clearness, elevation, and a certain purified and weighty wisdom. It is true that they do not unseal those deep-hidden fountains of thought and feeling and music, which flow so freely at the waving of Shakespeare's wand. We are not swiftly carried from a scene of clowns up to some sublime pinnacle of the seventh heaven, whence we see the dark abysses that lie about the path of human action, as well as all its sweet and shadowed places. Only let us not unjustly suppose that we are deciding the merits of the old French dramaturgy, its severe structure and stately measure, by answering the question, which no English nor German writer can ever seriously put, as to the relative depth and vision in poetic things of Shakespeare and Voltaire. Nor can we be expected to be deeply moved by a form of art that is so unfamiliar to us. It is not a question whether we ought to be so deeply moved. The too susceptible Marmontel describes how on the occasion of a visit to Ferney, Voltaire took him into his study and placed a manuscript into his hands. It was Tancrède, which was just finished. Marmontel eagerly read it, and he tells us how he

returned to the author, his face all bathed in tears.
'Your tears,' said Voltaire, 'tell me all that it most
concerns me to know.'[1]   The most supercilious critic
may find this very Tancrède worth reading, when he
remembers that Gibbon thought it splendid and interesting,[2] and that Goethe found it worth translating.
One could hardly be convicted now of want of sensibility, if all Voltaire's tragedy together failed to bathe
one's face in tears, but this is a very bad reason for
denying that it has other merits than pathos.

We cannot, indeed, compare the author of Zaïre
and Tancrède with the great author of Cinna and
Polyeucte, any more than in another kind we can
compare Gray with Milton. Voltaire is the very
genius of correctness, elegance, and grace, and if the
reader would know what this correctness means, he
will find a most wholesome exercise in reading Voltaire's notes on some of the most celebrated of
Corneille's plays.[3] But in masculine energy and in
poetic weightiness, as well as in organ-like richness of
music, Voltaire must be surely pronounced inferior to
his superb predecessor. There is a certain thinness
pervading the whole of his work for the stage, the
conception of character, the dramatic structure, and
the measure alike. Undoubtedly we may frequently
come upon weighty and noble lines, of fine music and

---

[1] *Mém. de Marmontel*, liv. vii. ii. 245. For Diderot's criticism, see his *Mémoires et Œuvr. Inédites*, i. 234 (1830). For
D'Alembert's, cf. Voltaire's *Œuv.* lxxv. p. 118.

[2] *Decline and Fall*, c. 52, note 83.

[3] *Œuvres*, vols. x. and xi.

lofty sense. But there is on the whole what strikes one as a fatal excess of facility, and a fatal defect of poetic saliency. The fluent ease of the verse destroys the impression of strength. 'Your friend,' wrote Madame du Châtelet once of her friend, 'has had a slight bout of illness, and you know that when he is ill, he can do nothing but write verses.'[1] We do not know whether the Marquise meant alexandrines, or those graceful verses of society of which Voltaire was so incomparable a master. It is certain that he wrote Zaïre in three weeks and Olympie in six days, though with respect to the latter we may well agree with the friend who told the author that he should not have rested on the seventh day. However that may be, there is a quality about his tragic verse which to one fresh from the sonorous majesty and dignified beauty of Polyeucte, or even the fine gravity of Tartufe, vibrates too lightly in the ear. Least of all may we compare him to Racine, whose two great tragedies of Iphigénie and Athalie Voltaire himself declared to mark the nearest approach ever made to dramatic perfection.[2] There is none of the mixed austerity and tenderness, height and sweetness, grace and firmness, that blend together with such invisible art and unique contrivance in the poet whose verses taught Fénelon and Massillon how to make music in their prose. To this Voltaire could only have access from without, for he lacked the famous master's internal depth, seriousness, and veneration

[1] Desnoiresterres, p. 342.		[2] Œuvres, ix. p. 382.

of soul. We know how little this approach from without can avail, and how vainly a man follows the harmonious grace of a style, when he lacks the impalpable graces of spirit that made the style live. It is only when grave thoughts and benignant aspirations and purifying images move with even habit through the mind, that a man masters the noblest expression. De Maistre, to whom Voltaire's name was the symbol for all that is accursed, admitted the nobleness of his work in tragedy, but he instantly took back the grudged praise by saying that even here he only resembles his two great rivals as a clever hypocrite resembles a saint.[1] Malignantly expressed, there is in this some truth.

It was one of the elements in the plan of dramatic reform that sprang up in Voltaire's mind during his residence in England, that the subjects of tragedy should be more masculine, and that love should cease to be an obligatory ingredient. 'It is nearly always the same piece, the same knot, formed by jealousy and a breach, and untied by a marriage; it is a perpetual coquetry, a simple comedy in which princes are actors, and in which occasionally blood is spilt for form's sake.'[2] This he counted a mistake, for, as he justly said, the heart is but lightly touched by a lover's woes, while it is profoundly softened by the anguish of a mother just about to lose her son. Thus in Mérope we have maternal sentiment made the spring of what is probably the best of Voltaire's tragedies,

[1] *Soirées*, 4ième entretien.   [2] *Œuvres*, v. p. 189.

abounding in a just vehemence, compact, full of
feeling at once exalted and natural, and moving with
a sustained energy that is not a too common mark of
his work. It was the same conviction of the propriety of making tragedy a means of expressing other
emotions than that which is so apt to degenerate into
an insipidity, which dictated the composition and
novel treatment of the Roman subjects, Brutus and
La Mort de César. Here the French drama first
became in some degree truly political. His predecessors when they handled a historic theme did so,
not from the historic or social point of view, but as
the illustration, or rather the suggestion, of some
central human passion. In the Cinna of Corneille the
political bearings, the moral of benevolent despotism
which Bonaparte found in it, were purely incidental,
and were distinctly subordinate to the portrayal of
character and the movement of feeling. In Brutus
the whole action lies in the region of great public
affairs, and of the passions which these affairs stir in
noble characters, without any admixture of purely
private tenderness. In La Mort de César we are
equally in the heroics of public action. Rome Sauvée,
of which the subject is the conspiracy of Catiline, and
the hero the most eloquent of consuls or men—a part
that Voltaire was very fond of filling in private
representations, and with distinguished success—is
extremely loose and spasmodic in structure, and the
speeches sound strained even when put into Cicero's
mouth. But here also private insipidities are banished,

though perhaps it is only in favour of public insipidities.
It is impossible to tell what share, if any, these plays
had in spreading that curious feeling about Roman
freedom and its most renowned defenders, which is so
striking a feature in some of the great episodes of the
Revolution. We cannot suspect Voltaire of any
design to stir political feeling. He was now essentially aristocratic and courtly in his predilection,
without the smallest active wish for an approach to
political revolution, if indeed the conception of a
change of that kind ever presented itself to him. He
was indefatigable in admiring and praising English
freedom, but, as has already been said, it was not the
laudation of a lover of popular government, but the
envy of a man of letters whose life was tormented by
censors of the press and the lieutenant of police. Perhaps the only approach to a public purpose in this fancy
for his Roman subjects was a lurking idea of arousing
in the nobles, for whom we must remember that his
dramatic work was above all designed, not a passion for
freedom from the authority of monarchic government,
but a passion of a more general kind for energetic
patriotism. Voltaire's letters abound with expressions of the writer's belief that he was the witness of
an epoch of decay in his own country. He had in
truth far too keen and practical and trained an eye not
to see how public spirit, political sagacity, national
ambition, and even valour had declined in the great
orders of France since the age of the Grand Monarch,
and how much his country had fallen back in the

race of civilisation and power. We should be guilty
of a very transparent exaggeration of the facts, if
any attempt were made to paint Voltaire in the attitude and colours of one transcendentally aspiring to
regenerate his countrymen. But there is no difficulty in believing that a man who had lived in England,
and knew so much of Prussia, should have seen the
fatal enervation which had come upon France, and
that with Voltaire's feeling for the stage, he should
have dreamt, by means of a more austere subject and
more masculine treatment, of reviving the love of
wisdom and glory and devotion in connection with
country. In a word, the lesson of La Mort de César
or of Brutus was not a specific admonition to slay
tyrants, or to execute stern judgments on sons, but
a general example of self-sacrificing patriotism and
devoted public honour.

It is often said that Voltaire's Romans are mere
creatures of parade and declamation, like the figures
of David's paintings,[1] and it is very likely that the
theatre infected the French people with that mischievous idea of the Romans, as a nation of declaimers
about freedom and the death of tyrants. The true
Roman was no doubt very much more like one of our
narrow, hard, and able Scotchmen in India, than the
lofty talkers who delighted the parterre of Paris or
Versailles. Unluckily for truth of historical conception, Cicero was, after Virgil, the most potent of
Roman memories, and a man of words became with

[1] Strauss, p. 79.

modern writers the favourite type of a people of
action.   All this, however, is beside the question.
Voltaire would have laughed at the idea of any
obligation to present either Romans or other personages on the stage with realistic fidelity.   The tragic
drama with him was the highest of the imaginative
and idealistic arts.   If he had sought a parallel to it
in the plastic arts he would have found one, not in
painting, which by reason of the greater flexibility
of its material demands a more exact verisimilitude,
but in sculpture.   Considered as statuesque figures
endowed with speech, Brutus, Cæsar, and the rest
are noble and impressive.   We may protest as vigor-
ously as we know how against any assimilation of the
great art of action with the great art of repose.   But
we can only criticise the individual productions of a
given theory, provided we for the moment accept the
conditions which the theory lays down.   All art rests
upon convention, and if we choose to repudiate any
particular set of conventions, we have no more right
to criticise the works of those who submit to them
than one would have to criticise sculpture, because
marble or bronze is not like flesh and blood.   Within
the conditions of the French classic drama Voltaire's
Romans are high and stately figures.

Voltaire's innovations extended beyond the introduction of more masculine treatment.   Before his
time romantic subjects had been regarded with dis-
favour, and Corneille's Bajazet was considered a bold
experiment.   Racine was more strictly classic, and

dramatists went on handling the same ancient fables,
'Thebes, or Pelops' line, or the tale of Troy divine,'
just as the Greeks had done, or just as the painters
in the Catholic times had never wearied of painting
the two eternal figures of human mother and divine
child. Voltaire treated the classic subjects as others
treated them, and if Œdipe misses the depth, delicate
reserve and fateful gloom of the Greeks, Mérope at any
rate breathes a fine and tragic spirit. But his restless
mind pressed forward into subjects which Racine
would have shuddered at, and every quarter of the universe became in turn a portion of the Voltairean stage.
L'Orphelin de la Chine introduces us to China and
Genghis-Khan, Mahomet to Arabia and its prophet,
Tancrède to Sicily; in Zulime we are among Moors,
in Alzire with Peruvians. This revolutionary enlargement of subject was significant of a general and very
important enlargement of interest which marked the
time, and led presently to those contrasts between
the condition of France and the imaginary felicity
and nobleness of wilder countries, which did so much
to breed an irresistible longing for change. Voltaire's
high-minded Scythians, generous Peruvians, and the
rest, prepared the way along with other influences
for that curious cosmopolitanism, that striking eagerness to believe in the equal virtuousness and devotion
inherent in human nature, independently of the religious or social form accidentally imposed upon them,
which found its ultimate outcome, first in an ardent
passion for social equality, and a depreciation of the

special sanctity of the current religion, and next in the ill-fated emancipating and proselytising aims of the Revolution, and in orators of the human race.

It has usually been thought surprising that Voltaire, consummate wit as he was, should have been so markedly unsuccessful in comedy. Certainly no one with so right a sense of the value of time as Voltaire himself had, will in our day waste many hours over his productions in this order. There are a dozen of them more or less, and we can only hope that they were the most rapid of his writings. Lines of extraordinary vivacity are not wanting, and at their best they offer a certain bustling sprightliness that might have been diverting in actual representation. But the keynote seems to be struck in farce, rather than in comedy; the intrigue, if not quite as slight as in Molière, is too forced; and the characters are nearly all excessively mediocre in conception. In one of the comedies, Le Dépositaire, the poet presented the aged patroness of his youth, but the necessity of respecting current ideas of the becoming prevented him from making a great character out of even so striking a figure as Ninon de l'Enclos. La Prude is a version of Wycherly's Plaindealer, and is in respect of force, animation, and the genuine spirit of comedy, very inferior to its admirable original. L'Indiscret is a sparkling and unconsidered trifle, L'Ecossaise is only a stinging attack on Fréron, and L'Enfant Prodigue, though greater pains were taken with it, has none of the glow of dramatic feeling. The liveliest of all is

La Femme qui a Raison, a short comedy of situation, which for one reading is entertaining in the closet, and must be excellent on the stage. It is very slight, however, and as usual verges on farce.

This inferiority of Voltaire's ought not to astonish any one who has reflected how much concentrated feeling and what profundity of vision go to the production of great comedy, and how in the mind of the dramatist, as in the movement of human life, comedy lies close to portentous tragedy. The author of the Bourgeois Gentilhomme and L'Avare was also the creator of the Misanthrope, that inscrutable piece, where, without plot, fable, or intrigue, we see a section of the polished life of the time, men and women paying visits, making and receiving compliments, discoursing upon affairs with easy lightness, flitting backwards and forwards with a thousand petty hurries, and among these one strange, rough, hoarse, half-sombre figure, moving solitarily with a chilling reality in the midst of frolicking shadows. Voltaire entered too eagerly into the interests of the world, was by temperament too exclusively sympathetic and receptive and social, to place himself even in imagination thus outside of the common circle. Without capacity for this, there is no comedy of the first order. Without serious consciousness of contrasts, no humour that endures. Shakespeare, Molière, and even Aristophanes, each of them unsurpassed writers of mere farce, were each of them, though with vast difference of degree, master of a tragic breadth of vision. Voltaire had moods of petulant spleen, but who feels that he ever saw, much less brooded over, the dark cavernous regions of human nature ? Without this we may have brilliant pleasantry of surprise, inimitable caricature, excellent comedy of society, but of the veritable comedy of human character and life, nothing.

In dazzling and irresistible caricature Voltaire has no equal. There is no deep humour, as in Don Quixote, or Tristram Shandy, which Voltaire did not care for,[1] or Richter's Siebenkäs, which he would not have cared for any more than De Stael did. He was too purely intellectual, too argumentative, too geometrical, and cared too much for illustrating a principle. But in Candide, Zadig, L'Ingénu, wit is as high as mere wit can go. They are better than Hudibras, because the motive is broader and more intellectual. Rapidity of play, infallible accuracy of stroke, perfect copiousness, and above all a fresh and unflagging spontaneity, combine with a surprising invention, to give these stories a singular quality, of which we most effectively observe the real brilliance, by comparing them with the too numerous imitations that their success has unhappily invited since.

It is impossible to omit from the most cursory study of Voltaire's work, that too famous poem which was his favourite amusement during some of the best years of his life, which was the delight of all who could by any means get the high favour of sight or hearing of so much as a canto of it, and which is now always

[1] *Œuvres,* xviii. p. 250.

spoken of, when it happens to be spoken of at all, with extreme abhorrence.[1] The Pucelle offends two modern sentiments, the love of modesty, and the love of the heroic personages of history. The moral sense and the historic sense have both been sharpened in some respects since Voltaire, and a poem which not only abounds in immodesty, and centres the whole action in an indecency of conception, but also fastens this gross chaplet round the memory of a great deliverer of the poet's own country, seems to offer a double outrage to an age when relish for licentious verse has gone out of fashion, and reverence for the heroic dead has come in. Still the fact that the greatest man of his time should have written one of the most unseemly poems that exist in any tongue, is worth trying to understand. Voltaire, let us remember, had no special turn, like Gibbon or Bayle, least of all like the unclean Swift, for extracting a malodorous diversion out of grossness or sensuality. His writings betray no irresistible passion for flying to an indelicacy, nor any of the vapid lasciviousness of some more modern French writers. The Pucelle is at least the wit of a rational man, and not the prying beastliness of a satyr. It is wit worse than poorly employed, but it is purity itself compared with some of the nameless abominations with which Diderot besmirched his imagination. The Persian Letters contain what we should now account passages of extreme licentious-

[1] Commenced soon after 1730 ; published surreptitiously in 1755 ; published by Voltaire himself in 1762.

ness, yet Montesquieu was assuredly no libertine.
Voltaire's life again was never indecent or immoderate
from the point of view of the manners of the time.
A man of grave character and untarnished life, like
Condorcet, did not scruple to defend a poem, in which
it is hard for us to see anything but a most indecorous
burlesque of a most heroic subject. He insists that
books which divert the imagination without heating
or seducing it, which by gay and pleasurable images
fill up those moments of exhaustion that are useless
alike for labour and meditation, have the effect of
inclining men to gentleness and indulgence. 'It was
not such books as the Pucelle that Gérard or Clément
used to read, or that the satellites of Cromwell carried
at the saddle-bow.'[1]

The fact is that in amusing himself by the Pucelle,
Voltaire was only giving literary expression to a kind
of view which had already in the society of the time
found for itself a thoroughly practical expression.
The people among whom he lived had systematised
that freedom from law or restraint in the relations of
the sexes, of which his poem is so vivid a representation.   The Duke of Richelieu was the irresistible
Lovelace of his time, and it was deemed an honour,
an honour to which Madame du Châtelet among so
many others has a title, to have yielded to his fascina-
tion.   A long and profoundly unedifying chronicle
might be drawn up of the memorable gallantries of
that time, and for our purpose it might fitly close

[1] *Vie de Voltaire,* p. 89.

with the amour with Saint Lambert that led to Madame du Châtelet's death. Of course, these countless gallantries in the most licentious persons of the day, such as Richelieu or Saxe, were neither more nor less than an outbreak of sheer dissoluteness, such as took place among English people of quality in the time of the Restoration. The idle and luxurious, whose imagination is uncontrolled by the discipline of labour and purpose, and to whom the indulgence of their own inclinations is the first and single law of life, are always ready to profit by any relaxation of restraint, which the moral conditions of the moment may permit.

The peculiarity of the licence of France in the middle of the eighteenth century is, that it was looked upon with complacency by the great intellectual leaders of opinion. It took its place in the progressive formula. What austerity was to other forward movements, licence was to this. It is not difficult to perceive how so extraordinary a circumstance came to pass. Chastity was the supreme virtue in the eyes of the church, the mystic key to Christian holiness. Continence was one of the most sacred of the pretensions by which the organised preachers of superstition claimed the reverence of men and women. It was identified, therefore, in a particular manner with that Infamous, against which the main assault of the time was directed. So men contended, more or less expressly, first, that continence was no commanding chief among virtues, then that it was a very superficial and easily practised virtue, finally that it was no virtue at all, but if sometimes a convenience, generally an impediment to free human happiness. These disastrous sophisms show the peril of having morality made an appendage of a set of theological mysteries, because the mysteries are sure in time to be dragged into the open air of reason, and moral truth crumbles away with the false dogmas with which it had got mixed.

'If,' says Condorcet, 'we may treat as useful the design to make superstition ridiculous in the eyes of men given to pleasures, and destined, by the very want of self-control which makes pleasures attractive to them, to become one day the unfortunate victims or the mischievous instruments of that vile tyrant of humanity; if the affectation of austerity in manners, if the excessive value attached to purity, only serves the hypocrites who by putting on the easy mask of chastity can dispense with all virtues, and cover with a sacred veil the vices most pernicious to society, hardness of heart and intolerance; if by accustoming men to treat as so many crimes faults from which honourable and conscientious persons are not exempt, we extend over the purest souls the power of that dangerous caste, which to rule and disturb the earth, has constituted itself exclusively the interpreter of heavenly justice;—then we shall see in the author of the Pucelle no more than a foe to hypocrisy and superstition.'[1]

[1] *Vie de Voltaire*, p. 88. On the same subject of chastity, cf. Condorcet's Works, vi. p. 264, and pp. 523-26; also a passage in his correspondence, i. p. 221.

It helps us to realise the infinite vileness of a system, like that of the Church in the last century, which could engender in men of essential nobleness of character like Condorcet, an antipathy so violent as to shut the eyes of their understanding to the radical sophistry of such pleading as this. Let one reflection out of many, serve to crush the whole of it. The key to effective life is unity of life, and unity of life means as much as anything else the unity of our human relations. Our identity does by no means consist in a historic continuity of tissues, but in an organic moral coherency of relation. It is this, which alone, if we consider the passing shortness of our days, makes life a whole, instead of a parcel of thrums bound together by an accident. Is not every incentive and every concession to vagrant appetite a force that enwraps a man in gratification of self, and severs him from duty to others, and so a force of dissolution and dispersion? It might be necessary to pull down the Church, but the worst church that has ever prostituted the name and the idea of religion cannot be so disastrous to society, as a gospel that systematically relaxes self-control as being an unmeaning curtailment of happiness. The apologists for the Pucelle exhibit the doctrine of individualism in one of its worst issues. 'Your proof that this is really the best of all possible worlds is excellent,' says Candide for his famous last word, 'but we must cultivate our garden.' The same principle of exclusive self-regard, applied to the gratification of sense, passed for a satisfactory defence of libertinage. In the first form it destroys a state, in the second it destroys the family.

It is easier to account for Voltaire's contempt for the mediæval superstition about purity, than his want of respect for a deliverer of France. The explanation lies in the conviction which had such power in Voltaire's own mind and with which he impregnated to such a degree the minds of others, that the action of illiterate and unpolished times can have no life in it. His view of progress was a progress of art and knowledge, and heroic action which was dumb, or which was not expressed in terms of intellect, was to the eighteenth century, and to Voltaire at least as much as to any other of its leaders, mere barbaric energy. In the order of taste, for instance, he can find only words of cool and limited praise for Homer, while for the polish and elegance of Virgil his admiration is supreme. The first was the bard of a rude time, while round the second cluster all the associations of a refined and lettered age. A self-devotion that was only articulate in the jargon of mystery and hallucination, and that was surrounded with rude and irrational circumstance, with ignorance, brutality, visions, miracle, was encircled by no halo in the eyes of a poet who found no nobleness where he did not find a definite intelligence, and who rested all his hopes and interests on the long distance set by time and civilisation between ourselves and such conditions and associations as belong to the name of Joan of

Arc. The foremost men of the eighteenth century despised Joan of Arc, whenever they had occasion to think of her, for the same reason which made them despise Gothic architecture. 'When,' says Voltaire in one place, 'the arts began to revive, they revived as Goths and Vandals; what unhappily remains to us of the architecture and sculpture of these times is a fantastic compound of rudeness and filigree.'[1] Just so, even Turgot, while protesting how dear to every sensible heart were the Gothic buildings destined to the use of the poor and the orphan, complained of the outrage done by their rude architecture to the delicacy of our sight.[2] Characters like Joan of Arc ranked in the same rude and fantastic order, and respect for them meant that respect for the middle age which was treason to the new time. Men despised her, just as they despised the majesty and beauty of the great church at Rheims where she brought her work to a climax, or the lofty grace and symmetry of the church of St. Ouen, within sight of which her life came to its terrible end.

Henry the Fourth was a hero with Voltaire, for no better reason than that he was the first great tolerant, the earliest historic indifferent. The Henriade is only important because it helped to popularise the type of its hero's character, and so to promote the rapidly-growing tendency in public opinion towards a still wider version of the policy of the Edict of Nantes.

[1] Essai sur la Poésie Epique. *Œuvres*, xiii. p. 474.
[2] *Œuvres*, ii. p. 591.

The reign of Lewis XIV. had thrown all previous
monarchs into obscurity, and the French king who
showed a warmer and more generous interest in the
happiness of his subjects than any they ever had, was
forgotten, until Voltaire brought him into fame. It
was just, however, because Henry's exploits were so
glorious, and at the same time so near in point of
time, that he made an indifferent hero for an epic poem.
'He should never choose for an epic poem history,'
said Hume very truly, 'the truth of which is well
known; for no fiction can come up to the interest of
the actual story and incidents of the singular life of
Henry IV.'[1] These general considerations, however,
as to the propriety of the subject are hardly worth
entering upon. How could any true epic come out of
that age, or find fountains in that critical, realistic, and
polemical soul? To fuse a long narrative of heroic
adventure in animated, picturesque, above all, in
sincere verse, is an achievement reserved for men with
a steadier glow, a firmer, simpler, more exuberant and
more natural poetic feeling, than was possible in that
time of mean shifts, purposeless public action, and
pitiful sacrifice of private self-respect. Virgil was
stirred by the greatness of the newly-united empire,
Tasso by the heroic march of Christendom against
pagan oppressors, Milton by the noble ardour of our
war for public rights. What long and glowing inspiration was possible to a would-be courtier, thrust
into the Bastille for wanting to fight a noble who

[1] Burton's *Life of David Hume*, ii. 440.

had had him caned by lackeys? Besides, an epic, of
all forms of poetic composition, most demands concentrated depth, and Voltaire was too widely curious
and vivacious on the intellectual side to be capable
of this emotional concentration.

But it is superfluous to give reasons why Voltaire's
epic should not be a great poem. The Henriade
itself is there, the most indisputable of arguments.
Of poems whose names are known out of literary
histories and academic catalogues, it is perhaps the
least worth reading in any language by any one but
a professional student of letters. It is less worth
reading than Lucan's Pharsalia, because it is more
deliberately artificial and gratuitously unspontaneous.
Paradise Regained, which it is too ready a fashion
among us to pronounce dull, still contains at least
three pieces of superb and unsurpassed description,
never fails in grave majestic verse, and is at the worst
free from all the dreary apparatus of phantom and
impersonation and mystic vision, which have never
jarred so profoundly with sense of poetic fitness, as
when associated with so political and matter-of-fact a
hero as Henry the Fourth. The reader has no illusion in such transactions as Saint Lewis taking Henry
into heaven and hell, Sleep hearing from her secret
caves, the Winds at sight of him falling into Silence,
and Dreams, children of Hope, flying to cover the
hero with olive and laurel. How can we overcome
our repugnance to that strange admixture of real and
and unreal matter which presents us with a highly-

coloured picture of the Temple of Love, where in the
forecourt sits Joy, with Mystery, Desire, Complaisance,
on the soft turf by her side, while in the inner sanc-
tuary haunt Jealousy, Suspicion, Malice, Fury ; while
the next canto describes

> L'église toujours une et partout étendue,
> Libre, mais sous un chef, adorant en tout lieu,
> Dans le bonheur des saints, la grandeur de son Dieu.
> Le Christ, de nos péchés victime renaissante,
> De ses élus chéris nourriture vivante,
> Descend sur les autels à ses yeux éperdus,
> Et lui découvre un Dieu sous un pain qui n'est plus.[1]

Voltaire congratulated himself in his preface that
he had come sufficiently near theological exactitude,
and to this qualification, which is so new for poetry,
the critic may add elegance and flow; but neither
elegance nor theological exactitude reconciles us to an
epic that has neither a stroke of sublimity nor a touch
of pathos, that presents no grandeur in character, and
no hurrying force and movement in action. Frederick
the Great used to speak of Voltaire as the French
Virgil, but then Frederick's father had never permitted him to learn Latin, and if he ever read Virgil
at all, it must have been in some of the jingling
French translations. Even so, with the episodes of
Dido and of Nisus and Euryalus in our minds, we
may wonder how so monstrous a parallel could have
occurred even to Frederick, who was no critic, between
two poets who have hardly a quality in common. If

[1] Henriade, x. 485-491.

the reader wishes to realise how nearly insipid even Voltaire's genius could become when working in unsuitable forms, he may turn from any canto of the Henriade to any page of Lucretius or the Paradise Lost. A French critic quotes the famous reviewer's sentence, concluding an analysis of some epic, to the effect that on the whole, when all is summed up, the given epic was 'one of the best that had appeared in the course of the current year;' and insists that Voltaire's piece will not at any rate perish in the oblivion of poetic annuals like these. If not, the only reason lies in that unfortunate tenderness for the bad work of famous men, which makes of so much reading time worse than wasted. 'The unwise,' said Candide, 'value every word in an author of repute.'

CHAPTER IV.

BERLIN.

THE Marquise du Châtelet died under circumstances that were tragical enough to herself, but which disgust the grave, while they give a grotesque amusement to those who look with cynical eye upon what they choose to treat as the great human comedy. In 1749 the friendship of sixteen years thus came to its end, and Voltaire was left without the tie that, in spite of too frequent breaking away from it, had brought him much happiness and good help so far on the road. He was now free, disastrously free as the event proved, to accept the invitations with which he had so long been pressed to take up his residence with the king who may dispute with him the claim to be held the most extraordinary man of that century.

Neither credit nor peace followed Voltaire in his own land. Lewis XV., perhaps the most worthless of all the creatures that monarchy has ever corrupted, always disliked him. The whole influence of the court and the official world had been uniformly exerted against him. Many years went by before he

could even win a seat in the academy, a distinction,
it may be added, to which Diderot, hardly second to
Voltaire in originality and power, never attained to
the end of his days. Madame de Pompadour, the
protectress of Quesnay, was Voltaire's first friend at
court. He said of her long afterwards that in the
bottom of her heart she belonged to the philosophers,
and did as much as she could to protect them.[1] She
had known him in her obscurer and more reputable
days, and she charged him with the composition of a
court-piece (1745), to celebrate the marriage of the
dauphin. The task was satisfactorily performed, and
honours which had been refused to the author of
Zaïre, Alzire, and the Henriade, were at once given
to the writer of the Princess of Navarre, which
Voltaire himself ranked as a mere farce of the fair.
He was made gentleman of the chamber and historio-
grapher of France. He disarmed the devout by the
Pope's acceptance of Mahomet, and by a letter which
he wrote to Father Latour, head of his former school,
protesting his affection for religion and his esteem for
the Jesuits. Condorcet most righteously pronounces
that, in spite of the art with which he handles his
expressions in this letter, it would undoubtedly have
been far better to give up the academy than to write
it.[2] It answered its purpose, and Voltaire was
admitted of the forty (May 1746). This distinction,
however, was far from securing for him the tranquillity which he had hoped from it, and worse libels

---

[1] *Œuvres*, lxxv. p. 266.　　　　[2] *Vie de Voltaire*, p. 60.

tormented him than before. The court sun ceased
to shine. Madame de Pompadour gave to Crébillon a
preference which Voltaire resented with more agitation than any preference of Madame Pompadour's
ought to have stirred in the breast of a strong man.

We cannot, however, too constantly remember not
to ask from Voltaire the heroic. He was far too
sympathetic, too generously eager to please, too susceptible to opinion. Of that stern and cold stuff
which supports a man in firm march and straight
course, giving him the ample content of self-respect,
he probably had less than any one of equal prominence has ever had. Instead of writing his tragedy
as well as he knew how, and then leaving it to its
destiny, he wrote it as well as he knew how, and then
went in disguise to the café of the critics to find out
what his inferiors had to say about his work. Instead
of composing his court-piece, and taking such reward
as offered, or disdaining such ignoble tasks—and
nobody knew better than he how ignoble they were
—he sought to catch some crumb of praise by fawn-
ingly asking of the vilest of men, *Trajan est-il content ?*
Make what allowance we will for difference of time
and circumstance, such an attitude to such a man,
whether in Seneca towards Nero, or Voltaire towards
Lewis xv., is a baseness that we ought never to
pardon and never to extenuate. Whether or no
there be in the human breast that natural religion of
goodness and virtue which was the sheet-anchor of
Voltaire's faith, there is at least a something in the

hearts of good men which sets a fast gulf between
them and those who are to the very depths of their
souls irredeemably saturated with corruption.

We may permit ourselves to hope that it was the
consciousness of the humiliation of such relations as
these, rather than the fact that they did not answer
their own paltry purpose, that made Voltaire resolve
a second time to shake the dust of his own country
from off his feet. In July 1750 he reached Potsdam,
and was installed with sumptuous honour in the court
of Frederick the Great, twenty-four years since he
had installed himself with Mr. Falkener, the English
merchant at Wandsworth. Diderot was busy with
the first volume of the Encyclopædia, and Rousseau
had just abandoned his second child in the hospital
for foundlings. If the visit to London did everything
for Voltaire, the visit to Berlin did nothing. There
was no Prussia, as there was an England. To travel
from the dominion of George II. to the dominion of
his famous nephew, was to go from the full light of
the eighteenth century back to the dimness of the
fifteenth. An academy of sciences, by the influence
of Sophie-Charlotte, and under the guidance of
Leibnitz, had been founded at Berlin at the beginning
of the eighteenth century ; but Frederick William
had an angry contempt for every kind of activity except drill and the preaching of orthodox theology, and
during his reign the academy languished in obscurity.[1]

[1] See the late C. Bartholmess's *Histoire Philosophique de
l'Académie de Prusse*, bk. ii.

The accession of Frederick II. was the signal for
its reconstitution, and the revival of its activity
under the direction of Maupertuis.   To the sciences
of experiment and observation, which had been its
original objects, was added a department of speculative philosophy.   The court was materialist, sceptical,
Voltairean, all at the same time ; but the academy as
a body was theologically orthodox, and it was wholly
and purely metaphysical in its philosophy.   We
may partly understand the distance at which Berlin
was then behind Paris, when we read D'Alembert's
just remonstrances with Frederick against giving as
subjects for prize-essays such metaphysical problems
as 'The search for a primary and permanent force, at
once substance and cause.'[1]

Whatever activity existed outside of the court and
the academy was divided between the dialectic of
Protestant scholasticism, and Wolf's exposition and
development of Leibnitz.   In literature proper there
arose with the accession of Frederick a small group
of essentially secondary critics, of whom Sulzer was
the best, without the vivid and radiant force of either
Voltaire or Diderot, and without the deep inspiration
and invention of those who were to follow them, and
to place Germany finally on a level with England and
France.   Lessing, the founder of the modern German
literature, was at this time a youth of twenty-two,
and by a striking turn of chance was employed by
Voltaire in putting into German his pleadings in the

[1] *Histoire Philosophique de l'Académie de Prusse*, bk. i. 230.

infamous Hirschel case. It was not then worth while
for a stranger to learn the language in which Lessing
had not yet written, and Voltaire, who was a master
of English and Italian, never knew more German
than was needed to curse a postilion.[1] Leibnitz
wrote everything of importance in Latin or French,
the Berlin academy conducted its transactions first in
Latin, next and for many years to come in French,
and one of its earliest presidents, a man of special
competence,[2] pronounced German to be a noble but
frightfully barbarised tongue. The famous Wolf had
done his best to make the tongue of his country literate,
but even his influence was unequal to the task.

Society was in its foundations not removed from
the mediæval. The soldiers with whom Frederick
won Zorndorf and Leuthen, like the Russians and
Austrians whom he defeated on those bloody days,
were not more nor less than serfs. Instead of philosophers like Newton and Locke, he had to find the
pride and safety of his country in swift rushing
troopers like Winterfield and Ziethen. A daring
cavalry-charge in season was for the moment more to
Prussia than any theory why it is that an apple falls,
and a new method of drill much more urgent than a
new origin for ideas. She was concerned not with
the speculative problem of the causes why the earth
keeps its place in the planetary system, but with the
practical problem how Prussia was to make her place
in the system of Europe. Prussia was then far more

[1] Corr. 1750. *Œuvres*, lxiv. p. 447.   [2] Jablonski.

behind France in all thought and all arts, save the
soldier's, than England was in front of France.

Voltaire had nothing to learn at Berlin, and may
we not add, as the king was a rooted Voltairean long
before this, he had nothing to teach there? The
sternest barrack in Europe was not a field in which
the apostle of free and refined intelligence could sow
seed with good hope of harvest. Voltaire at this
time, we have to recollect, was in the public mind
only a poet, and perhaps was regarded, if not altogether
by Frederick, certainly by those who surrounded him,
as much in the same order of being with Frederick's
flute, fitted by miracle with a greater number of stops.
'I don't give you any news of literature,' D'Alembert
wrote from Potsdam in 1763, 'for I don't know any,
and you know how barren literature is in this country,
where no one except the king concerns himself with
it.'[1] There is no particular disgrace to Berlin or its
king in this. Their task was very definite, and it
was only a pleasant error of Frederick's rather fantastic
youth to suppose that this task lay in the direction
of polite letters. The singer of the Henriade was
naturally of different quality and turn of mind from
a hero who had at least as hard an enterprise in his
hand as that of Henry IV. Voltaire and Frederick
were the two leaders of the two chief movements then
going on, in the great work of the transformation of
the old Europe into the new. But the movements
were in different matter, demanded vastly different

[1] *Œuvres,* lxxv. p. 224.

methods, and, as is so often the case, the scope of each was hardly visible to the pursuer of the other. Voltaire's work was to quicken the activity and proclaim the freedom of human intelligence, and to destroy the supremacy of an old spiritual order. Frederick's work was to shake down the old political order. The sum of their efforts was the definite commencement of that revolution in the thought and the political conformation of the West, of which the momentous local revolution in France must, if we take a sufficiently wide survey before and after, be counted a secondary phase. The conditions of the order which was established after the confusion of the fall of the Roman power before the inroads of the barbarians, and which constituted the Europe of the early and middle ages, are now tolerably well understood, and the historic continuity or identity of that order is typified in two institutions, which by the middle of the eighteenth century had reached very different stages of decay, and possessed very different powers of resisting attack. One was the German Empire, and the other was the Holy Catholic Church Frederick dealt a definite blow to the first, and Voltaire did the same to the second.

Those who read history and biography with a sturdy and childish pre-conception that the critical achievements in the long course of the world's progress must of necessity have fallen to the lot of the salt of the earth, will find it hard to associate the beginning of the great overt side of modern movement with

the two men who versified and wrangled together
for some two and a half years in the middle of the
eighteenth century at Berlin. It is hard to think of the
old state, with all its memories of simple enthusiasm
and wild valour and rude aspiration after some better
order, finally disappearing into the chaos for which it
was more than ripe, under the impulse of an arch
cynic. And it is hard, too, to think that the civilising
religion which was founded by a Jew, and first seized
by Jews, noblest and holiest of their race, got its first
and severest blow from one who was not above using
a Jew to cheat Christians out of their money. But
the fact remains of the vast work which this amazing
pair had to do, and did.

The character of the founder of the greatness of
Prussia, if indeed we may call founder one rather
than another member of that active, clear, and far-
sighted line, can have no attraction for those who
require as an indispensable condition of fealty that
their hero shall have either purity, or sensibility, or
generosity, or high honour, or manly respect for
human nature. Frederick's rapidity and firmness of
will, his administrative capacity, his military talent,
were marvellous and admirable enough; but on the
moral side of character, in his relations to men and
women, in his feeling for the unseen, in his ideas of
truth and beauty, he belonged to a type which is not
altogether uncommon. In his youth he had much of
a sort of shallow sensibility, which more sympathetic

usage might possibly have established and to some small extent even deepened, but which the curiously rough treatment that his pacific tastes and frivolous predilections provoked his father to inflict, turned in time into the most bitter and profound kind of cynicism that the world knows. No cynic is so hard and insensible as the man who has once had sensibility, perhaps because the consciousness that he was in earlier days open to more generous impressions persuades him that the fault of any change in his own view of things must needs lie in the world's villainy, which he has now happily for himself had time to find out. Sensibility of a true sort, springing from natural fountains of simple and unselfish feeling, can neither be corrupted nor dried up. But at its best, Frederick's sensibility was of the literary and æsthetic kind, rather than the humane and social. It concerned taste and expression, and had little root in the recognition as at first-hand of those facts of experience, of beauty and tenderness and cruelty and endurance, which are the natural objects that permanently quicken a sensitive nature. In a word, Frederick's was the conventional sensibility of the French literature of the time; a harmless thing enough in the poor souls that only poured themselves out in bad romance and worse verse, but terrible when it helped to fill with contempt for mankind an absolute monarch, with the most perfect military machine in Europe at his command. Frederick is constantly spoken of as a man typical of his century. In truth he was through-

out his life in ostentatious opposition to his century
on its most remarkable side. There has never been
any epoch whose foremost men had such faith and
hope in the virtues of humanity. There has never
been any prominent man who despised humanity so
bitterly and unaffectedly as Frederick despised it.

We know what to think of a man who writes a
touching and pathetic letter condoling with a friend
on the loss of his wife, and on the same day makes
an epigram on the dead woman [1]; who never found
so much pleasure in a friendly act as when he could
make it the means of hurting the recipient; whose
practical pleasantries were always spiteful and sneering
and cruel. As we read of his tricks on D'Argens or
Pöllnitz, we feel how right Voltaire was in borrowing
a nickname for him from a mischievous brute whom
he kept in his garden. He presented D'Argens with
a house; when D'Argens went to take possession he
found the walls adorned with pictures of all the most
indecent and humiliating episodes of his own life.
This was a type of Frederick's delicacy towards some
of those whom he honoured with his friendship. It
is true that, except Voltaire and Maupertuis, most of
the French philosophers whom Frederick seduced
into coming to live at Berlin were not too good for
the corporal's horse-play of which they were the
victims. But then we know, further, what to think
of a man whose self-respect fails to proscribe gross
and unworthy companions. He is either a lover of

[1] Corr. 1750. *Œuvres*, lxiv. p. 443.

parasites, which Frederick certainly was not, or else
the most execrable cynic, the cynic who delights in
any folly or depravity that assures him how right he
is in despising 'that damned race.'

Frederick need not have summoned the least
worthy French freethinkers, men like D'Argens and
La Mettrie and De Prades, in their own way as little
attractive in life and in doctrine as any monk or
Geneva preacher, to warrant him in thinking meanly
of mankind.　If any one wants to know what manner
of spirit this great temporal deliverer of Europe was
of, he may find what he seeks in the single episode
of the negotiations at Klein-Schnellendorf in 1741.
There, although he had made and was still bound by
a solemn treaty of alliance with France, he entered
into secret engagements with the Hungarian Queen,
to be veiled by adroitly pretended hostilities.　Even
if, as an illustrious apologist of the Prussian King is
reduced to plead, this is in a certain fashion defensible,
on the ground that France and Austria were both
playing with cogged dice, and therefore the other
dicer of the party was in self-defence driven to show
himself their superior in these excellent artifices, there
still seems a gratuitous infamy in hinting to the
Austrian general, as Frederick did, how he might
assault with advantage the French enemy, Frederick's
own ally at the moment.[1]　This was the author of
the plea for political morality, called the Anti-
Machiavel, whose publication Voltaire had superin-

---

[1] Carlyle's *History of Frederick*, bk. xiii. ch. 5.

tended the year before, and, for that matter, had
done his best to prevent. Still, as Frederick so
graciously said of his new guest and old friend : ' He
has all the tricks of a monkey ; but I shall make no
sign, for I need him in my study of French style.
One may learn good things from a scoundrel : I want
to know his French ; what is his morality to me ?'
And so a royal statesman may have the manners of
the coarsest corporal, and the morality of the grossest
cynic, and still have both the eye to discern, and the
hand to control, the forces of a great forward movement.

Frederick had the signal honour of accepting his
position, and taking up with an almost perfect forti-
tude the burden which it laid upon him. ' We are
not masters of our own lot,' he wrote to Voltaire,
immediately after his accession to the throne ; 'the
whirlwind of circumstances carries us away, and we
must suffer ourselves to be carried away.'[1]   And
what he said in this hour of exaltation he did not
deny nearly twenty years later, when his fortunes
seemed absolutely desperate.   ' If I had been born a
private person,' he wrote to him in 1759, ' I would
give up everything for love of peace ; but a man is
bound to take on the spirit of his position.'[2]   'Philosophy teaches us to do our duty, to serve our country
faithfully at the price of our blood and our ease, to
sacrifice for it our whole existence.'[3]   Men are also

[1] Œuvres de Voltaire, lxxiii. p. 456.
[2] Ib. p. 813.   [3] Ib. p. 807.

called upon by their country to abstain from sacri-
ficing their existence, and if Frederick's sense of duty
to his subjects had been as perfect as it was excep-
tionally near being so, he would not have carried a
phial of poison round his neck.[1] Still on the whole
he devoted himself to his career with a temper that
was as entirely calculated for the overthrow of a
tottering system, as Voltaire's own. It is difficult to
tell whether Frederick's steady attention to letters
and men of letters, and his praiseworthy endeavours
to make Berlin a true academic centre, were due to
a real and disinterested love of knowledge, and a
sense of its worth to the spirit of man, or still more
to weak literary vanity, and a futile idea of universal
fame so far as his own productions went, and a purely
utilitarian purpose so far as his patronage of the
national academy was concerned. One thing is certain, that the philosophy which he learnt from French
masters, which Voltaire brought in his proper person
to Berlin, and to which Frederick to the end of his
days was always adding illustrative commentaries,
never made any impression on Germany. The teaching of Leibnitz and Wolf stood like a fortified wall
in the face of the French invasion, and whatever
effective share French speculation had upon Germany,
was through the influence of Descartes upon Leibnitz.

The dissolution of the outer framework of the
European state-system, for which Frederick's seizure

---

[1] For Voltaire's admirably expressed remonstrance, see Corr.
Oct. 1757. *Œuvres*, lxxiii. p. 768.

of Silesia was the first clear signal, followed as it was
by the indispensable suppression of the mischievous
independence, so called, of barbaric and feudal Poland,
where bishops and nobles held a people in the most
oppressive bondage, can only concern us here slightly,
because it was for the time only indirectly connected
with the characteristic work of Voltaire's life. But,
though indirect, the connection may be seen at our
distance of time to have been marked and unmistakable. The old order and principles of Europe
were to receive a new impress, and the decaying
system of the middle age to be replaced by a polity
of revolution, which should finally change the relations of nations, the types of European government,
and the ideas of spiritual control.

In 1733 the war of the Polish succession between
Austria and Russia on the one hand, and France and
Spain on the other, had given the first great shock
to the house of Austria, which was compelled to re-
nounce the pretensions and territory of the Empire
in Italy, or nearly all of them, in favour of the Spanish
Bourbons, as well as to surrender Lorraine to Stanislas,
with reversion to the crown of France. We may notice
in passing that it was at Stanislas' court of Lunéville
that Voltaire and the Marquise du Châtelet passed
their last days together. The wars of the Polish
succession were remarkable for another circumstance.
They were the first occasion of the decisive interference
of Russia in Western affairs, an only less important
disturbance of Europe than the first great interference

of Prussia a few years later. The falling to pieces of
the old Europe was as inevitable as, more than twelve
centuries before, had been the dissolution of that yet
older Europe whose heart had been not Vienna but
Rome. Russia and Prussia were not the only novel
elements. There was a third from over the sea, the
American colonies of France and England.

Roman Europe had been a vast imperial state, with
slavery for a base. Then, after the feudal organisation had run its course, there was a long and chaotic
transition of dynastic and territorial wars, frightfully
wasteful of humanity and worse than unfruitful to
progress. In vain do historians, intent on vindicating
the foregone conclusions of the optimism which a distorted notion about final causes demands or engenders
in them, try to show these hateful contests as parts
of a harmonious scheme of things, in which many
diverse forces move in a mysterious way to a common
and happy end. As if any good use, for instance,
were served by the transfer, for one of the chief
results of the war of the Polish succession, of the
Italian provinces of the Empire of the Spanish Bourbons. As if any good or permanent use were served
by the wars which ended in the Peace of Utrecht,
when victorious England conceded, and with much
wisdom conceded, the precise point which she had for
so many years been disputing. From the Peace of
Westphalia to the beginning of the Seven Years' War,
it is not too much to say that there was a century of
purely artificial strife on the continent of Europe, of

wars as factious, as merely personal, as unmeaning, as
the civil war of the Fronde was all of these things.
In speaking roundly of this period, we leave out of
account the first Silesian War, because the issue between Prussia and Austria was not decisively fought
out until the final death-struggle from 1756 to 1763.
It was the entry of Frederick the Great upon the
scene, that instantly raised international relations into
the region of real matter and changed a strife of
dynasties, houses, persons, into a vital competition
between old forces and principles and new. The aim-
less and bloody commotions which had raged over
Europe, and ground men's lives to dust in the red
mill of battle, came for a time to an end, and their
place was taken by a tremendous conflict, on whose
issue hung not merely the triumph of a dynasty, but
the question of the type to which future civilisation
was to conform.

In the preliminary war which followed immediately
upon the death of Charles VI. in 1740, and which had
its beginning in Frederick's invasion of Silesia, circumstances partially marched in the usual tradition, with
France and Austria playing opposite sides in an accustomed game. Before the opening of the Seven Years'
War the cardinal change of policy and alliances had
taken place. We are not concerned with the court
intrigues that brought the change about, with the
intricate manœuvres of the Jesuits, or the wounded
vanity of Bernis, whose verses Frederick laughed at,
or the pique of Pompadour, whom Frederick declined

to count an acquaintance. When conflicting forces of
tidal magnitude are at work, as they were in the
middle of the last century, the play of mere personal
aims and ambitions is necessarily of secondary importance ; because we may always count upon there being
at least one great power that clearly discerns its own
vital interest, and is sure therefore to press with
steady energy in its own special direction. That
power was Austria. One force of this kind is enough
to secure a universal adjustment of all the others in
their natural places.

The situation was apparently very complex. There
were in the middle of the century two great pairs of
opposed interests, the interests of France and England
on the ocean and in America, and the interests of
Austria and Prussia in Central Europe. The contest
was in each of the two cases much more than a superficial affair of dynasties or division of territory, to
meet the requirements of the metaphysical diplomacy
of the balance of power. It was a re-opening in far
vaster proportions of those profound issues of new
religion and old which had only been dammed up, and
not permanently settled, by the great Peace of Westphalia in 1648. In vaster proportions, not merely
because the new struggle between the Catholic and
Protestant powers extended into the new world, but
because the forces contained in these two creeds had
been widened and developed, and a multitude of
indirect consequences, entirely apart from theology
and church discipline, depended upon the triumph of

Great Britain and Prussia. The Governments of
France and Austria represented the feudal and military idea, not in the strength of that idea while it
was still alive, but in the narrow and oppressive form
of its decay. No social growth was possible under its
shadow, for one of its essential conditions was discour-
agement, active and passive, of commercial industry,
the main pathway then open to an advancing people.
Again, both France and Austria represented the old
type of monarchy, as distinguished alike from the
aristocratic oligarchy of England, and the new type
of monarchy which Prussia introduced into Europe,
frugal, encouraging industry, active in supervision,
indefatigable in improving the laws. Let us not
omit above all things the splendid religious toleration,
of which Prussia set so extraordinarily early an example
to Europe. The Protestants whom episcopal tyranny
drove from Salzburg found warm hospitality among
their northern brethren. While the professors of the
reformed faith were denied civil status in France,
and subjected to persecution of a mediæval bloodiness,
one Christian was counted exactly as another in
Prussia. While England was revelling in the infliction of atrocious penal laws on her Catholic citizens,
Prussia extended even to the abhorred Jesuit the
shelter which was denied him in Spain and at Rome.
The transfer of territory from Austria to Prussia
meant the extension of toleration in that territory.
Silesia, for instance, no sooner became Prussian, than
the University of Breslau, whose advantages had

hitherto been rigidly confined to Catholics, was at
once compulsorily opened to Protestants and Catholics
alike. In criticising Frederick's despotism let us recognise how much enlightenment, how much of what is
truly modern, was to be found in the manner in which
this despotic power was exercised, long before the same
enlightened principles were accepted in other countries.

We cannot understand the issues of the Seven
Years' War, nor indeed of the eighteenth century on
any of its more important sides, without tolerably
distinct ideas about the ages before and behind it,
about the sixteenth century and the twentieth; without
ideas as to the conditions of the break-up of the
Catholic and the feudal organisation, and, next, as to
the attitude proper to be assumed, and the methods
to be followed, in dealing with the more or less
anarchic circumstances in which their break-up and
its sequels leave us. There are two ways of regarding
these questions. You may say, as Comte says, that
the ultimate type of society, perfected on a basis of
positive knowledge, will in the essential features of
its constitution correspond to the ancient or mediæval
constitution which it replaces; because that gave the
fullest possible satisfaction to those elements of human
nature which are deepest and permanent, and to those
social needs which must always press upon us; that
anything which either seriously retards the dissolution
of the old, or draws men aside from the road which
leads on to the same organisation transformed, must
therefore be an impediment in the way of the new

N

society, and a peril to civilisation. Hence, they say, the mischievousness of Protestantism, Voltairism, and all the minor manifestations of the critical spirit, because they inspire their followers with a contempt, as mistaken towards the past as it is pernicious to the future, for those fundamental principles of social stability and individual happiness, to which alone we have to look for the establishment of a better order ; because they give to the unguided individual judgment the force and authority that can only come with safety from organisation and tradition, that is from a certain definite form of shaping and expressing the common judgment ; and because, moreover, they tend directly and indirectly to detach effort from social aims and the promotion of the common weal, to the attainment of mean and unwholesome individual ambitions. From this point of view, we should have to regard the acquisition of colonies, for instance, which was one of the chief objects of Lord Chatham's policy, as the mischievous transfer, in the interests of commercial cupidity, of an activity, hopefulness, and power, that ought to have been devoted to the solution of the growing social difficulties of Europe ; and that ought to have been bent from a profoundly mean egotism, in the nation and the traders whose interest was the key of the policy, into a generous feeling for the public order.

There is, however, another and a very different way of looking at all this. You cannot be sure, it is said, that the method of social advance is to be a return upon the old framework and the old lines ; to

be sure of this implies an impatient confidence that
social forms have all been exhausted, or else an unsupported assumption that the present transitory
form is so full of danger to the stability of civilisation,
as to make the acceptance of almost any firm order
better than the prolonged endurance of a social state
which, on that theory, ought hardly to be accounted
much better than the social state of Bedouin Arabs.
Is it not far better and safer to refrain from com-
mitting ourselves to a given type of social reconstruction, and to work forward patiently upon the only
principle that can be received with entire assurance ;
namely, that faithful cultivation of the intelligence,
and open-minded investigation of all that the intelligence may present to us, is the only certain method
of not missing the surest and quickest road to the
manifold improvements of which the fundamental
qualities of human nature, as well as the relations of
man in society, are susceptible ? There is no good
ground for supposing that this steadfast regard to
the fruitfulness and variety of the individual intelligence tends specially to lead to the concentration
of energy upon individual aims. For what lesson
does free intelligence teach us more constantly or more
impressively than that man standing alone is impotent,
that every unsocial act or sentiment tends to overthrow that collectivity of effort to which we owe all,
and, most important of all, that this collectivity is
most effectively secured by the just culture of the
impulses and affections ? No degree nor kind of

organisation could lead us further than this, and ought it not to be the prime object and chief hope of those who think about society, that this truth shall stand rooted in every one's own reason? If it does not so stand, you have no security for your spiritual organisation, and if it does, then you have no necessity. It is to the spread of this conviction, by the ever-pressing consciousness of urgent social circumstances, that we must look to suffuse industrial and egotistic energy with a truly moral and social sentiment.

This is the point of view from which we may justly regard the violent change that was the result of the Seven Years' War, as a truly progressive step. We cannot be as reasonably sure that the old conditions of men's relations in society are in whatever new shape destined to return, as we are sure that it was a good thing to prevent a feudal and jesuitical government like Austria from retaining a purely obstructive power in Europe, and a jesuitical government like France from establishing the same obstructive kind of power in America. The advantages of the final acquisition of America by Protestantism, and the decisive consolidation of Prussia, were not without alloy. History does not present us with these clean balances. It is not at all difficult to see the injurious elements in this victory of the northern powers, and nobody would be less willing than the present writer to accept either the Prussian polity of Frederick, or the commercial polity of England and her western colonies, as offering final types of wholesome social states.

But the alternative was the triumph of a far worse polity than either, the polity of the Society of Jesus.

Even those who claim our respect for the Jesuits as having in the beginning of their course served the very useful purpose of honestly administering that spiritual power which had fallen from the hands of the Popes, who had mischievously entered the ranks and followed the methods of temporal princes, do not deny that within a couple of generations they became a dangerous obstacle to the continuity of European progress. Indeed, it is clear that they grew into the very worst element that has ever appeared in the whole course of European history, because their influence rested on a systematic compromise with moral corruption. They had barely seized the spiritual power in the Catholic countries when it was perceived that as an engine of moral control their supposed power was no power at all; and that the only condition on which they could retain the honour and the political authority which were needful to them was that they should connive at moral depravity. They had the education of the country in their hands, and from the confessor's closet they pulled the wires which moved courts. There was no counter-force, for the mass of the people was dumb, ignorant, and fettered. Say what we will of the need for a spiritual power, the influence of the Jesuits by the middle of the eighteenth century was cutting off the very root of civilisation. This was the veritably Infamous. And this was the influence which the alliance of England and

Prussia, a thing accidental enough to all appearance, successfully and decisively checked, because the triumph of the two northern powers was naturally the means of discrediting the Jesuit intrigues in the court of Versailles and elsewhere, and stripping them of those associations of political and material success, which had hitherto stood to them in the stead of true spiritual credit.

The peace of 1763 had important territorial consequences. By the treaty of Paris between France, England, and Spain, Great Britain was assured of her possessions on the other side of the Atlantic. By the treaty of Hubertsburg between Austria, Prussia, and Saxony, Prussia was assured of her position as an independent power in Europe. These things were much. But the decisive repulse of the great Jesuit organisation was yet more. It was the most important side of the same facts. The immediate occasions of this repulse varied in different countries, and had their origin in different sets of superficial circumstance, but the debility of the courts of Austria and France was the only condition on which such occasions could be seized. The very next year, after the treaties of Paris and Hubertsburg, the Society of Jesus was suppressed in France, and its property confiscated. Three years later it was expelled from Spain. Within ten years from the peace of 1763 it was abolished by the virtuous Clement XIV. In Canada, where the order had been extremely powerful,[1] their authority vanished, and with it the probability of establishing

[1] Martin's *Hist. de France*, xv. p. 468.

in the northern half of the new world those ideas of
political absolutism and theological casuistry which
were undoing the old. Whatever the accidents which
hurried the catastrophe, there were two general causes
which really produced it, the revolution in ideas, and
the revolution in the seat of material power. If this
be a true description of the crisis, we can see sufficiently plainly to what an extent Voltaire and
Frederick, while they appeared to themselves to be
fellow-workers only in the culture of the muses, were
in fact unconsciously co-operating in a far mightier
task. When the war was drawing to an end, and
Frederick was likely to escape from the calamities
which had so nearly overwhelmed him and his kingdom in irretrievable ruin, we find Voltaire writing to
D'Alembert thus: 'As for Luc' (the nickname bor-
rowed for the king of Prussia from an ape with a
trick of biting), 'though I ought to be full of resentment against him, yet I confess to you that in my
quality of thinking creature and Frenchman, I am
heartily content that a certain most devout house has
not swallowed Germany up, and that the Jesuits
don't confess at Berlin. Superstition is monstrously
powerful towards the Danube.' To which his correspondent replied that he quite agreed that the triumph
of Frederick was a blessing for France and for philosophy. 'These Austrians are insolent capucins,
whom I would fain see annihilated with the superstition they protect.'[1] Here was precisely the issue.

[1] *Œuvres*, lxxv. p. 207 and p. 210.

It would be a great mistake to suppose that Frederick consciously and formally recognised the ultimate ends of his policy. Such deliberate marking out of the final destination of their work, imputed to rulers, churchmen, poets, is mostly a figment invented by philosophers. Frederick thought nothing at all about the conformation of the European societies in the twentieth century. It was enough for him to make a strong and independent Prussia, without any far-reaching vision, or indeed without any vision at all, of the effect which a strong and independent Prussia would finally have upon the readjustment of ideas and social forces in western civilisation. We are led to a false notion of history, and of all the conditions of political action and the development of nations, by attributing to statesmen deep and far-reaching sight of consequences, which only completed knowledge and some ingenuity enable those who live after to fit into a harmonious scheme. 'Fate, for whose wisdom I entertain all imaginable reverence, often finds in chance, by which it works, an instrument not over manageable.'[1] And the great ruler, knowing this, is content to abstain from playing fate's part, feeling his way slowly to the next step. His compass is only true for a very short distance, and his chart has marks for no long course. To make Prussia strong was the aim of Frederick's life. Hence, although the real destiny of his policy was to destroy the house of Austria, he did not scruple in

[1] Goethe.

1741 to offer to assist Maria Theresa with his best help against all the other invaders of the famous Pragmatic Sanction, which they had solemnly sworn to uphold. Afterwards, and before the outbreak of the Seven Years' War, he sought the alliance of France, but happily for Europe, not until after Kaunitz and Maria Theresa had already secured that blind and misguided power, thus driving him into an alliance with Great Britain. And so chance did the work of fate after all.

It may be said that such a view of the operation of the great forces of the world is destructive of all especial respect and gratitude towards the eminent men, of whom chance and fate have made mere instruments. What becomes of hero-worship, if your hero after all only half knew whither he sought to go, and if those achievements which have done such powerful service were not consciously directed towards the serviceable end? We can only answer that it is not the office of history to purvey heroes, nor always to join appreciation of a set of complex effects with veneration for this or that performer. For this veneration, if it is to be an intelligent mood, implies insight into the inmost privacy of aim and motive, and this insight, in the case of those whom circumstance raises on a towering pedestal, we can hardly ever count with assurance on finding faithful and authentic. History is perhaps not less interesting for not being distorted into a new hagiographa.

It is equally unwarranted to put into Frederick's

mind conscious ideas as to the type of monarchy proper for Europe in the epoch of passage from old systems. Once more, he thought of his own country, and his own country only, in all those wise measures of internal government which have been so unjustly and so childishly thrust by historians into the second place behind his exploits as a soldier, as if the civil activity of the period between 1763, when peace was made, and 1786, when he died, was not fully as remarkable in itself, and fully as momentous in its results, as the military activity of the period between 1763 and 1740. There is in men of the highest governing capacity, like Richelieu, or Cromwell, or Frederick, an instinct for good order and regular administration. They insist upon it for its own sake, independently of its effects either on the happiness of subjects, or on the fundamental policy and march of things. If Frederick had acceded to the supreme power in a highly civilised country, he would have been equally bent on imposing his own will and forcing the administration into the exact grooves prescribed by himself, and the result would have been as pestilent there as it was beneficial in a backward and semi-barbarous country such as Prussia was in his time. This good internal ordering was no more than a part of the same simple design which shaped his external policy. He had to make a nation, and its material independence in the face of Austria and Russia was not more a part of this process than giving it the great elements of internal well-being, equal laws, just administration, financial thrift, and stimulus and encouragement to industry. Such an achievement as the restoration of the germs of order and prosperity, which Frederick so rapidly brought about after the appalling ruin that seven years of disastrous war had effected, is unmatched in the history of human government. Well might he pride himself, as we know that he did, on replacing this social chaos by order, more than on Rossbach or Leuthen. Above all, he never forgot the truth which every statesman ought to have burning in letters of fire before his eyes; *I am the procurator of the poor.*

It commits us to no general theory of government to recognise the merits of Frederick's internal administration. They constitute a special case, to be judged by its own conditions. We may safely go so far as to say that in whatever degree the social state of a nation calls for active government, whether, as the people of the American Union boast of themselves, they need no government, or whether, as is the case in Great Britain, the wretched lives of the poor beneath the combined cupidity and heartless want of thought of the rich cry aloud for justice, in this degree it is good that the statesmen called to govern should be in that capacity of Frederick's type, conceding all freedom to thought, but energetic in the use of power as trustees for the whole nation against special classes. To meet completely the demands of their office they should have, what Frederick neither had nor could under the circumstances of his advent and the time be expected to have, a firm conviction that the highest ultimate end of all kingship is to enable nations to dispense with that organ of national life, and to fit them for a spontaneous initiative and free control in the conduct of their own affairs.

Let us be careful to remember that, if Frederick was a great ruler in the positive sense, he sprang from the critical school. The traditions of his house were strictly Protestant, his tutors were Calvinistic refugees, and his personal predilections had from his earliest youth been enthusiastically Voltairean. May we not count it one of the claims of the critical philosophy to a place among the leading progressive influences in western history, that it tended to produce statesmen of this positive type? I do not know of any period of corresponding length that can produce such a group of active, wise, and truly positive statesmen as existed in Europe between 1760 and 1780. Besides Frederick, we have Turgot in France, Pombal in Portugal, Charles III. and D'Aranda in Spain. If Charles III. was faithful to the old creed, the three greatest, at any rate, of these extraordinary men drew inspiration from the centre of the critical school. D'Aranda had mixed much with the Voltairean circle while in Paris. Pombal, in spite of the taint of some cruelty, in so many respects one of the most powerful and resolute ministers that has ever held office in Europe, had been for some time in England, and was a warm admirer of Voltaire, whose works he caused to be translated into Portuguese. The

famous school of Italian publicists, whose speculations
bore such admirable fruit in the humane legislation
of Leopold of Tuscany, and had so large a share in
that code with which the name of the ever hateful
Bonaparte has become fraudulently associated, these
excellent thinkers found their oracles in that critical
philosophy, of which we are so unjustly bidden to
think only in connection with shallow and reckless
destruction. The application of reason to the ameli-
oration of the social condition was the device of the
great rulers of this time, and the father and inspirer
of this device was that Voltaire who is habitually
presented to us a mere mocker.

Psychologues like Sulzer might declare that the
scourge of right thinking was to be found in 'those
philosophers who, more used to sallies of wit than to
deep reasoning, assume that they have overthrown
by a single smart trope truths only to be known by
combining a multitude of observations, so delicate
and difficult that we cannot grasp them without the
aid of the firmest attention.'[1] How many of these
so-called truths were anything but sophistical propositions, the products of intellectual ingenuity run riot,
without the smallest bearing either on positive science
or social well-being? And is it not rather an abuse
of men's willingness to take the profundity of metaphysics on trust, that any one who has formulated a
metaphysical proposition, with due technicality of
sounding words, has a claim to arrest the serious

[1] Bartholmess, ii. 111.

attention of every busy passer-by, and to throw on this innocent and laudable person the burden of dis proof? If Duns Scotus or St. Thomas Aquinas had risen from the dead, Voltaire would very properly have declined a bout of school dialectic with those famous shades, because he was living in the century of the Encyclopædia, when the exploration of things and the improvement of institutions had taken the place of subtle manipulation of unverified words, important as that process had once been in the intellectual development of Europe. He was equally wise in declining to throw more than a trope or sprightly sally in the direction of people who dealt only in the multiplication of metaphysical abracadabras. It was his task to fix the eyes of men upon action. In the sight of Lutheran or Wolfian conjurors with words this was egregious shallowness. Strangely enough they thought it the climax of philosophic profundity to reconcile their natural spiritualism with the supernatural spiritualism of the scriptures, and rationalistic theism with the historic theism of revelation.[1] Voltaire repudiated the supernatural and pseudo-historic half of this hybrid combination, and in doing so he showed a far profounder logic than the cloudiest and most sonorous of his theologico-metaphysical critics. We may call him negative and destructive on this account if we please, yet surely the abnegation of barren and inconsistent speculation, and of fruitless effort to seize a vain abstract universality, was a very

[1] See Bartholmess, i. 168.

meritorious trait in a man who did not stop here, but by every means, by poetry, by history, by biography, and by the manifestation of all his vivid personal interests, drew every one who was within the sphere of his attraction to the consideration of social action as the first fact for the firm attention of the leaders of mankind.

It may be said that even from this side Voltaire was destructive only, and undoubtedly, owing to the circumstances of the time, the destructive side seemed to predominate in his social influence. To say this, however, is not to bring an end to the matter. The truth is that no negative thinking can stop at the negative point. To teach men to hate superstition and injustice is a sure, if an indirect, way of teaching them to seek after their opposites. Voltaire could only shake obscurantist institutions by appealing to man's love of light, and the love of light, once stirred, leads far. He appealed to reason, and it was reason in Frederick and the others, which had quickened and strengthened the love of good order, that produced the striking reforming spirit which moved through the eighteenth century, until the reaction against French revolutionary violence arrested its progress. It is one of the most difficult questions in all history to determine whether the change from the old order to the new has been damaged or advanced by that most memorable arrest of the work of social renovation in the hands of sovereign and traditional governments, administered by wise statesmen with due re-

gard to traditional spirit; and how far the passionate
efforts of those classes, whose only tradition is a tradition of squalor and despair, have driven the possessors of superior material power back into obstructive
trepidation. The question is more than difficult, it is
in our generation insoluble, because the movement is
wholly incomplete. But whether the French outbreak
from 1789 to 1794 may prove to have been the
starting-point of a new society, or only to have been
a detrimental interruption and parent of interruptions
to stable movement forwards, we have in either case
to admit that there was a most vigorous attempt made
in all the chief countries in Europe, between the
middle of the century and the fall of the French
monarchy, to improve government and to perfect
administration; that Frederick of Prussia was the
author of the most permanently successful of these
endeavours; and that Frederick learnt to break loose
from dark usage, to prefer equity of administration,
to abandon religious superstition, and to insist on
tolerance, from the only effective moral and intellectual masters he ever had, first the French Calvinists,
and then the French critical school, with Voltaire for
chief. It is true, as we shall presently see, that an
important change in the spirit of French writers was
marked by the Encyclopædia, which was so much besides being critical. But then this famous work only
commenced in the year when Voltaire reached Berlin,
and Frederick's character had received its final shape
long before that time.

With the exception of Voltaire, D'Alembert was
the only really eminent Frenchman whose work ever
struck Frederick, and we are even conscious, in comparing his letters to these two eminent men, of a
certain seriousness and deferential respect towards
the later friend, which never marked his relations
with Voltaire after the early days of youthful enthusiasm. Frederick's admiration for France, indeed,
has been somewhat overstated by French writers,
and by those of our own country who have taken
their word for granted. 'Your nation,' Frederick
once wrote to Voltaire, 'is the most inconsequent in
all Europe. It abounds in bright intelligence, but
has no consistency in its ideas. This is how it
appears through all its history. There is really an
indelible character imprinted on it. The only exception in a long succession of reigns is to be found in a
few years of Lewis XIV. The reign of Henry IV.
was neither tranquil enough nor long enough for us
to take that into account. During the administration
of Richelieu we observe some consistency of design
and some nerve in execution; but in truth they are
uncommonly short epochs of wisdom in so long a
chronicle of madnesses. Again, France has been able
to produce men like Descartes or Malebranche, but
no Leibnitz, no Lockes, no Newtons. On the other
hand, for taste, you surpass all other nations, and I
will surely range myself under your standards in all
that regards delicacy of discernment and the judicious
and scrupulous choice between real beauties and those

o

which are only apparent. That is a great point in polite letters, but it is not everything.'[1] Frederick, however, could never endure the least hint that he was not a perfect Frenchman in the order of polite letters. The article on Prussia in the Encyclopædia was full of the most flattering eulogies of his work as a soldier and an administrator, and even contained handsome praise for his writings; but Diderot, the author of this part of the article, delicately suggested that a year or two in the Faubourg St. Honoré would perhaps have dispersed the few grains of Berlin sand which hindered the perfect purity of note of that admirable flute. Frederick, who had hitherto been an ardent reader of the Encyclopædia, never opened another volume.

We can understand Voltaire's character without wading through the slough of mean scandals which sprung up like gross fungi during his stay at Berlin. Who need remember that Frederick spoke of his illustrious guest as an orange of which, when one has squeezed the juice, one throws away the skin? Or how Voltaire retorted by speaking of his illustrious host, whose royal verses he had to correct, as a man sending his dirty linen to him to wash? or, still worse, as a compound of Julius Cæsar and the abbé Cotin? Nor need we examine into stories, suspicious products of Berlin malice, how Frederick stopped his guest's supply of sugar and chocolate, and how Voltaire put

[1] *Œuvres de Voltaire*, lxxiii. p. 836.

his host's candle-ends into his pocket. It is enough
to know that the king and the poet gradually lost
their illusions, and forgot that life was both too short
and too valuable to waste in vain efforts of making
believe that an illusion is other than it is. Voltaire
took a childish delight in his gold key and his star,
and in supping as an intimate with a king who had
won five battles. His life was at once free and occupied, the two conditions of happy existence. He
worked diligently at his Siècle de Louis XIV., and
diverted himself with operas, comedies, and great en-
tertainments among affable queens, charming prin-
cesses, and handsome maids of honour. Yet he could
not forget the saying, which had been so faithfully
carried to him, of the orange-skin. He declared that
he was like the man who fell from the top of a high
tower, and finding himself softly supported in the
air, cried out, *Good, if it only lasts.*[1] Or he was like a
husband striving hard to persuade himself of the
fidelity of a suspected wife. He had fits of violent
nostalgia. 'I am writing to you by the side of a
stove, with drooping head and heavy heart, looking
on to the River Spree, because the Spree falls into
the Elbe, the Elbe into the sea, and the sea receives
the Seine, and our Paris house is near the River
Seine, and I say, Why am I in this palace, in this
cabinet looking into this Spree, and not in our own
chimney-corner? . . . How my happiness is poisoned,
how short is life! What wretchedness to seek happi-

[1] Corr. 1751. *Œuvres*, lxiv. p. 524.

ness far from you; and what remorse, if one finds it away from you.'[1] This was to Madame Denis, his niece; but a Christmas in the Berlin barrack made even a plain coquette in Paris attractive and homely. We may imagine with what tender regrets he would look back upon the old days at Cirey.

Even in respect of the very mischief from which he had fled, the detraction and caballing of the envious, he was hardly any better off at Berlin than he had been at Paris. D'Argental, one of the wisest of his friends, had forewarned him of this, and that he had fled from enemies whom at any rate he never saw, only to find other enemies with whom he had to live day after day. This was exactly what came to pass. Voltaire often compared the system of life at Berlin and Potsdam to that of a convent, half military, half literary. The vices of conventual life came with its other features, and among them jealousy, envy, and malice. The tale-bearer, that constant parasite of such societies, had exquisite opportunities, and for a susceptible creature like Voltaire, the result was wholly fatal. The nights and suppers of the gods became, in his own phrase, suppers of Damocles. Alexander the Great was transformed into the tyrant Dionysius. The famous Diatribe of Doctor Akakia, in the autumn of 1752, brought matters to a climax, because its publication was supposed to show marked defiance of the king's wishes.

Maupertuis had been one of the earliest and most

[1] Corr. 1751. *Œuvres*, lxiv. p. 453.

strenuous Newtonians in France, and had at his own
personal risk helped to corroborate the truth of the
new system. In 1735 the zeal for experimental
science, which was so remarkable a trait in this
century of many-sided intellectual activity, induced
the academy of sciences to despatch an expedition to
take the actual measure of a degree of meridian
below the equator, and the curious and indefatigable
De la Condamine, one of the most ardent men of
that ardent time, with two other inquirers went to
Peru. In 1736 Maupertuis and Clairaut under the
same auspices started for the north pole, where, after
undergoing the severest hardships, they succeeded in
measuring their degree, and verifying by observation
Newton's demonstration of the oblate figure of the
earth, a verification that was further completed by
La Caille's voyage to the Cape of Good Hope in 1750.[1]
Maupertuis commemorated his share in this excellent
work by having a portrait of himself executed, in
which the palm of a hand gently flattens the north
pole. He was extremely courageous and extremely
vain. His costume was eccentric and affected, his
temper more jealous and arbitrary than comports with
the magnanimity of philosophers, and his manner
more gloomily solemn than the conditions of human
life can ever justify. With all his absurdities, he
was a man of real abilities, and of a solidity of character beyond that of any of his countrymen at
Frederick's court. I would rather live with him,

[1] See Whewell's *Hist. Ind. Sci.* bk. vii. ch. 4, § 7.

Frederick wrote to the princess Wilhelmina, than with Voltaire; 'his character is surer,' which in itself was saying little. But then, the moment he came into collision with Voltaire, his absurdities became the most important thing about him, because it was precisely these which Voltaire was sure to drag into unsparing prominence. In old days they had been good friends, and a letter still remains, mournfully testifying to the shallowness of men's sight into the roots of their relations with others, for it closes by bidding Maupertuis be sure that Voltaire will love him all the days of his life.[1] The causes of their collision were obvious enough. As Frederick said, Of two Frenchmen in the same court, one must perish. Maupertuis, from the heights of the exact sciences, probably despised Voltaire as a scribbler, while Voltaire, with a heart flowing over with gay vivacity, assuredly counted Maupertuis arbitrary, ridiculously solemn, and something of an impostor. The compliances of society, he said of the president of the Berlin academy, are not problems that he is fond of solving. Maupertuis acted to König, in the matter of an academic or discoverer's quarrel, in a way that struck Voltaire, and all men since, as tyrannical, unjust, and childish, all in one. He unhappily wrote a book which gave Voltaire such an excuse for punishing the author's injustice to König, as even Voltaire's spleen could hardly have hoped for, and the result was the wittiest and most pitiless of all the

[1] *Œuvres*, lxiv. p. 53.

purely personal satires in the world. The temptation
was certainly irresistible.

Maupertuis, as has been said, was courageous and
venturesome, and this venturesomeness being uncor-
rected by the severe discipline of a large body of
accurate positive knowledge, such as Clairaut and
Lagrange possessed, led him into some worse than
equivocal speculation. He was in the depths of the
metaphysical stage, and developed physical theories
out of abstract terms. Of some of these theories the
worst that could be said was they were wholly un-
proved. He advanced the hypothesis, for instance,
that all the animal species sprang from some first
creature, prototype of all creatures since. Others of
his theories were right in idea, but wrong in form,
and without even an attempt at verification. The
famous principle of the minimum of action, for
example, in spite of the truth at the bottom of it,
was valueless and confused, until Lagrange connected
it with fundamental dynamic principles, generalised
it, and cleared the unsupported metaphysical notions
out of it.[1] All this, however, was wise and Newtonic
compared with the ideas promulgated in the Philosophic Letters, on which the wicked Akakia so swiftly
pounced. Here were notions which it needed more
audacity to broach, than to face the frosts and snows
of Lapland; strange theories that in a certain state
of exaltation of the soul one may foresee the future;
that if the expiration of vital force could only be pre-

[1] See Comte's *Phil. Pos.* i. 525-529.

vented, the body might be kept alive for hundreds of
years; that by careful dissection of the brains of
giants, Patagonian and other, we should ascertain
something of the composition of the mind; that a
Latin town if it were established, and this was not
an original idea, would be an excellent means of
teaching the Latin language. Voltaire knew exactly
what kind of malicious gravity and feigned respect
would surround this amazing performance and its
author with inextinguishable laughter, and his thousand turns and tropes cut deep into Maupertuis like
sharpened swords.

Voltaire was not by scientific training competent
to criticise Maupertuis. This is true; but then
Voltaire had what in such cases dispensed with special
competence, a preternatural gift of detecting an
impostor, and we must add that here as in every
other case his anger was set aflame not by intellectual
vapidity, but by what he counted gross wrong.
Maupertuis had acted with despotic injustice towards
König, and Voltaire resolved to punish him. This is
perhaps the only side of that world-famous and truly
wretched fray which it is worth our while to remember,
besides its illustration of the general moral that active
interest in public affairs is the only sure safeguard
against the inhuman egotism, otherwise so nearly
inevitable and in any wise so revolting, of men of
letters and men of science.

Frederick took the side of the president of his
academy, and had Doctor Akakia publicly burnt

within earshot of its author's quarters.[1] Voltaire
had long been preparing for the end by depositing
his funds in the hands of the Duke of Würtemberg,
and by other steps, which had come to the king's ears,
and had by no means smoothed matters. He sees
now that the orange has been squeezed, and that it is
his business to think of saving the skin. He drew
up for his own instruction, he said, a pocket-dictionary
of terms in use with kings : *My friend* means *my
slave; my dear friend* means that *you are more than
indifferent to me;* understand by *I will make you happy,
I will endure you, as long as I have need of you; sup
with me to-night* means *I will make fun of you to-night.*[2]
Voltaire, though he had been, and always was, the
most graceful of courtiers, kept to his point, and
loudly gave Frederick to understand that in literary
disputes he recognised no kings. An act of tyranny
had been committed towards König, who was his friend,
and nothing would induce him to admit either that it
was anything else, or that it was other than just to
have held up the tyrant to the laughter of Europe.

Frederick was profoundly irritated, and the terms
in which he writes of his French Virgil as an ape who
ought to be flogged for his tricks, a man worse than
many who have been broken on the wheel, a creature

[1] It may be worth mentioning that there actually existed in
the sixteenth century a French physician, who changed his real
name of Sans-Malice into Akakia, and left descendants so called.
See M. Jal's *Dictionnaire Critique de Biographie et d'Histoire*,
p. 19 (1869).

[2] Corr. 1752. *Œuvres*, lxv. p. 138.

who may deserve a statue for his poetry but who certainly deserves chains for his conduct, seem to imply
a quite special mortification and resentment.   He
had no doubt a deep and haughty contempt for all
these angers of celestial minds.   The cabals of men of
letters, he wrote to Voltaire, seemed to him the lowest
depth of degradation.[1]   And he would fain have flung
a handful of dust on the furious creatures.   After
three months of vain effort to achieve the impossible,
Voltaire being only moderately compliant, the king
in March 1753 gave him leave to depart, though with
a sort of nominal understanding for politeness' sake
that there was to be a speedy return.

Voltaire, however, was not a man in whose breast
the flame of resentment ever flickered away in politeness, until his adversary had humbled himself. Though
no one ever so systematically convinced himself each
day for thirty years that he was on the very point of
death, no one was less careful to measure the things
that were worth doing from the point of view of a
conventional *memento mori*.   Nobody spoke about
dying so much, nor thought about it so little.   The
first use he made of his liberty was to shoot yet
another bolt at Maupertuis from Leipzig, more piercing than any that had gone before.   Frederick now
in his turn abandoned the forms of politeness, and the
renowned episode of Frankfort took place.   Voltaire,
on reaching Frankfort, was required by the Prussian
resident in the free city to surrender his court decora-

[1] Desnoiresterres, 394.

tions, and, more important than these, a certain volume
of royal verse containing the Palladium, a poem of
indecencies which were probably worse than those of
the Pucelle, because an indecent German is usually
worse than an indecent Frenchman.   The poems,
however, were what was far worse than indecent in
Frederick's eyes; they were impolitic, for they contained bitter sarcasm on sovereigns whom he might
be glad to have, and one of whom he did actually
have, on his side in the day of approaching storm.
Various delays and unlucky mishaps occurred, and
Voltaire underwent a kind of imprisonment for some
five weeks (May 31 to July 7, 1753), under extremely
mortifying and humiliating circumstances.   There
was on the one part an honest, punctual, methodic,
rather dull Prussian subordinate, anxious above all
other things in the world, not excepting respect for
genius and respect for law, to obey the injunctions
of his master from Berlin.   On the other part Voltaire,
whom we know; excitable as a demon, burning with
fury against enemies who were out of his reach now
that he had spent all his ammunition of satire upon
them, only half understanding what was said to him
in a strange tongue, mad with fear lest Frederick
meant to detain him after all.   It would need the
singer of the battle of the frogs and mice to do justice
to this five-weeks' tragi-comedy.   A bookseller with
whom he had had feuds years before, injudiciously
came either to pay his respects, or to demand some
trivial arrears of money; the furious poet and philo-

sopher rushed up to his visitor and inflicted a stinging
box on the ear, while Collini, his Italian secretary,
hastily offered this intrepid consolation to Van Duren,
'Sir, you have received a box on the ear from one of
the greatest men in the world.' A clerk came to
settle this affair or that, and Voltaire rushed towards
him with click of pistol, the friendly Collini again in-
terfering to better purpose by striking up the hand
that had written Mérope and was on the point of
despatching a clerk. We need not go into the minute
circumstances of the Frankfort outrage. Freytag, the
subordinate, clearly overstrained his instructions, and
his excess of zeal in detaining and harassing Voltaire
can only be laid indirectly to Frederick's charge. But
Frederick is responsible, as every principal is, who
launches an agent in a lawless and tyrannic course.
The German Varnhagen has undoubtedly shown that
Voltaire's account, witty and diverting as it is, is not
free from many misrepresentations, and some tolerably
deliberate lies. French writers have as undoubtedly
shown that the detention of a French citizen by a
Prussian agent in a free town of the Empire was a
distinct and outrageous illegality.[1] We, who are
fortunately not committed by the exigencies of
patriotism to close our eyes to either half of the
facts, may with facile impartiality admit both halves.
Voltaire, though fundamentally a man of exceptional
truth, was by no means incapable of an untruth when

---

[1] Desnoiresterres, *Voltaire et Frédéric*, cc. 9 and 10. Carlyle's
Frederick, bk. xvi. ch. 12.

his imagination was hot, and Frederick was by no means incapable of an outrage upon law, when law stood between him and his purpose. Frederick's subordinates had no right to detain Voltaire at all, and they had no right to allow themselves to be provoked by his impatience into the infliction of even small outrages upon him and his obnoxious niece. On the other hand, if Voltaire had been a sort of Benjamin Franklin, if he had possessed a well-regulated mind, a cool and gentle temper, a nice sense of the expedient, then the most grotesque scene of a life in which there was too much of grotesque, would not have been acted as it was, to the supreme delight of those miserable souls who love to contemplate the follies of the wise.

Any reader who takes the trouble to read the documents affecting this preposterous brawl at Frankfort between a thoroughly subordinate German and the most insubordinate Frenchman that ever lived,— this adventure, as its victim called it, of Cimbrians and Sicambrians,—will be rather struck by the extreme care with which Frederick impresses on the persons concerned the propriety of having Voltaire's written and signed word for such parts of the transaction as needed official commemoration. In one place he expressly insists that a given memorandum should be written by Voltaire's own hand from top to bottom. This precaution, which seems so strange in a king who had won five battles, dealing with the author of a score of tragedies, an epic, and many other fine things, sprang in truth from no desire to cast a

wanton slight on Voltaire's honour, but from the
painful knowledge that the author of the fine things
was not above tampering with papers and denying
patent superscriptions. Voltaire's visit had not been
of long duration, before the unfortunate lawsuit with
Abraham Hirschel occurred. Of this transaction we
need only say this much, that Voltaire employed the
Jew in some illegal jobbing in Saxon securities; that
he gave him bills on a Paris banker, holding diamonds
from the Jew as pledge of honest Christian dealing;
that his suspicions were aroused, that he protested his
bills, then agreed to buy the jewels, then quarrelled
over the price, and finally plunged into a suit, of which
the issues were practically two, whether Hirschel had
any rights on one of the Paris bills, and whether the
jewels were fairly charged. Voltaire got his bill back,
and the jewels were to be duly valued; but the proceedings disclosed two facts of considerable seriousness
for all who should have dealings with him : first, that
he had interpolated matter to his own advantage in a
document already signed by his adversary, thus making
the Jew to have signed what he had signed not ; and
second, that when very hard pushed he would not
swerve from a false oath, any more than his great
enemy the apostle Peter had done.[1] Frederick had
remembered all this, just as every negotiator who had
to deal with Frederick remembered that the great

---

[1] See Desnoiresterres, *Voltaire et Frédéric*, pp. 124-153, including a facsimile of the fraudulently altered agreement. Also
Carlyle's *Frederick*, bk. xvi. ch. 7.

king was not above such infamies as Klein-Schnellendorf, nor such meanness as filching away with his foot
a letter that had slipped unseen from an ambassador's
pocket.[1]

And so there was an end, if not of correspondence,
yet of that friendship, which after all had always
belonged rather to the spoken order than to the deep
unspeakable. There was now cynical, hoarse-voiced
contempt on the one side, and fierce, reverberating,
shrill fury on the other. The spectacle and the sound
are distressing to those who crave dignity and admission of the serious in the relations of men with one
another, as well as some sense of the myriad indefinable relations which encompass us unawares, giving
colour and perspective to our more definable bonds.
One would rather that even in their estrangement
there had been some grace and firmness and self-
control, and that at least the long-cherished illusion
had faded away worthily, as when one bids farewell
to a friend whom a perverse will carries from us over
unknown seas until a far day, and we know not if we
shall see his face any more. It jars on us that the
moon which has climbed into the night and moved
like sound of music over heath and woodland, should
finally set in a gray swamp amid the harsh croaking
of amphibians. But the intimacy between Frederick
and Voltaire had perhaps been always most like the
theatre moon.

We may know what strange admixture of distrust

[1] Carlyle's *Frederick*, bk. xiii. ch. 5.

contempt, and tormenting reminiscence, mingled with the admiration of these two men for one another's genius, from the bitterness which occasionally springs up in the midst of their most graceful and amiable letters of a later date. For instance, this is Voltaire to Frederick; 'You have already done me ill enough; you put me wrong for ever with the king of France; you made me lose my offices and pensions; you used me shamefully at Frankfort, me and an innocent woman who was dragged through the mud and thrown into gaol; and now, while honouring me with letters, you mar the sweetness of this consolation by bitter reproaches. . . . The greatest harm that your works have done, is in the excuse they have given to the enemies of philosophy throughout Europe to say, "These philosophers cannot live in peace, and they cannot live together. Here is a king who does not believe in Jesus Christ; he invites to his court a man who does not believe in Jesus Christ, and he uses him ill; there is no humanity in these pretended philosophers, and God punishes them by means of one another." . . . Your admirable and solid wisdom is spoiled by the unfortunate pleasure you have always had in seeing the humiliation of other men, and in saying and writing stinging things to them; a pleasure most unworthy of you, and all the more so as you are raised above them by your rank and by your unique talents.'[1] To which the king answers that he is fully aware how many faults he has, and what great faults

[1] *Œuvres*, lxxiii. p. 830 (1760).

they are, that he does not treat himself very gently,
and that in dealing with himself he pardons nothing.
As for Voltaire's conduct, it would not have been
endured by any other philosopher. 'If you had not
had to do with a man madly enamoured of your fine
genius, you would not have got off so well with anybody else. Consider all that as done with, and never
let me hear again of that wearisome niece, who has
not so much merit as her uncle, with which to cover
her defects. People talk of the servant of Molière,
but nobody will ever speak of the niece of Voltaire.'

The poet had talked, after his usual manner, of
being old and worn out, and tottering on the brink
of the grave. 'Why, you are only sixty-two,' said
Frederick, 'and your soul is full of that fire which
animates and sustains the body. You will bury me
and half the present generation. You will have the
delight of making a spiteful couplet on my tomb.'[1]
Voltaire did not make a couplet, but he wrote a prose
lampoon on the king's private life, which is one of the
bitterest libels that malice ever prompted, and from
which the greater part of Europe has been content to
borrow its idea of the character of Frederick.[2] This
was vengeance enough even for Voltaire. We may
add that while Voltaire constantly declared that he
could never forget the outrages which the king of
Prussia had inflicted on him, neither did he forget to

[1] *Œuvres*, lxxiii. pp. 835-837.
[2] Printed in vol. i. of the Baudouin edition, as *Mémoires
pour servir à la vie de M. Voltaire*, p. 212.

draw his pension from the king of Prussia even in
times when Frederick was most urgently pressed.[1] It
may be said that he was ready to return favours ; 'If
things go on as they are going now,' he wrote with
sportive malice, 'I reckon on having to allow a pension
to the king of Prussia.'[2]

It was not surprising that Voltaire did not return
to Paris. His correspondence during his residence at
Berlin attests in every page of it how bitterly he
resented the cabals of ignoble men of letters, and the
insolence of ignoble men of authority. 'If I had
been in Paris this Lent,' he wrote in 1752, 'I should
have been hissed in town, and made sport of at
court, and the Siècle de Louis XIV. would have been
denounced, as smacking of heresy, as audacious, and
full of ill significance. I should have had to go to
defend myself in the anteroom of the lieutenant of
police. The officers would say, as they saw me pass,
There is a man who belongs to us. . . . No, my friend,
qui bene latuit, bene vixit.'[3] With most just anger,
he contrasted German liberality with the tyrannical
suspicion of his own government. The emperor, he
says, made no difficulty in permitting the publication
of a book in which Leopold was called a coward.
Holland gave free circulation to statements that the
Dutch are ingrates and that their trade is perishing. He was allowed to print under the eyes of the
king of Prussia that the Great Elector abased himself

---

[1] Corr. 1758. *Œuvres*, lxxv. p. 80.   [2] *Ib.* p. 31.
[3] Corr. lxv. p. 23. Cf. also p. 83.

uselessly before Lewis XIV., and resisted him as uselessly. It was only in France where permission was refused for an eulogy of Lewis XIV. and of France, and that, because he had been neither base enough nor foolish enough to disfigure his eulogy either by shameful silences or cowardly misrepresentations.[1] The imprisonment, nine years before this, of Lenglet Dufresnoy, an old man of seventy, for no worse offence than publishing a supplement to De Thou's history, had made a deep impression on Voltaire.[2] He would have been something lower than human if he had forgotten the treatment which he had himself received at the hands of the most feeble and incompetent government that ever was endured by a civilised people.

So he found his way to Geneva, then and until 1798 an independent republic or municipality. There (1755) he made himself two hermitages, one for summer, called the Délices, a short distance from the spot where the Arve falls into the Rhone, and the other near Lausanne (Monrion) for winter. Here, he says, I see from my bed this glorious lake, which bathes a hundred gardens at the foot of my terrace; which forms on right and left a stream of a dozen leagues, and a calm sea in front of my windows; and which waters the fields of Savoy, crowned with the

[1] Corr. lxv. p. 15.
[2] Corr. 1743. Œuv. lviii. p. 131. A very long and careful list of the oppressions practised on writers in this reign is given in Mr. Buckle's Hist. of Civilisation, i. 675-681.

Alps in the distance.[1] You write to me, replied
D'Alembert, from your bed, whence you command
ten leagues of the lake, and I answer you from my
hole, whence I command a patch of sky three ells
long.[2] To poor D'Alembert the name of the famous
lake was fraught with evil associations, for he had just
published his too veracious article on Geneva in the
Encyclopædia, in which he paid the clergy of that city
the unwelcome compliment, that they were the most
logical of all Protestants, for they were Socinians;
and he was now suffering the penalty of men who
stir up angry hives.

The enjoyment which Voltaire had then and for
twenty years to come in his noble landscape, and
which he so often commemorates in his letters, is a
proof that may be added to others, of the injustice of
the common idea that the Voltairean school of the
eighteenth century were specially insensible to the
picturesque. Morellet, for instance, records his delight
and wonder at the Alps and the descent into Italy,
in terms quite as warm, if much less profuse, as those
of the most impressible modern tourist.[3] Diderot
had a strong spontaneous feeling for nature, as he
shows not only in his truly remarkable criticisms on
the paintings of twenty years, but also in his most
private correspondence, where he demonstrates in
terms too plain, simple, and homely, to be suspected

[1] Foisset's *Corres. de Voltaire avec de Brosses*, etc., p. 318.
Also Corr. 1757. *Œuvres*, lxvi. pp. 1-50 passim.
[2] *Œuvres*, lxxv. p. 61.   [3] *Mémoires*, i. ch. iii. p. 55.

of insincerity, the meditative delight with which the
solitary contemplation of fine landscape inspired him.
He has no peculiar felicity in describing natural
features in words, or in reproducing the inner harmonies with which the soft lines of distant hills, or
the richness of deep embosoming woodlands, or the
swift procession of clouds driven by fierce or cheerful
winds, compose and strengthen the sympathising
spirit.   But he was as susceptible to them as men of
more sonorous word.[1]   And Voltaire finds the liveliest
pleasure in the natural sights and objects around him,
though they never quickened in him those brooding
moods of egotistic introspection and deep-questioning
contemplation in which Jean Jacques, Bernardin de
St. Pierre, and Sénancour, found a sort of refuge from
their own desperate impotency of will and of material
activity.   Voltaire never felt this impotency.   As
the very apostle of action, how should he have felt it?
It pleased him in the first few months of his settlement
in new scenes, and at other times, to borrow some of
Frederick's talk about the bestial folly of the human
race, and the absurdity of troubling oneself about it;
but what was a sincere cynicism in the king, was in
Voltaire only a bit of cant, the passing affectation of
an hour.   The dramatist whose imagination had
produced so long a series of dramas of situation, the
historian who had been attracted by such labours as
those of Charles XII. of Sweden and Peter the Great

---

[1] See for instance a letter to Mdlle. de Voland : *Mémoires,
Correspondance, et Ouv. inédites,* i. 99.

of Russia, as well as by the achievements of the
illustrious men who adorned the age of Lewis XIV.,
proved himself of far too objective and positive a
temperament to be capable of that self-conscious
despair of action, that paralysing lack of confidence
in will, which drove men of other humour and other
experience forlorn into the hermit's caves of a new
Thebaid. Voltaire's ostentatious enjoyment of his
landscape and his garden was only the expansion of a
seafarer, who after a stormful voyage finds himself in
a fair haven. His lines to Liberty[1] give us the keynote to his mood at this time. He did not suppose
that he had got all, but he knew that he had got
somewhat.

> Je ne vante point d'avoir en cet asile
> Rencontré le parfait bonheur :
> Il n'est point retiré dans le fond d'un bocage ;
> Il est encore moins chez les rois ;
> Il n'est pas même chez le sage ;
> De cette courte vie il n'est point le partage ;
> Il y faut renoncer ; mais on peut quelquefois
> Embrasser au moins son image.

'Tis a fine thing, is tranquillity,' he wrote; 'yes,
but ennui is of its acquaintance and belongs to the
family. To repulse this ugly relation, I have set up
a theatre.'[2] Besides the theatre, guests were frequent
and multitudinous. He speaks of sometimes having
a crowd of fifty persons at table.[3] Besides Les Délices
and Lausanne, he purchased from the President de

---

[1] L'Auteur arrivant à sa terre. *Œuv.* xvii. 194.
[2] Corr. 1757. *Œuv.* lxvi. p. 38.   [3] *Ib.* p. 32.

Brosses a life-interest in Tourney, and in the same
year (1758) he bought the lordship of Ferney, close
by. He was thus a citizen of Geneva, of Berne, and
of France, 'for philosophers ought to have two or
three holes underground against the hounds who chase
them.' If the dogs of France should hunt him, he
could take shelter in Geneva. If the dogs of Geneva
began to bay, he could run into France. By and by
this consideration of safety grew less absorbing, and
all was abandoned except Ferney; a name that will
always remain associated with those vigorous and terrible assaults upon the Infamous, which first definitely
opened when Voltaire became the lord of this little
domain.

CHAPTER V.

RELIGION.

I.

IN examining the Voltairean attack upon religion we have to remember that it was in the first instance prompted, and throughout its course stimulated and embittered, by antipathy to the external organisation of the religion. It was not merely disbelief in a creed, but exasperation against a church. Two distinct elements lay at the bottom of Voltaire's enmity to the peculiar form of monotheism which he found supreme around him. One of them was the intellectual element of repugnance to a system of belief that rested on miracles and mysteries irreconcilable with reason, and was so intimately associated with some of the most odious types of character and most atrocious actions in the Old Testament, which undoubtedly contains so many of both. The other was the moral element of anger against the expounders of this system, their intolerance of light and hatred of knowledge, their fierce yet profoundly contemptible struggles with one another, the scandals of their casuistry, their besotted cruelty. Of these two elements, the second

was, no doubt, if not the earlier in time, at least the
stronger in intensity. It was because he perceived
the fruit to be so deadly, that Voltaire laid the axe
to the root of the tree. It is easy to say that these
poisonous Jesuitries and black Jansenisms were no
fruit of the tree, but the produce of a mere graft,
which could have been lopped off without touching
the sacred trunk. Voltaire thought otherwise, and
whether he was right or wrong, it is only just to him
to keep constantly before us the egregious failure of
Catholicism in his day as a social force. This is a
fact as to which there can be no dispute among persons
with knowledge enough and mental freedom enough
to be competent to have an opinion, and Voltairism
can only be fairly weighed if we regard it as being in
the first instance no outbreak of reckless speculative
intelligence, but a righteous social protest against a
system socially pestilent. It was the revival of the
worst parts of this system in the cruelty and obscur-
antism which broke out after the middle of the century, that converted Voltaire into an active assailant
of belief. But for that he would pretty certainly
have remained tranquilly in the phase of deism of
which some of his early verses are the expression.
Philosophy is truly as Callicles says in the Gorgias,
a most charming accomplishment for a man to follow
at the right age, but to carry philosophy too far is
the undoing of humanity.

Voltaire no doubt deliberately set himself to overthrow the Catholic theology, as well as the ecclesi-

astical system which was bound up with it, and he did so for the very sufficient reason that it has always been impossible for men to become indulgent in act, while they remained fanatical in belief. They will not cease to be persecutors, he said, until they have ceased to be absurd.[1] The object was to secure tolerance, and tolerance could only be expected as the product of indifference, and indifference could be spread most surely by throwing the fullest light of reason and common sense on the mystical foundations of revealed religion. To stop short at the inculcation of charity and indulgence was to surrender the cause; for how should the mere homilies of a secular moralist soften those whom the direct injunctions of a deity and his inspired apostles, their own acknowledged masters, failed to make charitable? It was essential that the superstitions in which intolerance had its root should be proved detestable and ridiculous. When men had learnt to laugh at superstition, then they would perceive how abominable is the oppressive fanaticism which is its champion.

It is hardly possible to deny the service which Protestantism rendered in preventing the revolution from Catholicism to scientific modes of thought from being that violent, abrupt, and irreconcilable breach, which we now observe in France and Italy, when we remember that the cause of toleration was systematically defended in England by men who as systematically defended the cause of Christianity. The

[1] Corr. *Œuv.* lxxv. p. 249.

Liberty of Prophesying, in which the expediency of
tolerance was based on the difficulty of being sure
that we are right, was written by one of the most
devout and orthodox divines; while the famous
Letters on Toleration (1689), in which the truly remarkable step is taken of confining the functions of
civil government to men's civil interests and the
things of this world, were the work of the same
Locke who vindicated the Reasonableness of Christianity.[1] The English Deists pressed home in a very
effectual way the deduction of universal freedom of
speech from the first maxims of Protestantism, and
their inference was practically admitted.[2] Hence
there was no inseparable association between adherence to the old religious ideas and the prohibition of
free speech in spirituals, and on the other hand there
was no obligation on the part of those who claimed
free speech to attack a church which did not refuse
their claim.

In France the strictly repressive policy of the
church in the eighteenth century, sometimes bloody
and cruel as in the persecution of the Protestants,
sometimes minutely vexatious as in the persecution
of the men of letters, but always stubborn and lynx-

[1] It was to the last-named book, one may suppose, that
Voltaire referred, when he asked how it was that Locke, after
having so profoundly traced the development of the human
understanding, could so degrade his own understanding in another work. (Dict. Phil. s.v. Platon. *Œuv.* lvii. p. 369.)
[2] See Collins's Apology for Free Debate and Liberty of Writing, prefixed to the *Grounds and Reasons of Christianity.*

eyed, had the natural effect of making it a point of honour with most of those who valued liberty to hurl themselves upon the religious system, of which rigorous intolerance was so prominent a characteristic. The Protestant dilution of the theological spirit seems thus to be in the long run a more effective preparation for decisive abandonment of it, than its virulent dissolution in the biting acids of Voltairism, because within limits the slower these great transformations are in accomplishing themselves, the better it is for many of the most precious and most tender parts of human character. Our present contention is that the attitude of the religionists left no alternative. It is best that creeds, like men who have done the work of the day, should die the slow deaths of nature, yet it is counted lawful to raise an armed hand upon the brigand who seeks the life of another.

Voltaire to the end of his course contended that the church only was to blame for the storm which overtook her teaching in the later years, when his own courageous attack had inspired a host of others, less brilliant but not any less embittered, to throw themselves on the reeling enemy. The cause of the inundation of Europe by the literature of negativism and repudiation was to be sought first of all in the fierce theological disputes which revolted the best of the laity. Of this violent revulsion of feeling Voltaire himself was the great organ. He furnished its justification, and nourished its fire, and invested it with a splendid lustre. Even when with the timidity of ex-

treme age he seemed to deprecate the growing ferocity
of the attack, he still taunted the clerical party with
their own folly in allowing a mean and egotistic virulence to override every consideration of true wisdom
and policy. 'Now,' he wrote in 1768, 'a revolution
has been accomplished in the human mind, that nothing
again can ever arrest. They would have prevented this
revolution, if they had been sage and moderate. The
quarrels of Jansenists and Molinists have done more
harm to the Christian religion than could have been
done by four emperors like Julian one after another.'[1]

It cannot be too often repeated that the Christianity
which Voltaire assailed was not that of the Sermon
on the Mount, for there was not a man then alive
more keenly sensible than he was of the generous
humanity which is there enjoined with a force that
so strangely touches the heart, nor one who was on
the whole, in spite of constitutional infirmities and
words which were far worse than his deeds, more
ardent and persevering in its practice. Still less was
he the enemy of a form of Christian profession which
now fascinates many fine and subtle minds, and which
starting from the assumption that there are certain
inborn cravings in the human heart, constant, profound, and inextinguishable, discerns in the long religious tradition an adequate proof that the mystic
faith in the incarnation, and in the spiritual facts
which pour like rays from that awful centre, are the
highest satisfaction which a divine will has as yet

[1] Corr. 1768. *Œuv.* lxx. p. 140.

been pleased to establish for all these yearnings of the race of men. This graceful development of belief, emancipated from dogma and reducing so many substantial bodies to pale shades, so many articles once held as solid realities to the strange tenuity of dreams, was not the Christianity of Voltaire's time, any more than it was that of the Holy Office. There was nothing resembling the present popularity of a treatment which gives generals so immense a preponderance over particulars—somewhat to the neglect of the old saying about the snare that lies hidden in generals, many persons being tolerably indifferent about the *dolus* so long as they can make sure of the *latet*. He attacked a definite theology, not a theosophy. We may, indeed, imagine the kind of questions which he would have asked of one pressing such a doctrine on his acceptance ; how he would have sought the grounds for calling aspirations universal, which the numerical majority of the human race appear to have been without, and the grounds for making subjective yearnings the test and the measure of the truth of definite objective records ; how he would have prayed to be instructed of these cravings, whether they spring up spontaneously, or are the products of spiritual self-indulgence, and also of the precise manner in which they come to be satisfied and soothed by the momentary appearance of a humane figure far off upon the earth ; how he would have paused to consider the intelligibility of so overwhelming a wonder as the incarnation having been wrought, for the benefit

of so infinitesimally small a fragment of mankind.
We can imagine this and much else, but Voltaire
would never have stirred a finger to attack a mysticism which is not aggressive, and can hardly be
other than negatively hurtful.

If any one had maintained against Voltaire that
the aspirations after a future life, the longing for
some token that the deity watches over his creatures
and is moved by a tender solicitude for them, and
the other spiritual desires alleged to be instinctive in
men, constitute as trustworthy and firm a guide to
truth as the logical reason, we may be sure that he
would have forgiven what he must have considered
an enervating abnegation of intelligence, for the sake
of the humane, if not very actively improving, course
of life to which this kind of pietism is wont to lead.
He might possibly have entertained a little contempt
for them, but it would have been quiet contempt and
unspoken. There is no case of Voltaire mocking at
any set of men who lived good lives. He did not
mock the English Quakers. He doubtless attacked
many of the beliefs which good men hold sacred, but
if good men take up their abode under the same roof
which shelters the children of darkness and wrong,
it is not the fault of Voltaire if they are hit by the
smooth stones shot from his sling against their unworthy comrades. The object of his assault was that
amalgam of metaphysical subtleties, degrading legends,
false miracles, and narrow depraving conceptions of
divine government which made the starting-point and

vantage-ground of those ecclesiastical oppressors, whom
he habitually and justly designated the enemies of the
human race. The evil and the good, the old purity
and the superadded corruptions, were all so inextric-
ably bound up in the Catholicism of the eighteenth
century, that it was impossible to deal a blow to the
one without risk of harm to the other. The method
was desperate, but then the enemy was a true Chimæra,
a monster sodden in black corruption, with whom in
the breast of a humane man there could be no terms.

The popes during the Voltairean period were above
the average in virtue and intelligence, but their power
was entirely overshadowed by that wonderful order
which had assumed all effective spiritual supremacy
for something like two centuries. Nor was this order
the only retrogressive influence. The eighteenth century was the century not only of the Sacré Cœur, but
of the miracles of the dead abbé Pâris, transactions
in which Jansenist emulated Jesuit in dragging men
and women into the deepest slough of superstition.
A Roman augur fresh from the inspection of the
sacrificial entrails would have had a right to despise the
priests who invented an object for the adoration of men
in the diseased and hideous visions of Mary Alacoque.
The man who sells rain to savages may almost be held
to add to the self-respect of the race, if you contrast
him with the convulsionnaires and the fanatics who
were transported by their revolting performances.[1]

---

[1] The reader will find an account of them in M. Lanfrey's
L'Eglise et les Philosophes du 18ième Siècle, pp. 131-135.

France is the country where reactions are most rapid and most violent. Nowhere else can the reformer count so surely on seeing the completion of his reform followed so instantly by the triumph of its adversaries. The expulsion of the Jesuits, under circumstances of marked and uncompromising harshness, was not consummated, before the tide of religious bigotry flowed in from the opposite shore, and swelled to a portentous height. The exultation of the philosophers at the coming fall of their old foes, was instantly checked by the yet worse things which befell them and their principles at the hands of new enemies. The reign of the Jansenists was speedily pronounced more hateful than the reign of the Jesuits. Various accommodations were possible with heaven, so long as the Jesuits had credit, but the Jansenists were pitiless.[1]

The parliament or supreme judicial tribunal of Paris[2] was Jansenist, mainly out of political hatred of the Jesuits, partly from a hostility, very easily explained, to every manifestation of ultramontane feeling and influence, partly from a professional jealousy of the clergy, but partly also because the austere predestinarian dogma, and the metaphysical theology which brought it into supreme prominence, seem often to have had an unexplained affinity for serious minds trained in legal ideas and their applica-

[1] Corr. *Œuv.* lxvi. p. 100.
[2] For the composition of this body see Voltaire's Histoire du Parlement de Paris. *Œuv.* xxxiv. Or in Martin's *Hist. de France*, iv. 295 ; xii. 280 ; and xiii. 53.

tion. The Jesuits had systematically abstained as
far as was possible from purely speculative theology.
Suarez is pronounced one of the greatest writers in
speculative ethics and jurisprudence; but in the
technical metaphysics of theology the Jesuits with
all their literary industry did not greatly care to
exercise themselves. Their task was social and practical, and as confessors, directors, preachers, and
instructors, they had naturally paid less attention to
abstract thought than to the arts of eloquence, address,
and pliancy. Then, too, in doctrine they had uniformly clung to the softer, more amiable, more
worldly, less repulsive, interpretation of the eternally
embarrassing claims of grace, election, free-will. The
Augustinian, Calvinistic, or Jansenist view of the impotence of will and the saving importance of grace is
the answer of souls eager to feel immediate individual
contact with a Supreme Being. The Jesuits and their
power represented extremely different sentiments,
fundamentally religious, but still fundamentally social
also, the desire of men for sympathetic and consider-
ate guidance in conduct, and their craving for such a
unity of the external ordering of the faith as should
leave them undistracted to live their lives. The
former concentrated feelings upon the relations of
men directly and immediately with a Supreme Being;
the latter upon their relations with this Being only
mediately, through their relations with one another,
and with the church to which a measure of divinity
had been attributed. Hence the decline of the Jesuits

assumed the form of a depravation of morals, while the Jansenists held more and more tightly to a narrow and bigoted correctness of belief. The parliament was willing to resist a Molinist archbishop and his satellites, when they refused burial to all who should die without having received a certificate of conformity to the famous bull Unigenitus, which proscribed Jansenist opinion.[1] But none the less for this was it bent on suppressing the common enemy, who despised the bull and the Five propositions, Molina and Jansenius, archbishop Beaumont and Quesnel, all equally. Voltaire's natural sagacity made him alive to the fact, which perhaps remains as true now as then, that the professional and middle classes are a worse enemy of liberal opinion and are more intolerant than the remnants of the old aristocratic orders. He says to D'Alembert, 'You are right in declaring yourself the enemy of the great and their flatterers; still, the great protect one upon occasion, they despise the Infamous, and they will not persecute philosophers; but as for your pedants of Paris, who have bought their office, as for those insolent bourgeois, half fanatics, half imbecile, they can do nothing but mischief.'[2] He had not learnt to look away from both classes, professional and aristocratic alike, to that third estate where the voice of the reformer has always found the first response. Still what he said was true as against the lawyers, whose vision perhaps never extends be-

[1] Siècle de Louis xv. c. 36. *Œuvres*, xxix. p. 3.
[2] Corr. *Œuv.* lxxv. p. 145.

yond the improvement of that mere surface of order
with which their profession is concerned. The Parliament of Paris was the eager ally of the bigots of
the court in 1757, in fulminating deadly edicts against
the Encyclopædia and all concerned in its production
or circulation. In 1762, the year of the publication
of Emile and the Contrat Social, not all the influence
of Rousseau's powerful protectors could prevent the
launching of a decree of arrest against him. Bloodier
measures were not wanting.

In 1762 Morellet had published under the title of
a Manual for Inquisitors a selection of the most cruel
and revolting portions of the procedure of the Holy
Office, drawn from the Directorium Inquisitorium of
Eymeric, a grand inquisitor of the fourteenth century.
The cold-blooded cruelties of the regulations, which
were thus brought into the light of the eighteenth
century, created the most profound sensation among
the rapidly increasing adherents of tolerance and
humanity. Voltaire was intensely stirred by this
resuscitation of horrors that he mistook for dead. It
made the same impression upon him, he said, as the
bleeding body of Cæsar made upon the men of Rome.[1]
But he soon found that it was an error to impute a
special cruelty to the spiritual power. Malesherbes,
in giving Morellet the requisite permission to print
his Manual, had amazed his friend by telling him,
that though he might suppose he was giving to the
world a collection of extraordinary facts and unheard-

[1] Corr. *Œuvres*, lxvii. p. 166.

of processes, yet in truth the jurisprudence of Eymeric
and his inquisition was as nearly as possible identical
with the criminal jurisprudence of France at that
very moment.[1] This was very soon to be proved.

The bigots, infuriated by the blows which were
destroying the Jesuits, hunted out against heretical
enemies some forgotten portions of this terrible
jurisprudence. A protestant pastor, Rochette, was
hung for exercising his functions in Languedoc. The
Catholics on the occasion of the arrest of Rochette
were summoned by sound of tocsin, and three young
Protestants, who were brothers, fearing massacre in
the midst of the agitation, took up their arms: for
this offence they were convicted of rebellion, and had
their heads struck off.[2] It became painfully clear how
great a mistake it was to suppose the clergy touched
with some special curse of cruelty. Then, as usually,
for good or for evil, they were on about the same
moral level with an immense number of laymen, and
were not much more than the incarnation of the
average darkness of the hour. If Eymeric's procedure
only copied the ordinary criminal jurisprudence, the
bigotry of the ecclesiastics was accurately reflected in
the bigotry of the secular tribunals. The Protestant
Calas was broken on the wheel (1762), because his
son had been found dead, and some one chose to say
that the father had killed him, to prevent him from
turning Catholic. There was not the smallest fragment

[1] Mém. de Morellet, ch. iii. p. 62.
[2] Martin's *Hist. de France*, xvi. p. 139.

of evidence, direct or indirect, for a single link in the chain of circumstances on which the unfortunate man's guilt depended ; while there were many facts which made the theory of his guilt the most improbable that could have been brought forward. The widow and the children of Calas were put to the torture, and eventually fled to Geneva to take refuge with Voltaire. During the same year the same tribunal, the parliament of Toulouse, did its best to repeat this atrocity in the case of Sirven. Sirven was a Protestant, and his daughter had been with perfect legality snatched away from him, and shut up in a convent, there to be better instructed in the faith. She ran away, and was found at the bottom of a well. Sirven was accused of murdering his daughter, and he only escaped the wheel by prompt flight. His wife perished of misery amid the snows of the Cevennes, and he joined the wretched family of Calas at Geneva, where the same generous man furnished shelter and protection.

In the north of France the fire of intolerance burnt at least as hotly as in the south. At Abbeville a crucifix was found to have been mutilated in the night. Two lads of eighteen, to one of whom Frederick gave shelter in Prussia, were accused under cover of the sacrilege, and La Barre was condemned by the tribunal of Amiens, at the instance of the bishop, to have tongue and right hand cut off, and then be burnt alive ; a sentence that was presently commuted by the Parliament of Paris to decapitation (1766). There was no

proof whatever that either of the two youths was in
any way concerned in the outrage. The bishop of
the diocese had issued monitory proclamations, and
conducted a solemn procession to the insulted crucifix.
The imagination of the town was kindled, and the
sacrilege became the universal talk of a people growing
more and more excited. Rumour ran that a new sect
was being formed, which was for breaking all the
crucifixes, which threw the host on the ground and cut
it with knives. There were women who declared that
they had seen these things. All the horrible stories
were revived which had been believed against the
Jews in the middle ages. A citizen took advantage
of this fierce agitation to gratify a private grudge
against a relative of La Barre. He set inquiries
on foot among the lowest persons for proof that the
youth had been concerned in the original crime. By
one means or another he got together material enough
to support an indictment. Proceedings once begun, a
crowd of informers rose up. It was deposed that La
Barre and D'Etallonde had passed within thirty yards
of the sacred procession without removing their hats,
that La Barre had spoken irreverently of the Virgin
Mary, that he had been heard to sing unseemly songs
and recite ribald litanies. This testimony, given with
a vagueness that ought to have proved it legally
valueless, was the fruit of the episcopal monitory,
which as at Toulouse in the case of Calas, virtually
incited the dregs of the people to bring accusations
against their superiors, and menaced a man with the

pains of hell if he should refuse to put his neighbour
in peril of his life. The tribunal, as excited as the
witnesses and the rest of the public, relied on a royal
ordinance of 1682, directed against sacrilege and
superstition and designed to put down sorcery. In
the sentence inflicting so bloody a punishment, the
offence was described as consisting in singing abominable songs against the Virgin Mary.[1] To exact such
a penalty for such a delinquency was to make human
life a mere plaything for the ignorant passion of the
populace and the intellectual confusion of the tribunals.

These atrocities kindled in Voltaire a blaze of
anger and pity, that remains among the things of
which humanity has most reason to be proud. Everybody who has read much of the French writing of
the middle of the eighteenth century, is conscious
from time to time of a sound of mocking and sardonic
laughter in it. This laugh of the eighteenth century
has been too often misunderstood as the expression
of a cynical hardness of heart, proving the hollowness
of the humanitarian pretensions in the midst of which
it is heard. It was in truth something very different;
it was the form in which men sought a little relief
from the monotony of the abominations which op-
pressed them, and from whose taint they had such
difficulty to escape. This refrain, that after all a
man can do nothing better than laugh, apparently so
shallow and inhuman, in reality so penetrated with

[1] Relation de la Mort du Chevalier de la Barre, 1766; Le
Cri du Sang Innocent, 1775. *Œuv.* xxxix. p. 99.

melancholy, we may count most certainly on finding at the close of the narration of some more than usually iniquitous or imbecile exploit of those in authority. It was when the thought of the political and social and intellectual degradation of their country became too vivid to be endured, that men like Voltaire and D'Alembert would abruptly turn away from it, and in the bitterness of their impotence cry that there was nothing for it but to take the world and all that befalls therein in merriment. It was the grimacing of a man who jests when he is perishing of hunger, or is shrinking under knife or cautery. Thus D'Alembert having given Voltaire an account of the execution of the unfortunate La Barre, in words that show how intensely his own narrative was afflicting him, suddenly concludes by saying that he will add no more on this auto-da-fé, so honourable to the French nation, for it made him ill-humoured, and he meant only to mock at whatever might happen.[1] But Voltaire could not rest thus. The thought of so hateful a crime, perpetrated by a tribunal of justice, clothed him in the shirt of Nessus. All aflame, he wrote to D'Alembert with noble impetuosity :

'This is no longer a time for jesting : witty things do not go well with massacres. What? These Busirises in wigs destroy in the midst of horrible tortures children of sixteen! And that in face of the verdict of ten upright and humane judges! And the victim suffers it! People talk about it for a

[1] Corr. July 16, 1766. *Œuv.* lxxv. p. 357.

moment, and the next they are hastening to the comic opera; and barbarity, become the more insolent for our silence, will to-morrow cut throats juridically at pleasure. Here Calas broken on the wheel, there Sirven condemned to be hung, further off a gag thrust into the mouth of a lieutenant-general, a fortnight after that five youths condemned to the flames for extravagances that deserved nothing worse than Saint Lazare. Is this the country of philosophy and pleasure? It is the country rather of the Saint Bartholomew massacre. Why, the Inquisition would not have ventured to do what these Jansenist judges have done.'[1] When he had received D'Alembert's letter, ending as we have seen, his remonstrance waxed vehement: 'What, you would be content to laugh? We ought rather to resolve to seek venge-ance, or at any rate to leave a country where day after day such horrors are committed. . . . No, once more, I cannot bear that you should finish your letter by saying, I mean to laugh. Ah, my friend, is it a time for laughing? Did men laugh when they saw Phalaris's bull being made red-hot?'[2]

This revival in the tribunals of Paris and the provincial towns alike, of the ignorant fanaticism and the unscientific jurisprudence of the most unenlight-ened times, was the more bitter and insupportable from the new light which shone around such horrors. Beccaria's treatise on Offences and Penalties had just been translated into French by Morellet, and furnished

[1] Corr. *Œuv.* lxxv. p. 359.   [2] *Ib.* p. 361.

a strange commentary upon the atrocities of Toulouse
and Abbeville. It seemed, men said, as if at every
striking vindication of the rights of humanity the
genius of cruelty broke its chains, and, to prove the
futility of all such vindications, inspired new acts of
barbarism and violence.[1] The philosophic group had
yielded to a premature exultation, and in their inex-
perience supposed that they who planted the tree
should see the gathering-in of the fruit. The reign
of reason was believed to be close at hand, and this
belief made the visible recrudescence of fanatical un-
reason signally insupportable. It is a high honour to
Voltaire and his disciples that the trial did not prove
too strong for their faith, and that when they saw
how far too sanguine they had been, they were more
astonished than they were discouraged, and their
energy redoubled with the demands made upon it.
The meaner partisans of an orthodoxy which can only
make wholly sure of itself by injustice to adversaries,
have always loved to paint the Voltairean school in the
character of demons, enjoying their work of destruction with a sportive and impish delight. They may
have rejoiced in their strength so long as they cherished
the illusion that those who first kindled the torch
should also complete the long course and bear the
lamp to the goal. When the gravity of the enterprise
showed itself before them, they remained alert with
all courage, but they ceased to fancy that courage
necessarily makes men happy. The mantle of philo-

[1] Grimm, *Corr. Lit.* v. p. 133.

sophy was rent in a hundred places, and bitter winds
entered at a hundred holes, but they only drew it the
more closely around them.[1] At the very last Voltaire
seems to have seen something of the vast space which
every ray of light has to traverse before it reaches the
eye of the common understanding. 'I now perceive,'
he wrote the year before his death, 'that we must still
wait three or four hundred years. One day it cannot
but be that good men win their cause ; but before
that glorious day arrives how many disgusts have we
to undergo, how many dark persecutions, without
reckoning the La Barres, of whom from time to time
they will make an auto-da-fé.'[2] To speak thus was to
recognise the true character of the revolution, and the
many elements which go to the transformation of an
old society. To speak thus, too, was to mark the true
character of the sincere lover of human progress, the
soul of steadfast patience and strong hope, mingled with
many a pang for the far-off and slow-coming good.

It was a natural thing to identify the Jesuits with
the strongest part of the old society, because their
organisation was both the strongest and most striking
of its external supports. Their suppression, though
not to be dispensed with except on the condition of
an ultimate overthrow of morality and an extinction
of intellectual light, had one effect which the statesmen of the time could hardly be expected to see, and
which has not been enough considered. Just as the
papacy by the fourteenth century had become more

---

[1] Corr. 1774. *Œuv.* lxxv. p. 627.   [2] *Ib.* p. 696.

and more exclusively a temporal power, so the Jesuits by the middle of the eighteenth had become more and more a commercial power. They were a powerful trading corporation, and it was as merchants, rather than as casuists and directors of conscience, that they finally came into collision with secular authority in France, Portugal, and Spain. Now since the revival of the order it has been exclusively engaged in the contest for spiritual supremacy, and for as much of temporal power as has seemed essential to its security. This, however, is only one of the evils which counterbalance the advantages of every progressive measure; for, alas, when the statesman believes most confidently that he has advanced by a league, a very few years show him or others that his league was after all no more than an ell or two.

The reactionary outburst of fanaticism for which the humiliation of the Jesuits was a signal, only showed how well founded the Voltairean allegations as to the depraving effects of the existing system of religion had really been. It was the verification of all that Voltaire ever said against the system, and demonstrated both the virulence and the tenacity of the influences which Catholicism in the days of its degradation had exerted over the character of the nation. It was most illogical to expect a people who had been bred in the Catholic tradition suddenly to welcome its enemies. If Catholicism had trained men up to the temper which seeks the light and loves it, how should it have deserved animosity? Nearly all lovers of improvement are apt in the heat of a generous enthusiasm to forget that if all the world were ready to embrace their cause, their improvement could hardly be needed. It is one of the hardest conditions of things that the more numerous and resolute the enemies of reform, then the more unmistakably urgent the necessity for it. It was just because the cruelty, persecution, and darkness, in the last ten years of the reign of Lewis xv. were things possible, that the onslaught upon Catholicism was justifiable and praiseworthy. They showed the depth and strength of the forces of the old society, and they foreshadowed the violence which marked its dissolution. If people had remembered in 1789 how few years separated them from the wide-spread fanaticism which darkened the last days of Voltaire, they might have calculated better how few years separated them from the Napoleonic Concordat.

No permanent transformation of a society, we may be sure, can ever take place until a transformation has been accomplished in the spiritual basis of thought. Voltaire may have distinctly seen this and formulated it to himself, or not ; in any case, he steered his own course exactly as he would have done if he had seen it. As M. Guizot expresses it, the separation between the spiritual and temporal orders was never real in Europe except in the eighteenth century, when for the first time the spiritual order developed itself entirely apart from the temporal order.[1] Thus Vol-

---

[1] *Hist. de la Civilisation en Europe*, 14ième leçon, p. 405 Cf. also De Tocqueville's *Ancien Régime*, liv. iii. ch. I.

taire acquiesced without murmur or reproach in the
conditions of political absolutism, and the disgrace
and ruin which the nullity of the government brought
upon his country in the Seven Years' War, keenly as
he felt it, yet provoked no thought of temporal
changes. His correspondence in that fatal time is
marked by a startling apathy about public events, and
even Rossbach seems not to move him to seek its causes.
If we compare his joyful enthusiasm at the accession
of Turgot to power in 1774, we can have no doubt
that this strange numbness of feeling was only the
silence of a wise man despairing of saying or seeing
anything useful, and not the criminal folly of a bad
citizen to whom the welfare of his country is not dear.
The disasters of France were as serious to him as to
any one else, as may be plainly seen under the assumed
philosophy with which his vivacious spirit loved to
veil real feeling; but the impossibility of doing anything, even of taking a part in the process with which
we English are so familiar as the forming of public
opinion, drove him for consolation to the field where
he was certain of doing efficient work.[1] Writing in
1761, a year of crushing national loss, he says to one
of the oldest and most intimate of his correspondents :
'There is nothing to laugh at in all this. I am struck
to the heart. Our only resource is in the promptest
and most humiliating peace. I always fancy, when
some overwhelming disaster arrives, that the French
will be serious for six weeks. I have not yet been

[1] Corr. 1757-58. *Œuv.* lxvi. pp. 92, 102, 112, 185, etc.

able to disabuse myself of this notion.'[1] Voltaire was
penetrated by the spirit of action, and he perceived
and regretted that the organisation of France did not
permit of the effective action of private individuals
in the field of politics.[2] There are lines in the Henriade extolling the freedom of England,[3] and he sometimes indulges in the commonplaces of a literary re-
publicanism ; but turning to the portion of his works
which his editors have classified as political, we scarcely
find much beyond the documents, and they are important and interesting enough, still not truly political,
that relate to the various affairs of Calas, La Barre,
and others, in which he exposed the atrocities of the
tribunals. So far as they come into the region of
politics at all, it is only to assail the overt and direct
injustice done to society by the institutions, privileges,
and pretensions of the church. He constantly attacks
in a great variety of forms the material mischief inflicted on society by the vast numbers of monks,
mendicant or other ; their unproductive lives, the
burden of their maintenance weighing upon more
industrious subjects, the restriction of population
occasioned by their celibacy. The direct refusal of
the clergy in 1750 to consent to pay their share of the
taxes like other citizens, though owning as much as
a fifth of all the property in the realm, moved him to
insist in a vigorous pamphlet that the distinction in a
kingdom between spiritual and temporal powers is a

[1] Corr. *Œuv.* lxvii. p. 174 ; also lxxv. p. 170.
[2] See ante, p. 19.   [3] Chant i. v. 306.

relic of barbarism; that it is monstrous to permit a
body of men to say, Let those pay who work, we
ought not to pay because we are idle; that superstition inevitably tends to make bad citizens, and therefore princes ought to protect philosophy which destroys
superstition.[1]

Voltaire's task, however, was never directly political,
but spiritual, to shake the foundations of that religious
system which professed to be founded on the revelation
of Christ. Was he not right? If we find ourselves
walking amid a generation of cruel and unjust and
darkened spirits, we may be assured that it is their
beliefs on what they deem highest that have made
them so. There is no counting with certainty on the
justice of men who are capable of fashioning and
worshipping an unjust divinity, nor on their humanity
so long as they incorporate inhuman motives in their
most sacred dogma, nor on their reasonableness while
they rigorously decline to accept reason as a test of
truth.

It is necessary to admit from the point of view of
impartial criticism, that Voltaire had one defect of
character, of extreme importance in a leader of this
memorable and direct attack. With all his enthusiasm
for things noble and lofty, generous and compassion-
ate, he missed the peculiar emotion of holiness, the
soul and life alike of the words of Christ and Saint
Paul, that indefinable secret of the long hold of mystic
superstition over so many high natures, otherwise

[1] La Voix du Sage et du Peuple (1750). *Œuv.* xxxviii. p. 53,

entirely prepared for the brightness of the rational
day. From this impalpable essence which magically
surrounds us with the mysterious and subtle atmosphere of the unseen, changing distances and proportions, adding new faculties of sight and purpose,
extinguishing the flames of disorderly passion in a
flood of truly divine aspiration, we have to confess
that the virtue went out in the presence of Voltaire.
To admire Voltaire, cried a man who detested him, is
the sign of a corrupt heart, and if anybody is drawn
to his works, then be very sure that God does not
love such an one.[1] The truth of which that is so
vehement a paraphrase amounts to this, that Voltaire
has said no word, nor even shown an indirect appreciation of any word said by another, which stirs or
expands the emotional susceptibility, indefinite exultation, and far-swelling inner harmony, which De
Maistre and others have known as the love of God,
and for which a better name, as covering most varieties
of form and manifestation, is holiness, deepest of all
the words that defy definition. Through the affronts
which his reason received from certain pretensions
both in the writers and in some of those whose actions
they commemorated, this sublime trait in the Bible, in
both portions of it, was unhappily lost to Voltaire. He
had no ear for the finer vibrations of the spiritual voice.

This had no concern in the fact that he hated and
despised, and was eager that others should hate and
despise, the religious forms that ruled France in his

[1] De Maistre, *Soirées de St. Pétersbourg*, 4ième.

day.   The Christianity which he assailed was as little
touched as Voltairism itself with that spirit of holiness which poured itself round the lives and words
of the two founders, the great master and the great
apostle.   The more deeply imbued a man was with
this spirit, the more ardently would he crave the demolition of that Infamous in belief and in practice, which
poisoned the stream of holiness in its springs, and
shed pestilence along its banks, and choked its issues
in barrenness and corruption.

The point where the failure of this quality in
Voltaire was especially a source of weakness to his
attack, is to be found in the crippling of his historic
imagination, and the inability which this inflicted
upon him of conceiving the true meaning and lowest
roots of the Catholic legend.   The middle age between
himself and the polytheism of the Empire was a
parched desert to him and to all his school, just as
to the Protestant the interval between the apostles
and Luther is a long night of unclean things.   He
saw only a besotted people led in chains by a crafty
priesthood; he heard only the unending repetition of
records that were fictitious, and dogmas that drew a
curtain of darkness over the understanding.   Men
spoke to him of the mild beams of Christian charity,
and where they pointed he saw only the yellow glare
of the stake; they talked of the gentle solace of
Christian faith, and he heard only the shrieks of the
thousands and tens of thousands whom faithful
Christian persecutors had racked, strangled, gibbeted,

burnt, broken on the wheel.   Through the steam of
innocent blood which Christians for the honour of
their belief had spilt in every quarter of the known
world, the blood of Jews, Moors, Indians, and all the
vast holocausts of heretical sects and people in eastern
and western Europe, he saw only dismal tracts of
intellectual darkness, and heard only the humming
of the doctors, as they served forth to congregations
of poor men hungering for spiritual sustenance the
draff of theological superstition.

This vehement and blinding antipathy arose partly
from the intense force with which the existing aspect
of Catholicism recalled all that was worst, and shut out
all that was best in its former history.   One cannot
fairly expect the man who is in the grip of a decrepit
tyrant, to do absolutely full justice to the seemly
deeds and gracious promises of his tormentor's youth.
But partly also this blindness arose from the fact that
Voltaire measured the achievements of Catholicism by
the magnitude of its pretensions.   He took its supernatural claims seriously, and his intelligence was
exasperated beyond control by the amazing dispro-
portion and incongruity between these claims and the
most conspicuous of the actual results.   Those who
have parted company with a religion, as Voltaire had
parted company with Christianity, can only be counted
upon to award the well-earned praise to its better
part, after they have planted themselves stably on the
assumption that the given religion is a human and
natural force like another.

The just historic calm on which our modern prides
himself, is only possible in proportion to the mature
completeness with which he takes for granted, and
believes that those to whom he speaks will take for
granted, the absence of supernatural intervention in
the processes of religious action and development.
He is absolutely undisturbed by the thought of that
claim, which was omnipotent until Voltaire came to
do deadly battle with it, of Christianity to be a
crowning miracle of divine favour, which should raise
men to be only a little lower than the angels, and
should be the instrument for pouring out upon them
an ever-flowing stream of special and extraordinary
grace. It is not until the idea has dropped out of
our minds of the great fathers of the church as saints,
that we are free to perceive what services they
rendered as statesmen, and it is only when men have
ceased to dispute whether Christianity was a revelation, that they have eyes to see what services it has
rendered as a system. But in Voltaire's time, if
Catholicism was justified historically, it was believed
dogmatically, and therefore was to be attacked dogmatically also. The surrender of the written legend
has never hindered its champions from taking ground
which implied some esoteric revelation, that proves to
be some special interpretation of the written legend.
So long as the thinker is busy disproving the position
that a man who happens to live on a certain part of
the globe is a being of such singular and exceptional
consequence in the universe as to be held worthy by

supreme heavenly powers of receiving a miraculous message and the promise of this and that unspeakable privilege in indescribable worlds to come, so long he is not likely to weigh very fairly the effects of the belief in such power, messages, and privileges, on the education and advancement of this world. The modern historic justice which is done to Catholicism is due to the establishment of a series of convictions that civilisation is a structure which man by his own right arm has raised for himself, that it has been exposed to many an era of storm and stress, and to manifold influences which have been perpetually destroying portions of the great edifice, adding fresh parts, modifying the old, by an interminable succession of changes, resounding and volcanic, or still and imperceptible; that the danger of destruction was never so terrible as in the days of the dissolution of the old Roman society; that in this prolonged crisis the Christian church emerged, first by its organisation and the ability of some of its chiefs, and next by the attraction of legends that harmonised with the needs of a dark, confused, and terror-stricken time; that the many barbarous and absurd articles of belief incorporated in the Christian profession by the sophists of the East, received from time to time humane modification in the hands of the wiser churchmen of the West, whose practical judgment was perpetually softening down the crude, savage, unilluminated doctrines which had naturally sprung up in the dismal age when the Catholic system acquired substance and shape,

A just recognition of all these things is only easy to one whose expectations from humanity are moderate, who perceives how tardy and difficult is the accom·plishment of each smallest step in the long process, and how helpful are even the simplest beliefs of rude times in transforming men from vagrant animals into beings with a consciousness of fixed common relations towards some object of common worship, and so planting the first germs of social consolidation and growth.

Voltaire was, from the circumstances in which he was placed, too busy proving the purely human origin of Catholicism to have a mind free to examine how much, if we suppose it to be of purely human origin, it has done for those who accepted it. Perhaps we ought rather to praise than blame him for abstaining from planting himself at the historic point of view, before settling the previous question whether the historic point of view is permitted in considering the religious movements of Europe. Until Voltaire and others had divested the current religion of its super-natural pretensions, it was impossible for any thinker, who declines to try to take the second step before he has already taken the first, to survey the operations of such a religion as a merely secular force. This surely is a field of thought where no serious inquirer could content himself with a mere working hypothesis. If the supernatural claims of Catholicism are well founded, then the historic method of treating it is either a frivolous diversion or else a grave and

mischievous heresy.   The issue being of this moment,
everybody who studies the philosophy of history with
effect must have made up his mind in one way or the
other.   Voltaire had made up his mind very definitely,
and the conclusion to which, for adequate or inadequate
reasons, he came in this matter was one of the most
influential agencies in preparing men's minds for the
construction and general reception of a sounder historical philosophy than was within his own reach.   That
he did not see the deduction from his work is a
limitation of vision that he shares with most of the
men to whom it has fallen to overthrow old sytems,
and clear the ground on which the next generation
has raised new.

II.

Having said thus much on the general causes and
conditions of Voltaire's attack, we may next briefly
examine his method.   A brief examination suffices,
because, like all his contemporaries, he was so very
imperfectly acquainted with the principles of scientific
criticism, and because his weapons, though sharp and
deadly enough for their purpose, are now likely to
become more and more thoroughly antiquated.   In
criticism he was, as has often been remarked, the
direct descendant of Bayle.   That is, his instruments
were purely literary and dialectical.   He examined
the various sacred narratives as if he had been
reviewing a contemporary historian.   He delights in

the minute cavils of literary pyrrhonism, and rejoices
in the artifice of imposing the significance of the letter,
where his adversaries strove for interpretation of the
spirit.   As if, for instance, anything could be more
childish than to attack baptism by asking whether
Christianity consists in throwing water on the head,
with a little salt in it.[1]   He is perfectly content with
the exposure of a fallacy in words, without seeking to
expose the root fallacy of idea.   Nothing short of the
blindest partisanship can pretend to find in this a
proper or adequate method.   The utmost that can be
said, and no just historian ought to forget to say it, is
that it was not more improper nor inadequate than
the orthodox method of defence.   Bayle's commentary on the words, 'Compel them to come in,' would
not satisfy the modern requirements of scriptural
exegesis, but it was quite good enough to confound
those who contended that the text was a direct
warrant and injunction from heaven for the bitterest
persecution on earth.   But the unfair parry of unfair
thrust, extenuate it as we may, count it inevitable as
we may, even reckoning up such advantages from it
as we can, and in the present case they were enormous,
can never be any pattern or masterpiece of retort;
and it is folly to allow admiration for the social merit
of Voltaire's end to blind us to the logical demerit of
his means.   It is deliberately to throw away the
advantage of our distance from the contest, and to sell
for a momentary self-indulgence in the spirit of party

[1] *Œuvres*, xxxv. p. 37

the birthright of a free and equitable historic vision.
Let men not fail to do justice to the gains of humanity
won by the emancipation of the eighteenth century;
but we shall be worse off than if they had never been
transmitted, if they are allowed to bind us to approve
of every detail of the many movements by which the
final triumph was obtained.

The key to his method of attack is given us in a
sentence in one of his letters to D'Alembert. 'It
is never by means of metaphysics,' he says, 'that you
will succeed in delivering men from error; you must
prove the truth by facts.'[1] In other words, the
sublime abstract reasoning of a Spinoza will do far
less to dispel the narrow ideas, unfounded beliefs, and
false restrictive conceptions which cripple the human
intelligence so long as it is in bondage to a theological
system, than a direct disproval of the alleged facts
on which the system professes to rest. It is only by
dealing immediately with these that you can make the
repulse of error a real question, substantially interesting
to ordinary men. Always remembering that Voltaire's
intelligence was practical rather than speculative,
and, besides this, that from the time when he commenced his attack in earnest the object which he had
at heart was the overthrow of a crushing practical
institution, we may agree that in such a humour and
with such a purpose the most effective way of
harassing so active and pestilent a foe was to carry
the war into the enemy's quarters, and to use those

[1] Corr. 1773. *Œuvres*, lxxv. p. 614.

kinds of arguments which the greatest number of men
would be likely to find cogent. We may complain
that Voltaire never rises from the ground into the
region of the higher facts of religion; and this is quite
true. It would have been controversially futile if he
had done so. There was no audience in those times
for the discussion of the higher facts; and the reason
of this was that the spiritual instructors and champions themselves thrust into the front place legends,
miracles, and the whole of the peculiarly vulgar part
of the theological apparatus, which it would have
been as absurd to controvert metaphysically, as it
would be to try to elevate a Gold-coast negro from
his fetish worship by the transcendental parts of
Plato.

It nearly always happens that the defenders of a
decaying system, when they find themselves surrounded by the wholly uncongenial atmosphere of
rationalistic method, fall back, not on the noblest,
but on the ignoblest parts of their system. Distressed
by the light, they shrink hurriedly into darkest
recesses of the familiar caves, partly because they
have a sense of especial security in a region that
they know so well, and partly because they have
misgivings lest the surrender of articles or practices
in which they only half believe, should by too
stringent process of logical compulsion lead to the
destruction of others in which they believe with all
their hearts. Such tactics may or may not be politic,
but we can at least be quite certain that they tend

neither to elevation of religion, nor discovery of truth, nor profit and sincerity of discussion. If a set of doctrines be attacked from many quarters in an unworthy manner, and taken at their worst instead of at their best, we may be quite sure that this is as much due to the defenders as to the assailants. It was not Voltaire's fault that the controversy turned on issues which a more modern opponent would not care to dispute. He is constantly flippant and trivial, and constantly manifests gross irreverence, but it was the writers whom he was combating, writers like Sanchez or the stercorists, who had opened frivolous and unbecoming questions that could hardly be exposed with gravity. He was making war on an institution, and it was not his concern to fight on ground which his adversary had never thought, and was too blind and demoralised to be able to think, of taking up. It was not his fault that the upholders of the creed he attacked, made a stand upon the letter of sacred documents, upon prophecy and miracle and special intervention, upon the virtues of relics and the liquefaction of the blood of Saint Januarius. The same wise man who forbade us to answer a fool according to his folly, also enjoined upon us to answer a fool according to his folly, and the moral commentator agrees that each prescription is as sage as its contradictory.

If truth means anything, it was worth while to put to rout the distortions of truth with which the church lowered the understanding of its votaries. If truth means anything, then it was worth while to reply to the allegation that the history of the Christian church is a long witness of the goodness of heaven and the ever-present guidance of its heavenly founder, by a record of the actual facts; of the simplicity, equality, absence of multiplied rites, orders, and dogmas, among the primitive members of the congregation, and of the radical differences between the use of apostolic times and of times since; of the incurable want of authority for all those tales of demons being cast out, pious inscriptions in letters of gold found graven on the hearts of martyrs, and the rest, which grow rare in proportion as we draw nearer to the times when the evidence for them would have been preserved; of the infamous character of many Christian heroes, from Constantine downwards, and of the promptitude with which the Christians, as soon as ever they had power, dyed their hands in the blood of their persecutors; of the stupefying circumstances that after a revelation was made to the human race by no less a prodigy than the incarnation of supreme power in a mortal body, and the miraculous maintenance of this event and its significance in the tradition, doctrine, discipline of the Catholic church, yet the whole of Asia, the whole of Africa, all the possessions of the English and Dutch in America, all the uncivilised Indian tribes, all the southern lands, amounting to one-fifth part of the globe still remain in the clutches of the

demon, to verify that holy saying of many being
called but few chosen.[1]

It may be said that this kind of argument really
proves nothing at all about the supernatural origin
or character of the Christian revelation, for which
you must seek the responses not of ecclesiastical
history but of the human heart. And that may be
a fair thing to say, but then this contention of the
new revelation being only a message to the heart
has only been heard since Voltaire thrust aside the
very different contention of his day. Those various
beliefs were universally accepted about the progress
of the church, which were true in no sense whatever,
literal or spiritual, mystical or historical. People
accepted traditions and records, sacred and profane,
as literal, accurate, categorical declarations and de-
scriptions of a long series of things done and suffered.
Moreover, the modern argument in favour of the
supernatural origin of the Christian religion, drawn
from its suitableness to our needs and its divine
response to our aspirations, must be admitted by
every candid person resorting to it to be of exactly
equal force in the mouth of a Mahometan or a fire-
worshipper or an astrolater. If you apply a subjective
test of this kind, it must be as good for the sincere
and satisfied votaries of one creed, as it is for those
of any other. The needs and aspirations of the
Mahometan would not be satisfied by fetishism or
polytheism, nor those of the developed polytheist by

[1] Cf. Dict. Phil. s.v. Eglise. *Œuv.* liv. pp. 221-248.

totem-worship. It would be ridiculous for so small a minority of the race as the professors of Christianity to assume that their aspirations are the absolute measure of those of humanity in every stage. The argument can never carry us beyond the relativity of religious truth.

Now the French apologist a hundred years ago dealt in the most absolute possible matter. Christianity to him meant a set of very concrete ideas of all sorts; any one who accepted them in the concrete and literal form prescribed by the church would share infinite bliss, and any one who rejected them, whether deliberately or from never having been so happy as to hear of them, would be infinitely tormented. If this theory be right, then Voltaire must naturally be abhorred by all persons who hold it, as a perverse and mischievous hinderer of light. If it be wrong, and we must observe that from its terms this is not one of the marvellously multiplying beliefs of which we hear that they may be half wrong and half right, then Voltaire may take rank with other useful expellers of popular error. Everybody must admit how imperfect is all such treatment of popular error; how little rich, how little comprehensive, how little full. Yet the surgeon who has couched his patient's cataract has surely done a service, even if he do not straightway carry him to enjoy the restored faculty on some high summit of far and noble prospect.

Voltaire's attack was essentially the attack of the English deists, as indeed he is always willing enough to admit, pursued with far less gravity and honest search for truth, but, it is hardly necessary to say, with far more adroitness, rapidity, and grace of manner than any of them, even than Bolingbroke. As we have seen, he insisted on throwing himself upon the facts in the records that are least easily reconciled with a general sense of probability and evidence, as gradually developed in men by experience. He placed the various incidents of the Bible, the interpretation of them by the church, the statement of doctrine, the characters of prominent actors, in the full light of common experience and of the maxims which experience has made second nature. 'I always speak humanly,' he says mockingly, 'I always put myself in the place of a man who, having never heard tell either of Jews or Christians, should read these books for the first time, and not being illuminated by grace, should be so unhappy as to trust unaided reason in the matter, until he should be enlightened from on high.'[1]

It is superfluous to detail the treatment to which he subjected such mysteries of the faith as the inheritance of the curse of sin by all following generations from the first fall of man; the appearance from time to time, among an obscure oriental tribe, of prophets who foretold the coming of a divine deliverer, who should wash away that fatal stain by sacrificial expiation; the choice of this specially cruel, treacherous, stubborn, and rebellious tribe, to be the favoured

[1] Dieu et les Hommes, c. xiv. *Œuvres*, xlv. p. 318.

people of a deity of spotless mercy and truth; the
advent of the deliverer in circumstances of extraordinary meanness and obscurity among a generation
that greeted his pretensions with incredulity, and
finally caused him to be put to death with ignominy,
in spite of his appeal to the prophets and to the many
signs and wonders which he wrought among them;
the rising of this deliverer from the dead; the ascrip-
tion to him in the course of the next three or four
centuries of claims which he never made in person,
and of propositions which he never advanced while
he walked on the earth, yet which must now be
accepted by every one who would after death escape
a pitiless torment without end; the truly miraculous
preservation amid a fiery swarm of heresies, intricate,
minute, subtle, barely intelligible, but very soul-de-
stroying, of that little fragile thread of pure belief
which can alone guide each spirit in the divinely
appointed path. Exposed to the light, which they
were never meant to endure, of ordinary principles of
evidence founded on ordinary experience, the immortal
legends, the prophecies, the miracles, the mysteries, on
which the spiritual faith of Europe had hung for so
many generations, seemed to shrivel up in unlovely
dissolution. The authenticity of the texts on which
the salvation of man depends, the contradictions and
inconsistencies of the documents, the incompatibility
between many acts and motives expressly approved
by the holiest persons, and the justice and mercy
which are supposed to sit enthroned on high in their

bosoms, the forced constructions of prophecies and their stultifying futility of fulfilment, the extraordinary frivolousness of some of the occasions on which the divine power of thaumaturgy was deliberately and solemnly exerted,—these were among the points at which the messenger of Satan at Ferney was permitted sorely to buffet the church. What is the date of the Apostles' Creed? What of the so-called Athanasian Creed? How were the seven sacraments instituted one after another? What was the difference between the synaxis and the mass? And so forth through many hundreds of pages.

Along with rationalistic questions in scriptural and ecclesiastical history, are many more as to doctrine, and the assumption on which a doctrine rests; questions as to the trinity, as to redemption by the shedding of innocent blood, as to the daily miracle of transubstantiation, as to the resurrection of the body, as to the existence of an entity called soul independently of that matter which, apart from miracle, seems an inseparable condition of its manifestation. His arguments on all these subjects contain a strange mixture of shallow mockery and just objection. The questions which he suggests for the doctors as to the resurrection of the body may serve for an example. Among them are these :

'A Breton soldier goes to Canada. It happens by a not uncommon chance that he falls short of food; he is forced to eat a piece of an Iroquois whom he has killed over night. The Iroquois had fed on

Jesuits for two or three months, a great part of his body had thus become Jesuit. So there is the body of the soldier with Iroquois, Jesuit, and whatever he had eaten before, entering into it. How then will each resume exactly what belongs to him?' 'In order to come to life again, to be the same person you were, you must have a lively and present recollection; it is memory that makes your identity. Having lost memory, how are you to be the same man?' Again, 'considering that only certain material elements are proper for the composition of the human body, where is earth enough to be found to remake all the bodies needed for so many hundreds of generations? And supposing that by a prodigious miracle the whole human race could be resuscitated in the Valley of Jehoshaphat, where are all the spirits meanwhile?'[1]

Another very favourite mode of approaching the beliefs, incidents, and personages of Jewish and Christian history was to show that they had counterparts in some pagan fables or systems, in the books of Chinese philosophers or Brahminical sages. The inference from this identity or correspondence between some Judaical practices and myths, and the practices and myths of Arabians, Egyptians, Greeks, Romans, Hindoos, was that they were in all cases equally the artificial creations of impostors preying on the credulity of men, 'the first prophet or diviner having been the first rogue who met the first fool.' It is curious

---

[1] Dict. Phil. s.v. Résurrection. *Œuvres*, lviii. p. 67.

to observe how the modern argument from constantly extending discoveries in comparative mythology tends to the demolition of the special pretensions of Judaical myths of all sorts, by the very opposite inference to that on which the Voltairean school rested. Voltaire urged that as these myths resembled one another in this and that important feature, therefore they were all equally spurious, false, and absurd. The modern, on the contrary, would hold them all equally genuine, equally free from the taint of imposture in priest or people, and equally faithful representations of the mental states which produced and accepted them. The weakening of the particular sanctity and objective reality of any one form of these common primitive ways of thinking about the action of non-human agents would be just as strong, whether we take the new or the old view of the generation of myths, but the difference of the effect of the two views upon the justice and fertility of historic spirit is immeasurable.

There is no sign, however, that Voltaire was ever seriously conscious of the importance of a right consideration of the mental conditions of primitive peoples. This study had been commenced in his own time by De Brosses, the inventor of the term fetishism, and pronounced by competent modern authorities to have been a powerful and original thinker upon the facts of the infancy of civilisation.[1] Yet Voltaire treated the speculations of this industrious inquirer with the same ignorant contempt and

[1] See, for instance, Tylor's *Primitive Culture*, i. 32, ii. 131, etc.

scorn that the theological enemies of geology were once accustomed to bestow on men who chipped bits of rock and cherished fossils.[1] Oddly enough, Voltaire's carelessness and want of thought on these matters left him with that very theory of the nature of the development of cultivation, on which the theological school insists to this day as against the scientific ethnologists. The question is whether the earliest men were savages, or partially civilised; in other words, whether civilisation has consisted in a certain uniform progression from a state a little above the brutes, or whether the savage is not a being who has degenerated from a partial degree of civilisation. The progression theory was no doubt in a general way a characteristic doctrine of the men of the eighteenth century, for which De Maistre, an ardent and most ingenious advocate of the degeneration theory, reviled them with his usual heartiness. Yet his eagerness to depress revelation by exalting natural theology led Voltaire to the essentially theological position that the earliest men had a clear and lofty idea of a Supreme Being, and a ready appreciation of justice and charity in their relations with one another, until the vile ambition of priestly and prophetic impostors succeeded in setting upon their necks the yoke of systems which corrupted the heart and conscience, and sophisticated a pure and simple faith.

[1] Corr. 1770. *Œuvres*, lxxv. pp. 522, 526, etc. This active spite prevented the accession of De Brosses to a seat in the academy.

He did not hold that men were conscious of the
one God as they were conscious of light, or that they
had perceptions of such a being, as they had perceptions of the ground they tilled.   The idea was derived
by process of natural logic from the contemplation of
astonishing natural effects, of harvest and dearth, of
fair days and tempests, of benefactions and scourges.
They saw all these things, and felt the work of a
master.[1]   Just as in each community there were men
who by the force of their reason found out that
triangles with the same base and of the same height
are equal, and others who in sowing and reaping and
tending their flocks perceived that the sun and moon
returned pretty nearly to the point from which they
had started, and that they never travelled beyond a
certain limit to north or south, so there was a third
man who considered that men, animals, stars could
not have made themselves, and who saw that therefore a Supreme Being must exist; while a fourth,
struck by the wrongs that men inflicted on one
another, concluded that if there exists a being who
made the stars, the earth, and men, such a being must
confer favour on the virtuous, and punishments on
the wicked.   This idea, Voltaire declares, is so natural
and so good that it was most readily embraced.[2]   The
various forms of revelations were only so many corruptions of that simple, serviceable, and self-proving
monotheism, and so were the conceptions of poly-

[1] Dict. Phil. s. v. Dieu. *Œuvres*, liv. p. 20.
[2] Dieu et les Hommes, c. iii. *Œuvres*, xlv. p. 270.

theism. He had no notion that monotheism is a later development of the theological spirit than polytheism. Unable to deny that the Greeks and Romans, about whom he knew so little and talked so much, had plurality of gods, he drew a distinction between one Supreme Being and all the rest, and contended that you may search all their records in vain for a single fact or a single word to counterbalance the many passages and monuments which attest their belief of the sovereignty of the one deity and his superiority over all the rest.[1] We do not know whether this was a fortuitous kind of growth in his own mind, or whether it was a scrap of recollection from the painstaking pages in which Cudworth had worked at the establishment of that explanation of polytheism. Voltaire too often writes on these weighty subjects, as if trusting to a memory that snatched effectively at plausible theories, while losing much of their evidence and all their deeper bearings.

It would be not a little extraordinary, if we did not constantly remember that Voltaire's strength did not lie in speculation or systematic thought, that he saw none of the objections to this account of things, and that he was content with so limited an observation of the facts. If De Brosses had magnanimously suffered himself to be cheated in the transaction of the fourteen cords of wood, Voltaire would perhaps have read his book candidly, and if he had read it otherwise than with a foregone resolution to despise it, he would

[1] Dict. Phil. s. v. Polythéisme. *Œuvres*, lvii. p. 391.

have come upon a number of circumstances entirely
fatal to his smooth theory that many gods are always
subordinate to the one, because he would have had to
consider those states of the human mind in which
there are no spiritual gods at all, but in which every
object whatever is invested with volition and power.
In one place he shows something like a recognition of
the true nature of the process. 'I have always been
persuaded,' he says in a letter to Mairan, 'that the
phenomena of the heavens have been in the main the
source of the old fables. Thunder was heard on the
inaccessible summit of a mountain; therefore there
must be gods dwelling on the mountain, and launching
the thunder. The sun seems to speed from east to
west, therefore he has fine coursers. The rain does
not touch the head of one who sees a rainbow, so the
rainbow is a token that there will never again be a
deluge.'[1] But then Voltaire was no systematic
thinker, and thus there was no security that any
given right idea which came into his mind would
either remain present to him, or would be followed
up and placed along with other ideas in a scientific
order. Apart from this, however, it is extraordinary
that Voltaire's extreme acuteness did not suggest to
him the question, how it was that the artless and clear
belief in one God became more and more obscured by
the growing multitude of other gods, just in proportion as the primitive tribes became more civilised
in all the arts of life. If the nomad progenitors of the

[1] Corr. 1761. *Œuvres*, lxvii. p. 186.

Greeks had only one god, how was it that, as knowledge, social feeling, love of beauty, and all the other
ennobling parts of man became more fully developed,
the power of superstition waxed greater, and temples
and images were multiplied?

Again, the theologist might, consistently with his
deliberate principle of resort to the miraculous, contend that this first conception of a single supreme
power, in the fact of the existence of which he is
entirely at one with Voltaire, was directly implanted
by a supernatural force. But Voltaire, debarred from
such an explanation as this, was driven silently to
assume and imply the truly incredible position that
the rudest savages, being what we know them,
urgently occupied in the struggle for means of sub-
sistence, leading lives purely animal, possessed of no
vocabulary for any abstract idea, should yet by one
leap of natural logic have risen to one of the very
highest pinnacles of speculation, and both felt and
expressed the idea of cause in the most general and
comprehensive of all its forms. Surely this assumption, measured by any of those standards of experience or probability to which he professed to appeal,
was as much of a miracle as those which he so decisively
repudiated.

In one of his letters Voltaire declared that Locke
was the only reasonable metaphysician that he knew,
and that next to him he placed Hume.[1] Did he ever
read, we may wonder, that masterly essay on the

[1] Corr. 1758. *Œuvres*, lxvi. p. 200.

Natural History of Religion, where Hume not only
combats with his usual vigour and effectiveness the
idea of the belief in one omniscient, omnipotent, and
omnipresent spirit being the primary religion of men,
and shows that polytheism precedes monotheism, but
also traces the origin of all religion to its rudiment,
in that 'universal tendency among mankind to conceive all beings like themselves, and to transfer to
every object those qualities with which they are
familiarly acquainted, and of which they are intimately conscious?'[1] The greater the knowledge we
acquire of the spiritual rudiments of primitive people,
the more certainly is it established that the idea of
theism as the earliest and most elementary belief,
which Voltaire had picked up from Bolingbroke and
Pope, is untenable, and that Hume has been more
and more fully warranted in saying that the only
point of theology on which the consent of mankind
is nearly universal is that 'there is an invisible, intelligent power in the world, but whether this power
be supreme or subordinate, whether confined to one
being or distributed among several, what attributes,
qualities, connections, or principles of action, ought to
be ascribed to these beings, concerning all these points
there is the widest difference in the popular systems
of theology.'[2] This might be placing natural theology
very low, but Hume at any rate placed it where he
did and described it as he did, because he had knowledge enough of the condition of various nations in

[1] *Nat. Hist. of Religion*, sect. iii.   [2] *Ib.* sect. iv.

various parts of their history, and was sufficiently penetrated with a cautious and scientific spirit, to abstain from the unsupported and purely metaphysical conjectures of men like Voltaire and Rousseau. Well might the keen-eyed De Maistre describe him from the Catholic point of view as the most dangerous and the guiltiest of all those pestilent writers,—the one who employed most talent with most coolness to do most mischief.[1]

If Voltaire had studied Hume, moreover, he might have learnt how futile and inappropriate it is in the long run to examine a religion otherwise than in its most fundamental and comprehensive general ideas, and how narrow and superficial would every philosophic appreciation ultimately find what he called refutation by facts. For his own immediate purpose, which was to cover the church and its creed with ridicule, the method of collecting all the ludicrous, immoral, and inconsistent circumstances in the Scriptures and their current interpretation, was, as we have already said, a weapon potent enough. Voltaire, however, not only did not use, he never understood nor perceived, the fact that a religion rests for its final base on a certain small number of ideas, or that it is only by touching these, by loosening the firmness of their hold, by revealing their want of coherency and consistency with other accepted ideas, that we can expect to shake the superstructure. For example, if only the official exponents of religion had not been

---

[1] *Soirées de St. Pétersbourg*, vi. p. 403.

so firmly bent on making the feeblest of all their
ramparts into their very citadel, it would have been
a very small thing to urge the truly singular quality
of such miracles as those of the water made wine at
Cana, of the cursing of the barren fig-tree, of the unfortunate swine who rushed violently down a steep
place and were choked. These were legends that
from the right point of view of religion were not
worth defending, any more than from the right point
of view of truth they were worth attacking. The
details of the use of a supernaturally conferred power
may best be let alone, until the probability of the
existence and bestowal of such power has been discussed and decided. The important issue and matter
of vital concern turned upon the general idea of the
miraculous; yet this was what Voltaire, perhaps from
an instinctive consciousness of the little capacity he
possessed for genuine speculation, postponed to the
really secondary purpose of disparaging particular
cases of miraculous performance.

We are now touching what, before Hume, was
the central defect of the eighteenth-century attack,
judged philosophically rather than practically. The
movement was a reaction against a certain set of ideas
which had been incorporated in the Christian system,
as that system was elaborated by the oriental sophisters.
Yet the exact conflict between the old ideas and the
new was never conceived, much less was it expressed,
in clear comprehensive formulas. Consequently the
most general terms for the debate were neither sought

nor found, and hence the oppressive narrowness, the
stifling want of free air, throughout the controversy.
The truth or falsehood which it is good for us to
discover in connection with a religion resides not in
detail, but in the largest general ideas of the subject.
These draw all else along with them.   Let us take an
illustration from a characteristic of the anti-christian
attack which has already been mentioned.   The Voltairean school, as we have before observed,[1] habitually
derided the sacred importance attached by the church
in all ages, from Saint Paul downwards, to the practice
of continence.   But there is no sign, so far as the
present writer's knowledge goes, that they ever were
near perceiving the origin of that superstition lying
deep down for so many centuries in the human mind.
The sanctity of continence was only one product of the
old far-spreading conviction of all the evil and unholi-
ness essentially inherent in matter.   This conviction,
which has itself a history and genesis well worth
tracing, probably accounts for more of the peculiar
manifestations contained in Christianity than any one
principle of belief besides.   From this metaphysical
idea sprang the whole theory of asceticism; it had
much to do indirectly with the first establishment of
the doctrine of the divinity of Christ; it entered into
the triumph of indispensable grace.[2]   The speculative
origin of practices and sentiments which the heads of

[1] Ante, ch. iii.
[2] See Milman's *Hist. of Latin Christianity*, bk. ii. chap. ii.
and iii.

the western church valued, modified, and sagaciously used for ecclesiastical or political reasons, ought never to be lost sight of, because their duration has depended on the circumstance of the original speculative idea remaining deeply sunk, though not often put into articulate form, in the minds of the faithful, and of all others whom these practices and sentiments have influenced.   One key to the central movement of the eighteenth century is the dispersion of this association of evil and corruption from matter.   There was energetic and triumphant progress in the discovery of the laws of matter, in their most stupendous, over-whelming, and majestic order.   There was a steady tendency to resolve mental manifestations into functions of matter.   There was a general inclination to forget those depressing facts connected with the decay and dissolution of matter, which, in the dismal times when the church was founded, had been thrust into a prominence so humiliating to human dignity.   The general movement was carried too far by extreme spirits, but on the whole it was a salutary and much-needed protest against the limitation of knowledge within airy cloudlands where no true knowledge was to be reached, and of emotion within transcendental aspirations where the deep reality of human relations faded into dim distance.

It is only when controversy is conducted with reference to ground ideas of this kind, that the parties to it can be sure of being on the same plane, and, if they are not on the same plane, one of the least mis-

chiefs is that their arguments fly over one another's
heads.   Voltaire failed, partly from want of historic
knowledge, partly from insufficient depth of nature,
to see what these ground ideas were, against which
he was fighting.   Thus, to take another instance, he
failed to see that the belief in the exertion of supernatural power, even on occasions which struck him as
so frivolous, and in a manner undoubtedly incompatible with justice, was merely an incidental result
of a profoundly rooted idea of the closeness, constancy,
and mixed holiness and majesty, of the relations
between man and an awful being other than man,
endowed with powers denied to us, and animated
by motives inscrutable to us.   He chose, if we are
not wrong in using a term that may imply much conscious deliberation, to identify his own conception of
deity with the conception of deity in the first four
centuries of the Christian era, simply because the
object of each was called by a common name.   He
found that the actions attributed to the Supreme
Being whom the church revered, were unworthy of
a personage endowed with the qualities which he
ascribed to a supreme power, in his own version of
of that culminating conception.   He was thus never
on the same plane of thought or argument, but he
never was near finding this out.   The God whom he
conceived was incapable, from the very nature attributed to him by his worshippers, of the various
transactions, lofty and mean, sublime and puerile,
described in the documents on which Catholicism

relied, and the tradition by which it corroborated
and interpreted them.   The ground idea of the belief
in the miraculous was an extremely anthropomorphic
notion of a divinity, possessed of complete power, but
using it in obedience to motives which finite under-
standings cannot pretend to fathom or measure.
Such a notion was the natural growth of the human
mind, amid such a set of circumstances as attended
the development and establishment of Christianity.
Men sat in darkness, forlorn and without hope, and
it is not hard for us to imagine the exultation with
which some greater spirit would produce, and all
others would embrace, the idea of this misery and
darkness being no more than an outer accident, the
mysterious and incomprehensible dispensation of a
divine being, ever alive to the destinies of men, but
holding them in the hollow of an unseen hand, and
guiding them in ways that are not as our ways ; ever
remote from corporeal vision, but operating at a multitude of points on the spirit of each man through
grace, and finally, by a consummating miracle repeated
daily some thousands of times, severing this spirit from
the probation of flesh, and prolonging its existence
independently of the body through all eternity in
modes of being, none the less real for being impossible to conceive.   To Voltaire this was unspeakable
foolishness.   The prodigies of grace, of the resurrection of the body, of the incarnation of divinity, were
inconsistent with the qualities which he imputed to
the creator of the universe, and hence he contented

himself with mocking at them; the real state of the
case was simply that a number of influences had drawn
men aside from that conception of the creator, with
which such prodigies were not inconsistent, but
were on the contrary logically and inseparably associated.

This failure to rise to the highest ideas involved
in the great debate explains, along with much besides,
two striking facts connected with it. It explains the
intense acerbity of the conflict, and the flaming depth
of the chasm which divided and divides the two camps
in France. For the best natures are most violently
irritated and outraged by mocking and satiric attack
upon the minor details, the accidents, the outside of
the objects of faith, when they would have been
affected in a very different way by a contrast between
the loftiest parts of their own belief and the loftiest
parts of some other belief. Many persons who would
listen to a grave attack on the consistency, reasonableness, and elevation of the currently ascribed attributes of the godhead, with something of the respect
due to the profound solemnity of the subject, would
turn with deaf and implacable resentment upon
one who should make merry over the swine of
Gadara.

The same circumstance, secondly, explains the
absence of permanent quality about all that Voltaire
wrote upon religion. For instance, men who sympathise with him in his aims, and even for their
sake forgive him his method, who have long ago

T

struck the tents under which they once found shelter
in the lands of belief, to whom Catholicism has
become as extinct a thing as Mahometanism, even
they will turn with better chance of edification to
the great masters and teachers of the old faith, than
to the fiery precursor of the new. And why, if
not for the reason that while he dealt mainly with
the lower religious ideas, or with the higher ideas
in their lowest forms, they put these into the second
place, and move with an inspiring exultation amid
the loftiest and most general conceptions that fine
imagination and a soaring reason could discover
among the spiritual treasures of their religion. They
turned to the diviner mind, and exercised themselves
with the weightiest and most universal circumstances
of the destiny of mankind. This is what makes their
thought and eloquence of perpetual worth, because
the circumstances with which they deal are perpetually
present, and the elements of life and character to
which they appeal perpetually operative. The awful
law of death, the impenetrable secret of the first
cause, the fierce play of passion and universal distribution of pain, the momentariness of guilt and
eternity of remorse, the anguish of bereavement that
chokes and rends, the hopeless inner desolation which
is the unbroken lot of myriads of the forlorn of the
earth,—these ghostly things ever laying siege to the
soul were known to a Bossuet or a Pascal, and resolved by a series of ideas about the unknowable
power and the government of the world, which are no

longer the mighty weapons of exorcism they once
were, but they are at any rate of due magnitude and
proportion, sublime, solemn, never unworthy. We
touch the hands of those who have walked with the
most high, and they tell us many moving wonders;
we look on faces that have shone in rays from the
heaven of noble thoughts; we hear solemn and melo-
dious words from men who received answers from
oracles that to us are very mute, but the memory of
whose power is still upon us. Hence the work of
these glowing mortals lives even for those to whom
their faith is dead, while the words that Voltaire
wrote on religion are lifeless as the Infamous which
they so meritoriously slew. As we have said, he
never knew the deeper things of Catholicism. This
is what he wrote about the immortal Dante: 'Everybody with a spark of good sense ought to blush at
that monstrous assemblage in hell of Dante and
Virgil, of Saint Peter and Madonna Beatrice. There
are to be found among us, in the eighteenth century,
people who force themselves to admire feats of
imagination as stupidly extravagant and as barbarous as this; they have the brutality to oppose
them to the masterpieces of genius, wisdom, and
eloquence, that we have in our language. *O tempora, O judicium!*'[1] To which prodigy of criticism
we can only exclaim with the echo, *O tempora, O
judicium!*

---

[1] Corr. 1761. *Œuvres*, lxvii. p. 74.

III.

Let us see shortly what was Voltaire's own solution of those facts of life with which religion has to deal. The Catholic solution we know, and can definitely analyse and describe; but the vagueness of Voltairean deism defies any attempt at detailed examination. We can perceive a supernatural existence, endowed with indefinable attributes, which are fixed subjectively in the individual consciousness of each believer, and which therefore can never be set forth in a scheme of general acceptance. The Voltairean deist—and such persons exist in ample numbers to this day—hardly ever takes the trouble to reconcile with one another the various attributes which he imputes at various times to some great master power of the universe. There is scarcely one of these attributes to which, when it comes to be definitely described, he does not encounter affronting contradiction in the real occurrences that arise from time to time to search and try all our theories, deistical, or other. The phenomena of moral and physical evil on the earth, and the arrival of disasters which make no discrimination between their victims, are constantly dealing sore blows to the conceptions which the deist loves to erect in moments of optimistic expansion, of the clemency, justice, and illimitable power of a being who governs the universe, and is a something outside and independent of it. These

optimist conceptions, vague, unverified, free of definite relations with any moral or social system, and
furnishing no principle of active human association
as the Catholic idea of deity had done, constitute
the favourite religion or religiosity of those classes
in all modern countries, which have found the
Voltairean kind of objection to the Christian revelation insuperable, and which are so fortunate as to
enjoy a full measure of material prosperity.   To
these classes the black side of life is strange and a
matter of hearsay; and hence the awkwardness of
reconciling their complacent theory with the horror
of facts is never forced upon them.   In their own
happiness they love to superadd the luxury of thank-
fulness to the bounty of a being to whom they owe
all, and to swell the tide of their own emotions by
meditation on his infinite and unspeakable perfections.
Proof they require none, beyond the loveliness and
variety of external nature, the innocence and delight
of all young creatures, the order of the seasons bearing us their copious fruit, the vivid intelligence and
serviceable power of man, who is the divinely appointed recipient of all these multitudinous favours.
Hence in proportion as this sort of deism stirs the
soul of a man, the more closely are his inmost
thoughts reserved for contemplation of the relations
between the Supreme Being and his own individuality.
It is a creed which is specially adapted for, and has
been generally seized by, those with whom the
world has gone very well, owing to their own

laudable exertion, and who are inclined to believe
that the existing ordering of society is fundamentally
the best possible. It is the superlative decoration
of optimism.

The mass of men, those who dwell in dens and
whose lives are bitter, have never, in spite even of
Rousseau's teaching, accepted deism. An opportunity
for trying the experiment had occurred in the fourth
century, and the lesson should not be forgotten.
Deism had been the prevailing opinion in religion,
but, as the most instructive of all the historians of
the dissolution of the Empire observes, it was generally
felt that deism did not supply the void occasioned by
the absence of the multitude of sympathetic divinities
of the pagan system. Its influence was cold and in-
animate.[1] The common people are wont to crave
a revelation, or else they find atheism a rather better
synthesis than any other. They either cling to the
miraculously transmitted message with its hopes of
recompense, and its daily communication of the
divine voice in prayer or sacrament, or else they
make a world which moves through space as a black
monstrous ship with no steersman. The bare deistic
idea, of a being endowed at once with sovereign
power and sovereign clemency, with might that
cannot be resisted and justice that cannot be im-
pugned, who loves man with infinite tenderness, yet
sends him no word of comfort and gives him no way

[1] Finlay's *Greece under the Romans* (B.C. 146-A.D. 716), pp.
146 147.

of deliverance, is too hard a thing for those who have to endure the hardships of the brutes, but yet preserve the intelligence of men.

> Comment concevoir un Dieu, la bonté même,
> Qui prodigua ses biens à ses enfans qu'il aime,
> Et qui versa sur eux les maux à pleines mains?
> Quel œil peut pénétrer dans ses profonds desseins ?
> De l'être tout parfait le mal ne pouvait naître !
> Il ne vient point d'autrui puisque Dieu seul est maître :
> Il existe pourtant. O tristes vérités !
> O mélange étonnant de contrariétés !
> Un Dieu vint consoler notre race affligée ;
> Il visita la terre et ne l'a point changée !
> Un sophiste arrogant nous dit qu'il ne l'a pu ;
> Il le pouvait, dit l'autre, et ne l'a point voulu ;
> Il le voudra, sans doute ; et tandis qu'on raisonne,
> Des foudres souterraines engloutissent Lisbonne,
> Et de trente cités dispersent les débris,
> Des bords sanglans du Tage à la mer de Cadix.[1]

A bald deism has undoubtedly been the creed of some of the purest and most generous men that have ever trod the earth, but none the less on that account is it in its essence a doctrine of self-complacent individualism from which society has little to hope, and with which there is little chance of the bulk of society ever sympathising. In truth, one can scarcely call it a creed. It is mainly a name for a particular mood of fine spiritual exaltation ; the expression of a state of indefinite aspiration and supreme feeling for lofty things. Are you going to convert the new barbarians of our western world with this fair word of emptiness

[1] Poëme sur le Désastre de Lisbonne. *Œuvres*, xv. p. 53.

Will you sweeten the lives of suffering men, and take
its heaviness from that droning piteous chronicle of
wrong and cruelty and despair, which everlastingly
saddens the compassionating ear like moaning of a
midnight sea; will you animate the stout of heart
with new fire, and the firm of hand with fresh joy of
battle, by the thought of a being without intelligible
attributes, a mere abstract creation of metaphysic,
whose mercy is not as our mercy, nor his justice as
our justice, nor his fatherhood as the fatherhood of
men? It was not by a cold, a cheerless, a radically
depraving conception such as this, that the church
became the refuge of humanity in the dark times
of old, but by the representation, to men sitting
in bondage and confusion, of godlike natures moving among them under figure of the most eternally touching of human relations, a tender mother
ever interceding for them, and an elder brother
laying down his life that their burdens might be
loosened.

We have spoken of Voltairean deism, and the
expression is a convenient one to distinguish from the
various forms of mystic theology, which gloomily
disclaim any pretence to be rational, the halting-place
of spirits too deeply penetrated with the rationalistic
objections of Voltaire to accept revelation, and either
too timorous or too confident to acquiesce in a neutral
solution. It is unjust, however, to attribute to
Voltaire himself a perfect adherence to the deistical
idea. For the first half of his life there is no doubt

that it floated in his mind, as in so many others, in a random manner, as the true explanation of the world. His introduction to the teaching of Newton would give a firmer shape to such a belief. He has indeed told us that it was so. He mentions that in the course of several interviews he had with Doctor Samuel Clarke in 1726, this philosopher never pronounced the name of God without a curious air of awe and self-collection, and he commemorates the impression which the sight of this habit, and reflection upon its significance, made upon him.[1] Still it was not a very active or vital element of belief with him even then, but rather of the nature of the sublimest of poetic figures.

> Oui, dans le sein de Dieu, loin de ce corps mortel,
> L'esprit semble écouter la voix l'Eternel.[2]

Clearly this kind of expression means very little, and has no source in the deeper seats of the writer's feeling. A considerable number of Voltaire's deistical ejaculations, and on these occasions he threw into them a measure of real unction, may be fairly traced to the extraordinary polemical utility of an idea of spotless purity, entire justice, inexhaustible mercy, as an engine of battle against men who in the sacred name of this idea were the great practitioners of intolerance and wrong.

[1] Phil. de Newton. *Œuv.* xli. p. 46. See also the whole chapter.

[2] A Mdme. du Châtelet sur la Philosophie de Newton (1738). *Œuv.* xvii. p. 113.

> Ignorer ton être suprême,
> Grand Dieu! c'est un moindre blasphème,
> Et moins digne de ton courroux
> Que de te croire impitoyable,
> De nos malheurs insatiable,
> Jaloux, injuste comme nous.
> Lorsqu'un dévot atrabilaire
> Nourri de superstition,
> A par cette affreuse chimère,
> Corrompu sa religion,
> Le voilà stupide et farouche :
> Le fiel découle de sa bouche,
> Le fanatisme arme son bras :
> Et dans sa piété profonde
> Sa rage immolerait le monde
> A son Dieu, qu'il ne connaît pas.[1]

To have a conception of perfect goodness was a manifest convenience in confronting men who were to be proved masters of badness. But when the pressure of circumstance forced Voltaire to seek in earnest for an explanation of the world, which he had formerly been content to take in an easy way upon trust, then the deism, which had been barely more than nominal at best, was transformed into a very different and far sincerer mood. It would obviously be a gross blunder from a logical point to confound optimism with deism, but it is clear that what shook Voltaire's conviction of the existence of a deity was the awakening in him of a keener sense of the calamities that afflict the race of man. Personal misfortunes perhaps had their share. It was after the loss of Madame du Châtelet, and after the rude dispersion of his illusions as to

---

[1] Ode sur le Fanatisme. *Œuvres*, xvi. p. 331.

Frederick, when he barely knew whither to turn for
shelter or a home, that the optimism which he had
learnt in England began to lose its hold upon him.
We must do him the justice to add that he was yet
more sensible of disasters which affected others. The
horrid tide of war which devastated Europe and
America, the yet more hateful tide of persecution
for opinion which swept over France, and the cruel
maladministration of justice which disgraced her tribunals, stirred all that was best in him to the very
depths. The only non-dramatic poem of his which has
strength, sincerity, and profundity of meaning enough
firmly to arrest the reader's attention, and stimulate
both thought and feeling, is that fine and powerful
piece which he wrote on the occasion of the great
earthquake of Lisbon.[1] Here he threw into energetic and passionately argumentative verse the same
protest against the theory that whatever is is best,
which he afterwards urged in a very different form in
the 'refined insolence' of Candide.[2] He approaches
more nearly than a quarter of a century before he
would have thought possible, to the deep gloom of the
Pascal against whose terrible pictures he had then so
warmly protested. He sees mankind imprisoned in a
circle of appalling doom, from which there is no way
of escape. Unlike Pascal, he can find no solution,
and he denounces that mockery of a solution which

[1] *Œuvres*, xv. pp. 39-62.
[2] Aristotle's definition of εὐτραπελία, or wit, as ὕβρις πεπαι-
δευμένη marks one of Voltaire's chief talents with entire accuracy.

cries that all is well in accents stifled with lamentation.
He protests against the delusion of forcing the course
of the world's destiny into a moral formula, that shall
contain the terms of justice and mercy in their human
sense.

> Aux cris demi-formés de leurs voix expirantes,
> Au spectacle effrayant de leurs cendres fumantes,
> Direz-vous : C'est l'effet des éternelles lois,
> Qui d'un Dieu libre et bon nécessitent le choix ?
> Direz-vous, en voyant cet amas de victimes :
> Dieu s'est vengé, leur mort est le prix de leurs crimes ?
> Quelle crime, quelle faute ont commis ces enfans
> Sur le sein maternel écrasés et sanglans ?
> Lisbonne, qui n'est plus, eut-elle plus de vices
> Que Londres, que Paris, plongés dans les délices ?
> Lisbonne est abîmée, et l'on danse á Paris.

He equally refuses, though not in terms, to comfort
himself by the reflection that, in default of a better,
the current ragged theory of the providential government of the universe, because it may be possible, must
be true.   He can find no answer, and confesses his
belief that no answer is to be found by human effort.
Whatever side we take, we can only shudder ; there
is nothing that we know, nothing that we have not to
fear.   Nature is mute, and we interrogate her in vain ;
the book of destiny is closed to our eyes.

> L'homme, étranger à soi, de l'homme est ignoré.
> Que suis-je ? où suis-je ? où vais-je ? et d'où suis-je tiré ?
> Atomes tourmentés sur cet amas de boue,
> Que la mort engloutit, et dont le sort se joue,
> Mais atomes pensans, atomes dont les yeux,
> Guidés par la pensée, ont mesuré les cieux,

Au sein de l'infini nous élançons notre être,
Sans pouvoir un moment nous voir et nous connaître.

*   *   *   *   *

Le passé n'est pour nous qu'un triste souvenir ;
Le présent est affreux, s'il n'est point d'avenir,
Si la nuit du tombeau détruit l'être qui pense.

He abandons Plato and rejects Epicurus. Bayle knows more than they, as, with the balance in his hand, he teaches men to doubt; wise enough, great enough, to be without a system.

In a note he adds to this glorification of Bayle, whom he styles the advocate-general of the philosophers—the thinker in whose pages all opinions are set forth, all the reasons which shake them and all which uphold are equally investigated, while he abstains from giving any conclusions.[1] Elsewhere he explains that when he describes reason as having made immense progress in Germany, he does not refer to those who openly embrace the system of Spinoza; but the good folk who have no fixed principles on the nature of things, who do not know what is, but know very well what is not, these are my true philosophers.[2]

It would not be difficult to find a score of passages in which the writer assumes or declares certainty on this high matter to be attainable, and to be entirely in one direction. His opinions undoubtedly shifted with the veering of his moods, but on the whole these axioms of suspense mark the central point to which they constantly tended to return, and at which they rested longest. That dark word, Shut thine eyes and

[1] *Œuvres*, xv. p. 58.   [2] Corr. 1765. *Œuvres*, lxxv. p. 311.

thou shalt see, opened no road for him. The saying
that the Most High may be easily known, provided
one does not press for definition, offered no treasure
of spiritual acquisition to the man who never let go,
even if he did not always accurately appreciate,
Locke's injunction to us to be careful to define our
terms. We cannot label Voltaire either spiritualist
or materialist. The success with which he evades
these two appellations is one of the best available
tests of a man's capacity for approaching the great
problems with that care and positive judgment, which
are quite as proper to them as to practical affairs or
to physical science.

Thus with reference to the other great open
question, he habitually insisted that the immortality
of the soul can never possibly be demonstrated, and
that this is why it has been revealed to us by religion,[1]
which is perhaps Voltaire's way of saying that it is no
near concern of his. Sometimes he argued from considerations of general probability. The brutes feel
and think up to a certain point, and men have only
the advantage over them of a greater combination of
ideas; the more or less makes no difference in kind.
'Well, nobody thinks of giving an immortal soul to a
flea; why should you give one any the more to an
elephant, or a monkey, or my Champagne valet, or a
village steward who has a trifle more instinct than my
valet?'[2]   Again, he retorted significantly on those

[1] Lettres Ang. xiv. Œuvres, xxxv. p. 108.
[2] Corr. 1736. Œuvres, lxiii. p. 31.

who contended with a vehemence of prejudice known in some places even to this day, that belief in the immortality of the soul is an indispensable condition of probity : as if the first Jews accepted that dogma, and as if there were no honest men among them, and no instruction in virtue.[1]

In fine, then, we search Voltaire in vain for a positive creed, which logic may hold in coherent bonds, or social philosophy accept as a religious force. The old word about his faith must be pronounced true. It remains a creed of negation. But still, be it always understood, negation of darkness. And this inevitably leads in the direction of the day. It was an indispensable step in the process of transition. Men, it is constantly being said since the violent breaking-up of French society, will never consent to live on no better base than articles of denial and formulas of suspense, for are not the deepest parts of human character moved by strong yearning for relationship with the unknowable? It may be so, and if it be, the Voltairean movement was the great instrument in leading, not merely a scanty group of speculative intellects, but vast bodies, large nations, of common folk to perceive, or dimly to conjecture, that this object of adoration which their eyes strain after *is* unknowable, and that there is no attainable external correlative of their deep desire. Voltaire never went so far in the direction of assertion as Rousseau, and he never went so far in

[1] Dict. Phil. s. v. Locke. *Œuvres*, lvi. p. 338

the direction of denial as Holbach. And, whatever
we may say generally of the horror of the world for
the spirit that denies, all that was best and most truly
progressive in French society during the eighteenth
century, Turgot and Condorcet no less than Beaumar-
chais, showed itself content to follow him in this
middle path. His appreciation of religion was wanting in a hundred vital things, just as some may say
that Luther's was, but it contained the one idea which
the deepest spirit of the time prompted men to desire,
the decisive repudiation of the religious notions of the
past. We must call this negative, no doubt, but no
word should frighten us away from seeing how much
positive aspiration lay underneath. When men are
in the mood of France a century and a quarter since,
when all that an old civilisation has bestowed on
them of what is best and strongest, rises up against
all that the same civilisation has bequeathed to them
of what is pestilent and dangerous, they are never
nice critics. They do not decline a reinvigorating
article of faith, because it is not a system, nor do
they measure a deliverer by syllogism. The smallest
chink may shine like light of the sun to prisoners long
held in black and cavernous recesses.

When Bayle's Dictionary came out, we read, so
great was the avidity to have sight of it, that long
before the doors of the Mazarin library were open, a
little crowd assembled in the early morning of each
day, and there was as great a struggle for the first
access to the precious book, as for the front row

at the performance of a piece for which there is a
rage.[1] This was the beginning of an immense impulse
of curiosity, eager to fill the vacuum occasioned by the
slow subsidence of the old religion, which had once
covered not only faith, but science, history, dialectic,
and philosophy, all in a single synthesis. It was this
impulse which Voltaire both represented and acceler-
ated. In these periods of agitation, men forgive all
to one who represents without compromise or diminu-
tion their own dominant passions. Vehemence of
character counts for more than completeness of
doctrine, and they crave a battle-cry, not a disserta-
tion. They need to have their own sentiment aggres-
sively presented, and their own defects of boldness or
courage at once rebuked and supplemented by a leader
whose purpose can never be mistaken, and whose
words are never nipped by the frost of intellectual
misgiving. All through the century there was slowly
growing up an inner France, full of angry disgust
against the past. Its germ was the crowd eager to
read Bayle. Its outcome was the night of the Fourth
of August 1789, when the civil order of society was
overthrown between a sunset and a dawn. Voltaire,
as we have seen, studiously abstained from any public
word upon things political, but it was he who in the
long interval between these two events held men by
a watchword to which the political decay of the
country gave such meaning, that of hatred to the old.
And there was no such steadfast symbol of the old as

[1] Holberg, quoted in Sainte-Beuve's *Nouveaux Lundis*, ix. 26.

the church, to him and his school a lurid beacon on a monster-haunted shore.

Voltaire's selection of the church as the object of his attacks marks an important difference between him and the other great revolutionary precursor. Rousseau's Savoyard Vicar was perfectly willing to accept the cultus of Christianity, even when he had ceased to accept its dogma. He regarded all particular religions as so many salutary institutions, all good so long as they were the organs for a due service of God. He actually celebrated mass with more veneration after the acquisition of his new principles, than he had been accustomed to do when he supposed that the mass was an occasion of personal divine presence. This kind of teaching was clearly to perpetuate and transfix for ever the form of religion which each country, or any given set of men in it, might possess. It was to stereotype belief, as it is stereotyped among the millions in the East. Whence was reform to come, whence any ray of new light, whence a principle of growth and activity for the intelligence of men? How on these terms is truth to win the battle at a single point? This was the beginning of a fatal substitution of bland emotional complacency for robust cultivation of the reason, and firm reverence for its lessons as the highest that we can learn. Voltaire no doubt did in practice many a time come to terms with his adversary while he was yet on the way with him; but, disagreeable as these temporisings are to us who live in an easier day, they never deceived any one, nor could they ever be mistaken for the establishment of intellectual treason as a principle, or of philosophic indifference as a climax. As has been said, though he writes in the midst of the old régime, in the face of the Bastille, and with the fetters of the enemy in some sort actually upon him, he still finds a thousand means of reaching you.[1] He is always the representative of reason, and never of sentimentalism. He was not above superficial compromises in matters of conduct, and these it is hard or impossible to condone; but at any rate he is free from the deeper and more penetrating reproach of erecting hypocrisy into a deliberate doctrine.

We do not know how far he ever seriously approached the question, so much debated since the overthrow of the old order in France, whether a society can exist without a religion? He says in one place that to believe God and spirits corporeal is an old metaphysical error, but absolutely not to believe in any god would be an error incompatible with wise government. But even this much was said for the sake of introducing a taunt against the orthodox, who by a strange contradiction had risen up with fury against Bayle for believing it possible that a society of atheists could hold together, while they insisted with just as much violence that the empire of China was established on a basis of atheism.[2] His natural

---

[1] Quinet's *La Révolution*, i. 168.
[2] *Essai sur les Mœurs*, c. ii. *Œuvres*, xx. p. 344. See also c. clxxxii. *Œuv*. xxiv. p. 162.

sagacity would most likely have shown him that this
is one of the sterile problems, with which the obstructive defender of things as they are tries to draw the
soldier of improvement away from his strongest posts.
Whether a society can exist without religion or not,
at least its existence as a structure for whose duration
we can be anxious, must depend on the number of
men in it who deal honestly with their own under-
standings. And, further, is no man to be counted to
have a religion who, like Voltaire, left great questions
open, and put them aside, as all questions, that must
from the limitations of human faculty eternally remain
open, well deserve to be put aside? Must we ever
call an unknown God by one name? Are there so
few tasks for one on earth, that he must strain all his
soul to fix the regimen of high heaven?

Voltaire, there is every reason to think, did in an
informal kind of way suppose in the bottom of his
heart that there is nothing in human nature to hinder
a very advanced society from holding perfectly well
together, with all its opinions in a constant state of
analysis. Whatever we may think of it, this dream
of what is possible, if the activity of human intelligence were only sufficiently stimulated and the conditions of social union were once so adjusted as to give
it fair play, unquestionably lies at the root of the
revolutionary ideas with all those who were first
stirred by Voltaire rather than by Rousseau. Condorcet, for instance, manifestly depends with the firmest confidence upon that possibility being realised

It is the idea of every literary revolutionist, as distinguished from the social or economic revolutionist,
in France at the present day. The knowledge that
this was the case, added to the sound conviction
that men can never live by analysis alone, gave its
fire to De Maistre's powerful attack, and its immense
force to Burke's plea for what he called prejudice.
But the indispensable synthesis need never be immov-
ably fixed, nor can it soon again be one and single
for our civilisation; for progress consists in gradual
modifications of it, as increase of knowledge and un-
foreseen changes in the current of human affairs disclose imperfections in it, and wherever progress is a
law the stages of men's advance are unequal. Above
all, it is monstrous to suppose that because a man does
not accept your synthesis, he is therefore a being without a positive creed or a coherent body of belief
capable of guiding and inspiring conduct.

There are new solutions for him, if the old are
fallen dumb. If he no longer believes death to be
a stroke from the sword of God's justice, but the
leaden footfall of an inflexible law of matter, the
humility of his awe is deepened, and the tenderness
of his pity made holier, that creatures who can love
so much should have their days so shut round with a
wall of darkness. The purifying anguish of remorse
will be stronger, not weaker, when he has trained
himself to look upon every wrong in thought, every
duty omitted from act, each infringement of the inner
spiritual law which humanity is constantly perfecting

for its own guidance and advantage, less as a breach
of the decrees of an unseen tribunal, than as an un-
grateful infection, weakening and corrupting the future
of his brothers.   And he will be less effectually raised
from inmost prostration of soul by a doubtful subjective reconciliation, so meanly comfortable to his own
individuality, than by hearing full in the ear the sound
of the cry of humanity craving sleepless succour from
her children.   That swelling consciousness of height
and freedom with which the old legends of an omnipotent divine majesty fill the breast, may still remain ;
for how shall the universe ever cease to be a sovereign
wonder of overwhelming power and superhuman fixed-
ness of law?   And a man will be already in no mean
paradise, if at the hour of sunset a good hope can
fall upon him like harmonies of music that the earth
shall still be fair, and the happiness of every feeling
creature still receive a constant augmentation, and
each good cause yet find worthy defenders, when the
memory of his own poor name and personality has
long been blotted out of the brief recollection of men
for ever.

CHAPTER VI.

HISTORY.

THE activity of the foremost men of the eighteenth century in the composition of history is too remarkable a circumstance, not to deserve some attempt at explanation. There were historians in previous ages, but in the eighteenth century there was both in France, and afterwards in England, a special and extraordinary development in this direction. Partially no doubt this was due to the general movement of curiosity, the widespread desire for all kinds of knowledge, which was in the air. Men were emancipating themselves from the trammels of an authority which had not widened the limits of inquiry in the same proportion as human faculties had strengthened, and, amid the universal expansion of intelligent interest and the eager scrutiny of all the objects of knowledge which the new dawn was baring to sight, it was not possible that the order of political and social facts in former epochs should be neglected. This, however, does not sufficiently explain why such a man as Hume betook himself to the composition of history, or why Gibbon found himself best able to attack Christianity by tracing some of the most important parts of its annals, or why Voltaire, who lived so entirely and intensely in the present, should have thought it worth while to give so much labour to presentation of the past. It is a striking fact, which must be something more than an accident, that the best secular histories which remain from this period, one of them the most striking monument in historical literature, were written by the most marked assailants of reigning superstition.

Was it not, indeed, to be expected that as the dark clouds of an absorbing consciousness of the supernatural cleared away, men of understanding would be more and more drawn towards study of human action, and that the advance of society under purely natural and positive conditions would immediately seize a foremost place among the objects of experiential inquiry? It is too constantly maintained by persons with something of a vested interest in darkness, that those who do not worship the gods are indifferent to the happiness of men. Yet the history of intellectual progress would seem to show that it was not until the commencement of a rapid decline in the acceptance of terrorist and jealous deities and incomprehensible dogmas, that serious attention was given to some of the subjects in which a sound knowledge is among the most indispensable conditions of the advancing welfare of men. For instance, as soon as the hold of ancient versions of the supernatural was loosened over the stronger spirits, by the middle of the century there instantly took place an astonishing development of activity in the physical sciences. The interest of historic and economic studies was at least as pressing. Becoming aware that men had made their own world, thinkers found the consideration of the process by which this world is made, and the order of society established and developed, forced upon them with an entirely new significance. The dry bones of the ancient valley of annalists and chroniclers were made to live, and the great work of the reconstruction of the past was begun, with an alertness and perseverance that has not been surpassed even in an age of far purer and juster historical intelligence. It was quite reasonable that the conviction of each act in the universe, from the crash of an empire to the fall of a sparrow to the ground, being due to an arbitrary and inscrutable decree, should prevent the rise of history from the level of annals into the region of philosophy. The decay of this theory of the government of the universe was as reasonably the cause of a new mode of looking at the long records of the race, and we find ourselves moving in a day of historical masterpieces.

Voltaire has told us the circumstances under which he was led to approach the philosophy of history. Madame du Châtelet, whose mind would fain have reached every kind of knowledge, but who was especially apt for metaphysics and geometry, had conceived an aversion for history. 'What does it matter to me,' she would ask, 'a Frenchwoman living on my estate, to know that Egil succeeded Haquin

in Sweden, and that Ottoman was the son of Ortogrul!
I have read with pleasure the history of the Greeks
and the Romans; they offered me certain great
pictures which attracted me. But I have never yet
been able to finish any long history of our modern
nations. I can see scarcely anything in them but
confusion; a host of minute events without connection
or sequence, a thousand battles which settled nothing.
I renounced a study which overwhelms the mind
without illuminating it.' To this frank statement of
the case, to which so many thousands of persons in
all epochs would so heartily subscribe, Voltaire replied
by pointing out that perhaps the study of history
would be no waste of time, if by cutting away all the
details of wars, as tedious as they are untrustworthy,
all the frivolous negotiations which have been nothing
but pieces of purposeless cheating, all the minute
incidents which stifle great events, and by retaining
those which paint manners, you made of this chaos
a general and well-arranged picture ; in short, if you
tried to disengage from the concourse of events the
history of the human mind.[1] Not all the faults of
execution ought to blind us to the merit of this
notion of the true way of studying history, or to the
admirable clearness of vision with which Voltaire,
not only in this but in all his other historical pieces,
adhered to his own two leading principles ; first, that
laws, arts, manners, are the chief matter and concern
of history ; and second, that 'details which lead to

[1] Essai sur les Mœurs, pp. 1, 2.

nothing are in history what baggage is to an army, *impedimenta*, for we must look at things in large, for the very reason that the human mind is small and sinks under the weight of minutiæ.' Minutiæ ought to be collected by annalists, or in some kind of dictionaries where one might find them at need.[1] In this last point Voltaire, as might be expected, was more just than Bolingbroke, who had said somewhat petulantly that 'he had rather take the Darius whom Alexander conquered for the son of Hystaspes, and make as many anachronisms as a Jewish chronologer, than sacrifice half his life to collect all the learned lumber that fills the head of an antiquary.'[2] The antiquary's is a vocation like another, and the highest kind of history can only flourish on condition that the humbler ancillary kind flourishes also, and that there are patient and scrupulous men to mark the difference between Darius Codomannus and Darius the son of Hystaspes.

We may say that three kinds of men write history : the gazetteer or annalist, the statesman, and the philosopher. The annalist's business is to investigate and record events, and his highest merits are clearness, accuracy, and simplicity. The political historian seeks the superficial and immediate causes of great transactions, and he serves us by mixed penetration and soundness of judgment. The historical philosopher is concerned only with groups of events, the

---

[1] Essai sur les Mœurs, p. 9.
[2] *On the Study of History*, Letter i. ad finem.

changes and movements that transform communities, and with the trains of conditions that lead to such movements. The majority of historians, from the illustrious Bacon down to the compiler of a manual, illustrate the first kind. Thucydides and Tacitus, among the ancients, a Machiavelli or a Finlay, among moderns, may illustrate the second kind. As Voltaire was sometimes gazetteer and sometimes statesman, so Montesquieu took the statesman's point of view in his reflections on the decline of Rome, and that of the philosopher in the Spirit of Laws. It is the states-man or man of the world, who, after recounting Cæsar's failure on one occasion to comply with the etiquette of the senate, proceeds to make the follow-ing reflection, that ' we never offend men more, than when we shock their ceremonies and usages : seek to oppress them, and that is sometimes a proof of the importance you attach to them; but shock their customs, and that is always a mark of contempt.' [1] It is the philosopher, feeling for the causes of things and their order, who being led to inquire into the spirit or meaning of Laws, understands such an inquiry to involve a comparative investigation of the relations between laws and physical climate, the quality of ground, situation and extent of territory, the mode of life of the people, agricultural, hunting, or pastoral; between laws and the freedom of the constitution, the religion, wealth, trade, moral ideas, and manners, of the inhabitants; above all, historically, between

[1] *Grandeur et Décadence des Romains*, c. xi.

laws and their origin and the order of things on which
they were first founded.

In a similar way we may divide Voltaire's historical
pieces into two main classes. Indeed, if we count the
Annals of the Empire, which he wrote to please the
Duchess of Saxe-Gotha, he may rank also under the
third remaining head among the annalistic historians.
This, however, is too unsatisfactory a piece of work
for us to care either to classify or to remember it.
The subject was not of his own selection, he knew
comparatively little about it, his materials were extremely scanty and imperfect, and he composed it at
a time when his whole mind was violently perturbed
by his recent quarrel with Frederick, and torn by
anxiety where he should find a home in rest and
freedom. It was the only work he ever wrote, for
which he perhaps had no heart, and the least obser-
vant reader will notice how vast a difference this made
in the temper of its composition. Indeed, Voltaire
was not born to be a simple chronicler. The realistic
and practical leanings of his intellect naturally gave
him a distaste for the collection of mere uninterpreted
and unapplied facts. His clear comprehensiveness,
the product of a vigorous imagination with strong
sense, as naturally impelled him to group circumstances, and to introduce the widest possible gener-
ality among them. He has one of the peculiar gifts
of the historian, as distinguished from the gazetteer,
of throwing rapid glances over a wide field on the
suggestion of a minor fact as he passes by it, and of

converting what to others would be the mere unconsidered trifles of narrative into something possessed
of its due measure of vitality and significance.   He
fills his pages with reflections that are usually not
brought from very far depths, but which are almost
always lively, just, and in real matter.   Perhaps this
is not an unmixed good, for it is not unconnected
with an extraordinary evenness and light facility of
style, which tends to draw the reader somewhat too
rapidly and too smoothly over ground that had been
rugged enough to the actual travellers.   It tends
therefore tacitly to plant a false impression about the
tardiness, difficulty, peril, and infinitely varied possibilities of the social movements which are history's
object and material.   Perhaps a reader has a better
idea of the true manner in which events march, from
Comines or Clarendon, than from all the elegance and
manifold graces of Voltaire, and we sometimes feel
inclined to repeat De Maistre's angry demand for
that grave and unhasting dignity which is the life of
history.

We have already noticed one of the differences
between Voltaire and Rousseau, which arose from the
predominance of sentiment over reason in the latter.
In the present connection another fact well worth
noticing is that Rousseau was entirely wanting in
either taste or serious regard for history.   The past
seems to have been to him a kind of blurred tablet,
confused and indecipherable, interposed between the
vision of men and the only thought or knowledge

which it is good for them to possess. Voltaire's reading of this tablet was inadequate enough, in many
respects it was even a grave distortion of the truth;
but with that sound sense in which Rousseau was so
absolutely deficient, he felt how irrational it was, in
the first place, to shut our eyes deliberately to the
course and meaning of all the foregone action of the
race, and, in the second, to leave unattacked and
unturned the strong position which the traditional
parables of the past and their undisturbed interpretation conferred upon the champions of orthodoxy and
absolutism. Rousseau, being a sentimentalist, appears
to have discerned nothing of this. His ideas all involved a breach with the past, as Voltaire's did, but
Voltaire deserves credit for perceiving that, to make
this effective, you must at least find out as well as
you can what the past was.

For his four works in the class of political history
he had the best attainable authorities and material,
and no one was ever more diligent in putting them to
the best possible use.[1] His acute sense, strengthened
by contact with the world and its most active personages, made him what we may almost call prematurely
scientific in his demand for adequate evidence and
proof. It is rather striking, for example, to find him

[1] The dates of the publication of Voltaire's historical works
are these :—*Charles XII.*, 1731 ; *Siècle de Louis XIV.*, 1752 (a
portion of it in 1739) ; *Annales de l'Empire*, 1753-54; *Essai sur
les Mœurs*, 1757 (surreptitiously in 1754) ; *Histoire de Russie*,
Pt. I. in 1759, Pt. II. in 1763 ; *Précis du Siècle de Louis XV.*,
1768 ; *Histoire du Parlement de Paris*, 1769.

anticipating more recent objections to the trust-
worthiness of Tacitus, pointing out the extraordinary
improbabilities in his account of Tiberius, Nero, and
the others.   There is all the difference, he says,
between a faithful historian equally free from adula-
tion and hatred, and 'a malicious wit who poisons
everything through the medium of a concise and energetic style.'   Are we to believe, he asks elsewhere,
on the story of a man who lived long after Tiberius,
that this emperor, nearly eighty years old, who had
up to that time been decent almost to austerity, yet
passed all his time in debaucheries hitherto unknown,
and so monstrous as to need new names for them?[1]
And in the same way he questions the alleged atrocities of Nero and Caligula, as well as the motives
imputed to Domitian by Tacitus for the frequency
with which he sent to inquire after the health of
Agricola.   These historic doubts sprang from none
of the political judgment or feeling which propounds
them in more modern times, but purely from scientific
incredulity.   'History,' he once wrote, 'is after all
nothing but a parcel of tricks that we play the dead.'[2]
He did not hold this slightly splenetic theory, in
which assuredly there is a painful truth, to absolve
him from the duty of doing what he could to belie
it, and to make history as correct and as faithfully
representative of actual occurrences, as careful inquiry

[1] Le Pyrrhonisme de l'Histoire, cc. xii. xiii. *Œuvres,* xxxvi.
p. 346 ; also p. 428.

[2] Corr. *Œuvres,* lxvi. p. 17.

from those most likely to know the characters of the
most prominent actors could make it. In the composition of the Siècle de Louis XV. he had of course
the advantage of knowing all these leaders of the
public activity personally and at first hand, while if
he had not that advantage to the same extent in the
Siècle de Louis XIV., he at least mixed on intimate
terms with many who had been intimate with the
court of the great monarch. For the history of
Russia he was amply provided with documents and
authentic narratives from the Russian court, at whose
solicitation he undertook a work which was the first
full introduction of that hitherto barbarous and unknown country to the literature of civilised Europe.
His letters to Schouvalof, the imperial chamberlain,
attest the unremitting industry with which he sought
for every kind of information that might be useful
to him. 'The enlightened spirit which now reigns
among the principal nations of Europe, requires that
we should go to the bottom, where in former times a
historian barely thought it worth while to skim the
surface. People wish to know how a nation grew
together; what was its population before the epoch of
which you treat; the difference in the number of the
regular army then and in former times; the nature
and growth of its commerce; what arts have sprung
up within the country, and what have been introduced from elsewhere and been perfected there; what
used to be the ordinary average revenue of the state,
and what it is now; the birth and extension of its

X

navy; the proportion in numbers between its nobles and its ecclesiastics and monks, and between the latter and the cultivators of the soil, etc.'[1] Even importunities of this kind continued over a space of some years, and the copious responses which they brought, never consoled Voltaire for not having made the journey to the Russian capital in his proper person. 'I should have learnt more from you in a few hours of conversation,' he wrote to Schouvalof, 'than all the compilers in the world will ever teach me.'[2] In writing the History of Charles XII. of Sweden, one of the most delightful of his books, the art of which is none the less because it is so little ostentatious and striking and seems so easy, he had procured a large quantity of material from Fabrice, who knew the Swedish king during his detention at Bender and subsequently, and met Voltaire in London. This material was supplemented in later years by information picked up at Lunéville from the ex-Polish king Stanislas, who was indebted to Charles for his sovereignty, that true δῶρον ἄδωρον. 'As for the portraits of men,' Voltaire declared, 'they are nearly all the creations of fancy; 'tis a monstrous piece of charlatanry to pretend to paint a personage with whom you have never lived.'[3] Napoleon, in the memorable campaign of 1812, coming to various places which Voltaire had occasion to describe in his History of Charles XII., found his account weak and

---

[1] Corr. 1757. *Œuvres*, lxvi. p. 61.
[2] Corr. 1761. *Œuv.* lxvii. p. 228.   [3] *Œuvres*, xx. p. 10.

inaccurate, and threw it aside in favour of Adlerfeldt. This was to be expected from the very merit of the book; for how should a picture, painted in large for the general instruction of the world, satisfy the minute requirements of strategical topography? It was precisely Voltaire's object to separate history from geography, statistics, anecdote, biography, tactics, and to invest it with an independent character and quality apart from all these.

It is another of the distinctions of his new method of writing history that, with the exception of the book on Charles XII., he throws persons and personal interests into a second place, as being no more than instruments or convenient names for critical turning-points in the large movements of peoples. In the narration of the rise of Russia to a place among civilised nations, the character of Peter the Great inevitably comes into marked prominence, because when a population lies on the stagnant level of barbarism, the first man who summons them to undertake the task of national elevation constitutes an element of paramount importance in their annals. In proportion, however, as they rise to the fulfilment of this surpassing work, the importance of the heroic individual diminishes; as the national self-consciousness and collective powers become greater, the figure of the individual shows less.

Voltaire was always conscious, though not so clearly as writers are now, of the great historical principle that besides the prominent men of a generation there

is a something at work underneath, a moving current
on whose flood they are borne. He never fixed this
current by any of the names which now fall so glibly
from our lips,—tendency of the times, tenor of public
opinion, spirit of the age, and the like, by which we
give a collective name to groups of sentiments and
forces, all making in what seems to be a single direction. But although unnamed, this singular and invisible concurrence of circumstance was yet a reality
to him. The age was something besides its heroes,
and something besides its noisiest and most resounding occurrences. His divisions of the great epochs
of humanity are undoubtedly open to much criticism,
because the principles on which he drew the dividing
lines have lost their force in new generations. It was
to be expected that they would do so ; and his four
great epochs[1] were not likely to remain the four great
epochs of a posterity, which has partially learnt the
lesson that he had not learnt at all, that perfection
in the fine arts is not the highest mark of an age in
which humanity may glory. Nevertheless, we are
bound to recognise that a new way of regarding
human action, as well as a new way of composing
history, was being introduced by a writer whose first
paragraph declared that he proposed to himself a
greater object than an account of the life of Lewis
XIV. ; that he designed to paint for the instruction
of posterity, not the actions of a single man, but the
spirit of men ; and that while all periods must be

[1] Siècle de Louis XIV., c. i. Œuvres, xxv. p. 283.

alike to one who only desires to fill his memory with
facts, discrimination among them cannot be dispensed
with for one who thinks.

Hence also the propriety of discrimination among
the various kinds of fact which are at the historian's
disposal, and in this order Voltaire's whole soul
revolted against the reigning practice and prescription.
'I would rather have details,' he wrote to one of his
intimates so early in his career as 1735, 'about Racine
and Despréaux, Molière, Bossuet, Descartes, than I
would about the battle of Steinkirk. There is nothing
left but the names of men who led battalions and
squadrons. There is no return to the human race
from a hundred engagements; but the great men I
have spoken of prepared pure and everlasting pleasures
for mortals still unborn. A canal-sluice, a picture by
Poussin, a fine tragedy, a truth established, are all of
them things a thousand times more precious than the
whole mass of annals of the court, and than all the
narratives of campaigns.'[1] From this and from a
multitude of other passages, as well as from his actual
compositions, we perceive that the activity of a court
and the manœuvres of an army were no longer in
Voltaire's eyes the fit substance of history. One
reason for this might be his lively sense of the impossibility of knowing the character and motives of
people with whom one has not lived, or the real cause
of even the most momentous intrigues and negotiations
in which one has not taken a personal share. A still

[1] Corr. 1735. *Œuvres*, lxii. pp. 455, 456.

deeper reason would be his most rational conviction
that these matters are only of moment to us for their
larger results and unmistakable outcome, and from
the profoundly true and important principle that the
progress of intellectual enlightenment, material prosperity, and moral elevation is not only a feature in
the history of a nation, but does itself constitute that
history, while all records of other transactions in the
course of its annals, achievements in diplomacy, feats
of arms, revolutions in policy, have no true historic
value, except for the light they shed upon this
economic, intellectual, and moral progress, and are
not worth studying except in that light. We may
see the immediate effects of Voltaire's influence most
markedly of all in Gibbon, but in a less important
shape in the general account of the middle ages which
Robertson contributed to his History of Charles v.
(1769), and which remained for many years the most
instructive piece that our literature possessed upon
the character and spirit of the feudal system and
other features of the middle ages.   Adam Ferguson's
Essay on the History of Civil Society (1767) bears
traces of the same influence.   In both of these cases
much also must be added for the kindred authority of
Montesquieu.   One has some hesitation in adding
Hume to the list in the present connection, because
his history, the composition of which extended from
1752 to 1763, ought perhaps to be counted rather
the direct and independent outcome of the French
philosophic spirit, than of the French historic spirit

which itself proceeded from the philosophy; and
because, moreover, Hume, as a historian, has some of
Voltaire's most serious defects, without that breadth
and size which constituted his greatest merit, though
it is needless to point out how many merits Hume
had of his own. It is worth remarking that in some
pages which he wrote on Hume's History,[1] Voltaire
gave it a joyful welcome, as might be expected, and
particularly to those parts which we now esteem
most lightly, such as the contemptuous account of
Cromwell.

To return, however, to the point from which we
have digressed. One very direct consequence of the
historical principle we have described, and of the way
in which it was illustrated in the histories of Lewis
XIV. and Lewis XV., and most of all in the Essay on
Manners, was the degradation of war from the highest
to the lowest place among the objects of the historian's
regard. War began for the first time to be systematically considered and treated as a mere instrument
and means, and not as one of the most serious of
social ends. We can never honour Voltaire too long
nor too deeply for the vehemence and sincerity of his
abhorrence of the military spirit. Nowhere do we
feel more distinctly that he marked the end of the
mediæval temper, than in his noble protests against
the glory of bloodshed. The great orators of the
church to the very last donned the robes of their
most sumptuous rhetoric, when they were called to

[1] *Œuvres*, xxxvi. pp. 428-434 (1768).

consecrate the virtues of the victorious soldier. The pages of the Old Testament supplied them with a hundred baleful heroes to whom they might liken their warrior, and a hundred cruel and bloody tropes with which they might decorate the funeral oration. So long as the atrocities of the Hebrew chiefs and people, their treacheries and slaughters, were held sacred and celebrated with unction, it was not likely that the voice of the peacemaker could make itself heard.

Voltaire not only held up these demoralising records to the odium they deserve; he directly taxed the clergy with their failure to discharge the very highest part of their duty. Of the five or six thousand sermons of Massillon, he asked, are there a couple where you could pick out a word or two against the scourge and crime of war? Bourdaloue preached against impurity, but what sermon did he ever direct against the murder, rapine, brigandage, and universal rage, which desolate the world? 'Miserable physicians of souls, you declaim for five quarters of an hour against the mere pricks of a pin, and say no word on the curse which tears us into a thousand pieces! Philosophers and moralists, burn your books : so long as the caprice of a handful of men will cause the massacring in all loyalty of thousands of our brothers, the part of the human race which is devoted to heroism will contain all that is most frightful in human nature. What concern to me are humanity, benevolence, modesty, temperance, gentleness, wisdom, piety, so long as half an ounce of lead shatters my body, and I die at twenty

in torments unspeakable, surrounded by five or six
thousand dead or dying, while my eyes, opening for
the last time, see the town I was born in delivered
to fire and sword, and the last sounds that reach my
ears are the shrieks of women and children expiring
in the ruins—and the whole for the pretended interests of a man that we do not know?'[1] His rebuke
to Montesquieu is still more distinctively modern.
The author of the Esprit des Lois had said that among
societies it sometimes happens that natural defence
possibly involves the necessity of attack, when a nation
perceives that a longer peace would place another
nation in a position to destroy it.[2] 'If ever there
was a war evidently unjust,' Voltaire replies, 'it is
that which you propose ; it is to go and kill your
neighbour for fear your neighbour should be in a condition to attack you ; that is to say, you must run the
risk of ruining your country, in the hope of ruining
without reason some other country. . . . If your
neighbour grows too powerful during a time of peace,
what hinders you from growing powerful like him?
If he has made alliances, make alliances on your side.
If, having less religion, he has all the more manu-
facturers and soldiers for it, imitate him in so sage
an economy.   If he drills his sailors better, drill yours
too : all that is perfectly just.   But to expose your
people to the most horrible misery, in the idea, which
is so often chimerical, of crushing your dear brother,

[1] Dict. Phil. s.v. Guerre. Œuvres, lv. pp. 488, 489.
[2] Esprit des Lois, x. ii.

the most serene bordering prince—! 'twas never for
a president of a pacific order to give you such a piece
of counsel.'[1] The book in which this sound view of
justice and expediency in the dealings of nations with
one another was pressed upon the attention of France,
was published in 1764, five years before the birth of
the man who turned the tide back, and made the
international policy of France a synonym both for
iniquity and folly. On the 15th of August 1769
Voltaire concluded his letter to D'Alembert with his
usual vivacity: 'Adieu; my compliments to the devil,
for it is he who governs the world.'[2] If he had
known that, while he was writing, Napoleon Bonaparte had come into the world, and could at the
same time have foreseen the new-comer's destiny, he
might have said the same thing more seriously. Voltaire never played the sentimentalist. He knew that
there are complexities of affairs which only the sword
can cut. But he was the first influential writer—for
the abbé Saint-Pierre, so undeservedly laughed at for
his dreams of perpetual peace, had no influence to
speak of—who deliberately placed war among retrograde agencies, and deliberately dwelt upon peaceful industry as the true life of nations.[3]

Diplomacy and its complex subterranean processes,
which have occupied so extremely disproportionate a
space in written history, and which are in acted

---

[1] *Œuvres*, lv. p. 490.   [2] Corr. *Œuvres*, lxxv. p. 460.
[3] See a letter of the king of Prussia in Voltaire's *Works*, lxxiv
p. 144, etc.

history responsible for so much evil, were in the same
way informally relegated to the region of inhuman
occupations.   Its methods were the tortuous and
depressing methods of the same past, which had made
the many the playthings and unhappy instruments
of the few, and had never interrupted the triumphant manœuvres of craft and subtlety by a whisper for
the claims of humanity and justice.   Voltaire scarcely
ever speaks of negotiations between contending powers
without a shrewd thrust, half contemptuous and
half angry.   The plain where some negotiations took
place in the struggles among the descendants of
Charles the Great is still called the Field of Lies;
a name, he says, that might well be common to most
spots where men have negotiated.[1]   And this represents his general tone in speaking of a branch of
activity which may interest the professional diplomatist
in all its details, but which, as he thought, can only concern the historical student in its results.   Here Voltaire
represented a marked tendency, which waxes stronger
as societies grow more penetrated with popular forces,
to divest diplomacy of a professional quality, and to
throw the adjustment of the relations between nations
as entirely as possible into the hands of plain men of
firm and upright character, and full knowledge of the
special matters at issue.

It is, however, when we come to the ground idea
of the Essay on Manners,[2] that we feel the full breath

[1] C. xxiii.   Œuvres, xxi. p. 9.
[2] Mœurs, like ἦθη, is untranslatable by any single English

of the modern spirit, and perceive that at length we are nearing the wide expanse of the sea. There we emerge absolutely from the narrow conception of universal history, with which Bossuet had familiarised men's minds in the Discourse on Universal History. This famous piece, which has had at least as much praise as it merits, if we are to consider reason as well as eloquence, was fundamentally and in substance no more than a bit of theological commonplace splendidly decorated. Bossuet indeed spoke of 'the concatenation of human affairs,' but only in the same sentence with 'the sequence of the counsels of God.' The gorgeous rhetorician of the church was not likely to rise philosophically into the larger air of universal history, properly so called. His eloquent discourse is a vindication of divine foresight, by means of an intensely narrow survey of such sets of facts as might be thought not inconsistent with the deity's fixed purpose to make one final and decisive revelation to men. No one who looks upon the vast assemblage of stupendous human circumstances, from the first origin of man upon the earth, as merely the ordained antecedent of what, seen from the long procession of all the ages, figures in so diminutive a consummation as the Catholic church, is likely to obtain a very effective hold of that broad sequence and many-linked chain of events, to which Bossuet gave a right name,

word. The full title is *Essai sur les Mœurs et l'Esprit des Nations, et sur les principaux faits de l'Histoire depuis Charlemagne jusqu' à Louis XIII.*

but whose real meaning he never was even near seiz-
ing. His merit is that he did in a small and rhetorical
way, what Montesquieu and Voltaire afterwards did
in a truly comprehensive and philosophical way ; he
pressed forward general ideas in connection with the
recorded movements of the chief races of mankind.
For a teacher of history to leave the bare chronicler's
road so far as to declare, for example, the general
principle, inadequate and overstated as it is, that
'religion and civil government are the two points
on which human things revolve,' even this was a clear
step in advance—and to dismiss the long series of
emperors from Augustus to Alexander Severus in two
or three pages was to show a rare sense of large
historic proportion.   Again, Bossuet's expressions of
'the concatenation of the universe,' of the interde-
pendence of the parts of so vast a whole, of there
coming no great change without having its causes in
foregoing centuries, and of the true object of history
being to observe in connection with each epoch those
secret dispositions of events which prepared the way
for great changes, as well as the momentous conjunctures which more immediately brought them to
pass—all these phrases seem to point to a true and
philosophic survey.   But they end in themselves, and
lead nowhither.   The chain is an arbitrary and one-
sided collection of facts.   The writer does not cau-
tiously follow and feel after the successive links, but
forges and chooses and arranges them after a pattern
of his own, which was fixed independently of them.

A scientific term or two is not enough to disguise the purely theological essence of the treatise.

Bossuet's Discourse is moreover constructed wholly on the theory that a special revelation was delivered to the Jews, and in tracing their course we have fast hold of the chain by which it has pleased heaven to communicate to earth all the truths we possess as to the highest things. Such a conception stifles a modern reader. The first pages of the Essay on Manners, sometimes placed separately as the Philosophy of History, prove that we have escaped from the cave. The chosen people fell into rank with other peoples, that equally supposed themselves to be chosen by their own peculiar gods. They lose the towering pre-eminence in virtue and light and divine favour with which their own records and Bossuet's interpretation had so splendidly invested them. We find that their pretensions were not unique, but universal among nations in such a stage; that their virtues were not singular, though some of their vices seem so. In a word, if some of Voltaire's details are crude and rudimentary, at least he has the merit of showing to his unaccustomed readers what vast epochs of time, what uncounted multitudes of men, what varied movements of the human spirit, surround the little speck of Judaism.

The bulk of the Essay was composed in 1740, but it is probable that this preliminary examination of other oriental nations, their practices, institutions, and religious ideas, was suggested by Montesquieu's

memorable book, which appeared in 1748, some years
before the publication of the Essay on Manners.   It
is in point of execution much less satisfactory than
what follows, for Voltaire's knowledge of Greek and
Hebrew was inadequate, and he fell into various
errors which his adversaries happily possessed scholar-
ship enough to expose.   In the modern provinces of
the book, which constitute the important part of it,
he was much more entirely at home in his subject.
Here his familiarity with detail, considering the vast
quantity of his other employments, is extremely surprising, and perhaps in no other book of equal gener-
ality have there been discovered so few serious inac-
curacies, though none have encountered more hostile
critics.

Prejudice, alas, spares truth and light no more
when it narrows the vision of a free-thinker, than
when it distorts the faculty of the devout.   Being a
reaction against Bossuet's unreasonable exaltation of
the Jews and their history, Voltaire's conception of
the place due to them partook of the inevitable fault
of all reactions, and left out of sight considerations
which it is eminently unscientific not to remember.
'You never find,' he says, 'a generous action in the
annals of the Hebrews ; they knew neither hospitality
nor liberality nor clemency.   Their sovereign bliss is
to practise usury with foreigners, and this spirit of
usury is so rooted in their hearts, that it is the
continual object of the figures they employ in the
eloquence which is peculiar to them.   Their glory is

to deliver to fire and slaughter the small villages of which they may be able to take possession. They assassinate their masters when they are slaves, and they never know how to pardon when they are victorious; they are the enemies of the human race.'[1] This is as great an exaggeration on one side, as Bossuet's exaltation of them and their deeds was on the other side. We ought to admit what abominable traits the character and history of this race unfortunately present, without forgetting how much is owing to them for preserving in its sublimest shape, and investing with the most deeply impressive images and associations, that idea of monotheism which, if destined to be superseded by other ideas more commensurate with the limits of human intelligence, must still be counted the germ of much that is purest and loftiest and most inspiring among the ideals of western civilisation.

The same kind of extreme prejudice which drove Voltaire into maintaining of the Jews, not that they were a people whom we should do very ill either to imitate or admire, but nothing less than that they were the enemies of the human race, found vent in such assertions as that if any one could have restored the Empire to its strength, or at all events retarded its fall, that man was the Emperor Julian.[2] A historian may justly contend, if he thinks that the evidence warrants him, that Julian belongs to the type of vir-

[1] C. vi. *Œuvres*, xx. p. 396.
[2] C. xi. *Œuvres*, xx. p. 455.

tuous reactionists, just as we may say it of Wesley or
the chiefs of the Tractarians. But to make such an
assertion as that the repression of Christianity after
the middle of the fourth century, even supposing it
to have been possible of achievement, could have
given back to the rapidly declining empire a strength
of which all the roots were lifeless, was to falsify
history for the sake of exalting the name of an apos-
tate. A Roman aristocrat, blind to the real operation and comparative value of the forces at work,
might be pardoned for holding Christianity guilty of
the general dissolution around him; but it was a
strange phantasy for a philosopher of the eighteenth
century to suppose that the Christian system, in the
shape which it had assumed by Julian's time, did not
offer principles of firmer association, than the mere
rites of a paganism which was spontaneously decaying
with a rapidity that increased day by day.[1] There is
no stronger illustration of the twist which polemical
fury may give to the most acute intelligence, than
this belief of Voltaire's, that an organisation which
had attracted to itself every able and statesmanlike
intellect of the time, could do less for the regeneration of the Empire than the initiated disciple of
Platonist theurgy.

His account of the history of the church is composed in the same vein, and we may see where
Gibbon, who was a reader of Voltaire, drew the

[1] See on this interesting subject Finlay's *Greece under the
Romans* (B.C. 146-A.D. 716), pp. 156, 157.

inspiration of the solemn sneer with which he sapped
solemn creed.[1] 'So many frauds, so many errors, so
many disgusting absurdities,' says Voltaire, 'with
which we have been inundated for seventeen hundred
years, have been unable to do any harm to our religion. It is unquestionably divine, since seventeen
centuries of imposture and imbecility have not
destroyed it.'[2] Voltaire thought as ill as possible of
the century to which he belonged; we cannot therefore
charge him with the inconsistency which marks some
of his most prominent disciples, who while they
accepted such an account of the vileness of the church
as he had given them, did not scruple to believe that,
as if by miracle, seventeen centuries of steady depravation were *per saltum* to be followed by an eighteenth
and other centuries of boundless virtue and enlightenment. Still it is wonderful that he should have been
able to appreciate the admirable character of the best
sovereign of the thirteenth century, Lewis IX.,[3] and
to describe his motives and his achievements so
generously, and yet should never have thought of the
education and surrounding spiritual conditions by
which such a character had been formed. If the
power of Catholicism for evil was so great and decisive, it would have been reasonable to suppose that
it had some share also in moulding to good those who
came forth from it the very flower of humanity. But

[1] *Childe Harold*, iii. 106 and 107.
[2] C. ix. *Œuvres*, xx. p. 445.
[3] C. lviii. *Œuvres*, xxi. pp. 328-341.

Voltaire did not know how much a man is the product of a system operating on, and with, the individual predisposition, or he would not have chidden St. Lewis for remaining on the level of the prejudice of his time, instead of changing the spirit of his age.[1] How should St. Lewis have risen from the prejudice of his age, when it was exactly that prejudice which had formed him, and of which he represented the worthy side?

Even without this inconsistency, the fundamental error is bad enough. We get very wearied of the persistent identification of the church throughout the dark ages with fraud and imposture and sinister self-seeking, when we have once learnt, what is undoubtedly the most important principle in the study of those times, that it was the churchmen who kept the flickering light of civilisation alive amid the raging storms of uncontrolled passion and violence. The truth is that Voltaire never realised civilisation as an organism, which if not surrounded with the proper conditions of life will perish, and which will prosper and wax stronger exactly in proportion as it is nourished. That the light was more than once very near sinking in the west under the waves of barbarism, as it has actually sunk in the eastern portions of the Empire, seems to have been an all-important fact which he either never saw, or which, if he saw it, never impressed him as assuredly it ought to have done.

This is the more curious as he was able to perceive, in a way in which it were much to be wished

[1] Quelques petites Hardiesses, etc. *Œuvres*, xxxvi. p. 445.

that more recent historians might show an equal discernment, that we ought to use the terms of civilisation, with all their complex and accumulated associations, in an extremely modified sense in speaking of
the centuries between the fifth and the thirteenth,
just as it is the gravest mistake to suppose that,
because you can express the results of the various
contests of those times in terms of philosophy, therefore the actors in any one of them were both conscious of its most general bearings, and were animated
by large and philosophical inclinations.   For example,
after he has told us how William the Conqueror sent
to the Pope Harold's battle-standard and a small
portion of the small treasure that an English king
might possess in those times, he proceeds to reduce
the transaction to what he conceived to be its true
proportions, in the following manner : ' Thus,' he says,
' a barbarian, the son of a harlot, the murderer of a
legitimate king, shares the plunder of this king with
another barbarian ; for if you take away the names
of duke of Normandy, king of England, and pope, all
is reduced to the action of a Norman brigand and a
Lombard receiver of plunder.'[1]   This being the case,
the secular possessors of power being so rude, petty,
and barbarous, their contests being ' those of bears and
wolves,' their rapacity and violence being tempered by
few of those ideas of justice which form the bonds of
society in its more advanced stages, it ought to have
struck even the most ardent enemy of ecclesiastical

[1] C. xlii.   *Œuvres*, xxi. p. 143.

pretensions as a thing in the highest degree unphilo-
sophical, to pour all the ill epithets of usurpation upon
the virtuous efforts of the great churchmen, who were
least touched by the spirit of violence, to take away
as much power as they could from barbarous princes
and nobles, who were most impregnated with that
and all other dark spirits. The smaller the difference
between the least moral and the most moral orders in
a community, the more desirable it is that the order
with even a small advantage should acquire as much
power as possible; for the reason that so near an
approach to equality in morals is most likely to occur
when the average is low, and when therefore the need
to prevent it from falling any lower is most urgent.
Granting that the ecclesiastics were only slightly the
superiors of the barbarous laymen, this is all the better
ground for rejoicing that they succeeded in converting
their ascendancy of moral idea into an ascendancy of
political fact.

In short, Voltaire's great panorama, magnificent as
it is and most royally planned, is not drawn in lines
and with colour that explain the story or lay bare the
principles of its progress. The plan is imposed from
without, just as in Bossuet's case, not carefully sought
from within the facts themselves. What is meant
then by the assertion that Voltaire's Essay is one of
the foundations of modern history? If he gives no
explanation of the course of history, none to himself
probably, and none to us assuredly, what is his merit?
This, that he has fully placed before us the history

which is to be explained; that he has presented the long external succession of facts in their true magnitude and in a definite connection; that he did not write a history of France, or of the papacy, or of the Mahometan power, or of the crusades, but that he saw the advantage, as we see the unavoidable necessity, of comprehending in a single idea and surveying in a single work the various activities, the rise and fall of power, the transference from one to another of political predominance, the contributions to the art of living, among the societies which were once united in a single empire. The history of each of these societies, England, France, Spain, Italy, the Byzantine Empire, is followed in relation to the history of Europe, which is indeed composed of these co-ordinate parts. The movement of communities since the dissolution of the Roman Empire is exhibited in a collective form, and that it should be exhibited and accepted in this form was obviously a preliminary step to an organic treatment of the multiplied laws of social physics.

'There are some events,' he wrote in a note to his best poem, 'which have effects, and others which have none. It is with the chain of events as it is with a genealogical tree, where we perceive branches that become extinct at the first generation, and others that continue the race. Many events remain without any filiation. It is thus that in every machine there are effects necessary to the movement, while others are indifferent, following the operation of the first, and leading to nothing. The wheels of a vehicle serve to make it go; but whether they raise a little more or a little less dust, the journey is accomplished equally. Such is the general order of the world, that the links of the chain are not deranged by a little more or a little less of irregularity.'[1] The figures in this passage serve adequately to describe his own treatment. We see in the Essay the lines of the genealogical tree, but we do not learn the laws of the transmission of qualities from one stock to another; we see the links of the chain, but not the conditions which fastened each to the other; conditions, indeed, only to be grasped through a scientific study of human nature which Voltaire had never made; and finally we see the towering car drawn slowly along a devious road by sweat and strain of millions, but we know not why it went by this road rather than another. In a word, the inner machinery of societies and of their movement remains as far from our sight as it ever was. The study of those economic and material forces which have so profound an influence upon social transformations, was in its infancy, and the Economists, who really saw that there are definite laws regulating the play of these forces, unfortunately mixed up with their speculations a number of chimerical fancies, which Voltaire was too acute to accept, but not patient enough to sift.[2] In this respect he is as

[1] Notes sur le Désastre de Lisbonne. *Œuvres*, xv. p. 57.
[2] He ridiculed some of these in one of his most humane and otherwise excellent pieces, L'Homme aux Quarante Ecus (1767). *Œuv.* lix. p. 395.

defective as Gibbon, in whose book, so justly famous
for its splendid breadth of conception and industrious
elaboration of detail, we have much of that meagre
philosophy which consisted in the exposure of falsehood, but little of the true science which shows us the
numerous organs of society in connection with their
actual play and function.   Neither Gibbon nor Voltaire made any contribution, nor seems to have been
aware of the importance of contributing, to that study
of the fundamental conditions of the social union,
which Aristotle commenced, and which both Bodin
in the sixteenth century and Montesquieu in the
eighteenth had so meritoriously continued.[1] Nevertheless, it was much to lead men to study the history of
modern Europe as a whole, and we may say of Voltaire in connection with history what he said of Corneille in connection with tragedy—'It is so great a
merit to have opened the career, and inventors are so
much above other men, that posterity pardons their
greatest faults.'[2]

[1] *The Republic*, 1577.   *Esprit des Lois*, 1748.
[2] *Œuv.* lxvii. p. 94.

CHAPTER VII.

FERNEY.

VOLTAIRE, as we have seen, took possession of Ferney in 1758, and he lived here almost without a break for something like twenty years. His estate was a feudal seigniory in the district of Gex, on the very frontier of Switzerland, but in France, though enjoy·ing immunity from French taxation. He built a new manor-house, and in his capacity of lord of the manor replaced the dilapidated little church of the estate by a new one, very small, very plain, and about which, notwithstanding its famous inscription of which he so often boasted,—*Deo erexit Voltaire*,—much more noise has been made, than so simple and natural a proceeding at all calls for.[1] Madame Denis kept house for him, and according to the Paris gossips of the time, on an extravagant scale, which often produced ruptures between the two. Guests were incessant

---

[1] A drawing of Voltaire's château at Ferney is given in Blancheton's *Vues Pittoresques des Châteaux de France* (Paris, 1826), Part II. The château is still standing, and the prospect from the terrace repays a visit, apart from the interest of association. The church is now a receptacle for wine· casks.

and the hospitality ungrudging.[1] He complained during the Seven Years' War of the embarrassment of being a Frenchman, when he had to entertain daily at dinner Russians, English, and Germans.[2] He protests that he is weary of being hotel-keeper in general for all Europe, and so weary was he at one time of this noisy and costly post, that the establishment was partially suspended for upwards of a year. One of the most generous of Voltaire's many generous acts was his reception into his house of a child who had no other claim on him than that of being the great-grand-daughter of the uncle of Corneille. A soldier ought to succour the niece of his general, he said. He took the liveliest interest in the little maid's education, though she appears to have been a sulky pupil, and eventually he married her with due dower to one Dupuits. The bustle and expense of his establishment became greater than ever, and in the spring of 1768 Paris was as much electrified by news of a revolution at Ferney, as she has been since by some revolutions in her own streets. Madame Denis and the two Dupuits had suddenly made their way to Paris, and for a year and a half Voltaire was left in peace, part of which he employed sensibly in having his house cleaned from cellar to garret,—a bit of news

[1] The reader who is curious as to the most indifferent details, will find what he seeks in a singular monument of painstaking spleen, entitled *Ménage et Finances de Voltaire*, by M. Nicolardot (Paris, 1854).

[2] Corr. 1761. *Œuv.* lxvii. p. 190.

which is handed down to our times, since, according
to Grimm, the domestic arrangements of the manor-
house at Ferney interested at that moment more or
less every court in Europe.[1] In the autumn of 1769
Madame Denis returned, and with her the old stir
and extravagance were resumed, for Voltaire was one
of the best-humoured of men to his family and friends,
and could deny his niece nothing. We have more
than one description of this too immortal niece. They
are all equally unflattering. Her homeliness of appearance amounted to the ugliness that is bitter. She
was destitute of wit, and had a vulgar soul. Born to
be the insipid gossip of a bourgeois circle, says one
charitable writer, but having by chance the first man
in the nation for an uncle, she learnt to chatter about
literature and the theatre, as a parrot learns.[2] She
wrote a comedy ; but the players, out of respect for
Voltaire, declined to act in it. She wrote a tragedy ;
but the one favour, which the repeated entreaties of
years could never wring from Voltaire, was that he
would read it. She had histrionic as well as dramatic
ambition, and here worked a miracle, for her representation of Mérope once drew floods of tears from
some English ladies.[3] Her affectation of intellect
had not cooled the reality of simple sensation, and if
she loved art, she was said not to despise gallantry.
At any rate, though she was only sixteen years

[1] *Corr. Lit.* vi. p. 272 ; v. p. 385.
[2] Grimm, *Corr. Lit.* v. p. 393.
[3] Corr. 1761. *Œuv.* lxxv. p. 158.

younger than her uncle,[1] she needed continual festivities and crowds of guests.

Ferney was rather a difficult spot for a woman with a passion for the hum of cities. For five months in the year, says Voltaire, my deserts are, on the admission of Russians, worse than Siberia itself; we see thirty leagues of mountain, snow, and precipices: it is Naples in summer, Lapland in winter.[2] One year he marks with word of bitterness snow falling thick in the middle of May. Four feet of snow in the courtyard constituted a normal winter state. He commemorates with enthusiasm how one day, through these four feet of snow, he saw porters bringing him a hamper of Champagne from a friend; for the more generous sort of Burgundy with which he ordinarily recruited himself had fallen short, and he had been reduced to the humble vintage of Beaujolais.

Yet in the midst of a thousand discomforts and hardships we never hear him wishing to be back in Paris. It remained to him the accursed city, as it had been before his journey to England. He always thought with horror of its cabal, intrigue, frivolity, and sovereign indifference to the ruin of the kingdom and the shedding of innocent blood. There can be no doubt that this wise exile prolonged his days. He was constantly complaining of illness, and he passed

---

[1] Born 1710; lost her first husband 1744; married one Vivier in 1779; died 1790.

[2] Corr. 1770. *Œuv.* lxx. p. 175.

months at a time in bed, which may in truth have
been the best possible preservative of life for one of
his temperament.   Yet in spite of this avoidance of
society, this passion for his study, the man of ordinary
capacity, with no more than an ordinary working
day, may marvel how amid so many distractions the
master of the house contrived to write so many
scores of pieces, large and small, and so many hundreds
of letters, grave and gay.   Of these letters nearly
seven thousand are already in print, and M. Beuchot,
most carefully informed of all Voltaire's editors,
thinks there are likely to be quite as many more still
in undiscovered existence.   Ferney was the centre of
the most universal and varied correspondence that any
one man has ever carried on.   Frederick the Great
was not the only crowned head with whom Voltaire
interchanged royal communication.   Catharine II.
of Russia, of Anhalt-Zerbst by birth, was the helpful
patroness of Diderot and D'Alembert, and was always
eager to hear some word from the patriarch of
their encyclopædic church, only praying him not
to think her too importunate.   Christian VII. of
Denmark apologises for not being able at a stroke to
remove all the obstacles that lie in the way of the
civil liberty of his subjects.   Gustavus III. of Sweden
is elated by the thought that Voltaire sometimes casts
a glance on what is going on in the North, and protests
that this is their greatest encouragement to do as well
as they can in all ways.[1]   Joseph II. would fain have

---

[1] Corr. 1771-72.   Œuv. lxxiv. pp. 733 and 737.

called at Ferney while travelling incognito through France, but fear of his mother's displeasure held him back, the high and devout nature of Maria Theresa always finding Voltaire's mockery of sacred things deeply repugnant, as we may easily believe.

Beside sovereigns who wrote to him as to an equal, every young aspirant to literary distinction, however unknown and obscure, sought a criticism from Ferney. Twenty years before he settled down here, Voltaire had been consulted by Vauvenargues, and had replied with words of painstaking and generous counsel. It was always the same with him. No young author ever solicited advice in vain, and he was never sparing either of trouble or praise. The Marquis of Chastellux sent him a copy of his Félicité Publique, and was raised to the seventh heaven by a letter of thanks, in which Voltaire tells him: 'I covered the margin of my copy with notes, as I always do when a book charms and instructs me; I even took the liberty of not always sharing the author's opinion. I am very old and very feeble, but such reading makes me young again.' And the letter contains a large number of points where he thinks the author in error.[1]

Besides kings and the writers of books, plain men also besought his dictum on high matters. 'A burgomaster of Middleburg,' he informs Madame du Deffand, 'whom I do not know, wrote to me a little

[1] Corr. 1772. Œuvres, lxxi. p. 496. The marked copy is still in existence, along with the rest of Voltaire's books, at St. Petersburg; see Lavergne's Economistes du 18ième Siècle, p. 285

while since, to ask me in confidence whether there is
a God or not; whether, in case there be one, he takes
any heed of us; whether matter is eternal; whether
it can think; whether the soul is immortal; and
begging me to answer by return of post.'[1]   One may
suspect that a little colouring is added here by the
master hand, but the substantial facts are probable
enough.   He corresponded with cardinals, marshals
of France, and bishops, and he corresponded with
Helvétius and with Diderot, who, greatly to the
indignation of the business-like patriarch, had a bad
habit of leaving letters to answer themselves.[2]   If two
cavalry officers fell to disputing over the mess-table
as to the propriety of using some bit of old French,
it was to Ferney that the reference was instantly
made.[3]   We get an idea of the kind of imperial
authority which attached to Voltaire's judgment, from
the eagerness with which Turgot sought, without
revealing his name, an opinion from Ferney as to the
worth of a translation with which he lightened the
heavy burden of his intendance at Limoges, a translation of the Eclogues and Fourth Æneid into French
metric verse.   'They say,' wrote Turgot, 'that he is
so busy with his Encyclopædia as neither to speak
nor to write to any one.'   If Turgot could have seen
Voltaire's correspondence for 1770, he would have
found out how far this rumour was from the truth,

---

[1] Corr. 1761. *Œuvres*, lxvii. p. 166.
[2] *Œuvres*, lxxv. pp. 64, 69, etc.
[3] Corr. 1770. *Œuvres*, lxxi. p. 18.

and in fact he did get an answer to his own letter; but it can hardly have been very much more satisfactory than silence would have been, for Voltaire, while profuse in praise of the fidelity and spirit of the translation, unfortunately did not detect that it was meant for anything more ambitious than simple prose with enthusiasm in it.[1] As Turgot especially valued in the patriarch his 'superb ear,' the blow was as sharp as it well could be. He was little concerned or surprised on learning the fallacious reasoning of the poet in political economy. 'Reasoning,' he adds, 'has never been Voltaire's strong point.'[2] And that was true in matters of abstract science, but he was an unrivalled populariser of the results of other people's reasoning, from Newton's Principia down to Middleton's Free Enquiry, and this popularisation was what the conditions of the time caused to be most ardently demanded. The proof of the demand we may see in the extraordinary respect and curiosity, or dislike and alarm, with which Voltaire for the twenty crowning years of his life was regarded throughout the whole of civilised Europe.

It is impossible to read the multitudinous volumes of Voltaire's correspondence, and they are being added to every two or three years, with entire satisfaction. They are wittier than any other letters in the world. For lightness, swiftness, grace, spontaneity, you can find no second to them, at however long an interval. But they abound in many things which are disagree-

[1] *Œuvres de Turgot,* ii. pp. 814-825.   [2] *Ib.* p. 824.

able in the letters of an old man who had so true an
interest in the spread of virtue, knowledge, and the
other conditions of human dignity.   These, however,
may be passed over as the innocent and unconscious
unseemliness of a very gay nature living in a very
free age.   It is less easy to banish the unpleasant
impressions with which we find him playing the
equivocal part of being all things to all men.   One
would have been pleased to have a little more stiff-
ness, a little less pliancy of phrase.   We would not go
through the world insisting on grim Puritanic earnest-
ness at every moment of a man's life, but Voltaire's
lively complaisance with all sorts of unworthy people
is something worse than unedifying.   One can hardly
help sympathising with D'Alembert's remonstrance.
'You have rather spoilt the people who persecute us.
'Tis true you have had greater need than anybody else
to keep them quiet, and that you have been obliged
to offer a candle to Lucifer to save yourself from
Beelzebub, but Lucifer has only grown the prouder,
without Beelzebub growing the less malignant.'[1]   The
truth probably is that Voltaire did not always take
much thought of Lucifer or Beelzebub.   For one
thing, he was, as we have said more than once, intensely sympathetic by temperament, and in writing
to a friend, or even an acquaintance only, he was for
the moment animated by a lively good will and
anxiety to be in harmony with his correspondent.
There was nothing false in these purring pleasantries,

[1] *Œuvres*, lxxv. p. 331.

with which he amused all correspondents alike. They came as naturally from his mobile and genial constitution, as an equality of prosaic moroseness comes from persons of fundamentally different constitutions. For another thing, the old fashion of his youth never dropped away from him, and the elaborate courteousness and friendly ardour of manner, which he had learnt among the aristocratic friends of the days of the Regency and afterwards at Paris and Versailles, did not desert him in the solitudes of the Jura. He was to the last a man of quality, as well as a crusher of the Infamous, and to the last he kept up the tone of one who had been a gentleman of the chamber to one king, and court-chamberlain to another. Voltaire's temperament and earliest surroundings fully explain what was a more public, as well as more serious, falling away from the rigorous integrity which men are now accustomed to demand from the leaders of unpopular causes. His sins in this order are nearly as numerous as his public acts. Rousseau, perhaps we may say without breach of charity, as much from vanity as principle, prefixed his name to all that he wrote, and he paid the penalty in a life of wandering and persecution. Voltaire in his later days as invariably sheltered himself behind the anonymous, and not only disclaimed works of which it was notorious that he was the author, but insisted that his friends should impute them to this or that dead name. Nobody was deceived. While he got unwelcome credit for a multitude of pieces that were not his own, assuredly nothing really his ever failed to be set down to its true author. We can only say that this was the evil practice of the time, and that Voltaire was here little worse than Turgot and many another man of general virtuousness, to whom the ferocity of authority would not even allow freedom enough to plead for tolerance, much less to utter uncertified opinion. 'Time,' said D'Alembert, apologising for some whiff of orthodoxy which Voltaire scented in one or two articles in the Encyclopædia, 'will make people distinguish what we thought from what we said.'[1] Condorcet, as we know, deliberately defended these deceptions, which did not deceive, while they did protect. He contended that if you rob a man of his natural right of publishing his opinions, then you lose your own right to hear the truth from the man's lips.[2] Undoubtedly all laws admit that duress introduces new conditions into the determination of what is right and wrong in action, or at least that it mitigates pains and penalties, and the position of every claimant for free speech was in those days emphatically a position of duress. The choice lay between disavowal on the one hand, and on the other abstention from proclaiming truths by which only society could gain the freedom it so much needed ; between strict anonymity and leaving the darkness unbroken. And we must remember that disingenuous tricks to conceal authorship were not assuredly so unpardonable, when resorted to as pro-

---

[1] *Œuvres*, lxxv. p. 33.

[2] *Œuvres de Condorcet*, iv. pp. 33, 34, and vi. pp. 187-189.

tectives against imprisonment, confiscation, and possible peril of life, as they are now among ourselves, when they serve no more defensible purpose than sheltering men who have not the courage of their opinions, against one or two paltry social deprivations.

The monstrous proceedings against La Barre, and the ease with which in this and numerous other cases the jurisprudence of the tribunals lent itself to the cruelty of fanatics, no doubt excited in Voltaire a very genuine alarm for his own safety, and probably with good reason. We know that he could not venture to visit Italy, in consequence of his just fear lest the Inquisition should throw their redoubtable foe into prison, and the parliaments of Toulouse and Abbeville had perpetrated juridical murders as iniquitous as any of the proceedings of the Holy Office. And though it is easy and right for the young, who live in a time when you are not imprisoned or hung or decapitated for holding unpopular opinions, to call out for manliness to the uttermost in these things, one must make allowance for an occasional fit of timorousness in a man of eighty, whom nature had never cut out for a martyr. Yet, more than once, these fits committed Voltaire to acts which were as great a scandal to the devout as to the atheists. That he should rebuild the ruinous little chapel of his estate was not much more remarked, than it would be for a Protestant landlord to subscribe to repair the Catholic church on an Irish property containing only Catholic tenants. The gorgeous ceremony with which in his quality of lord he commemorated its opening, made everybody laugh, not excepting the chief performer, for he actually took the opportunity of lifting up his voice in the new temple and preaching a sermon against theft. The bishop of Annecy in Savoy, his diocesan, was furious at this mockery, and urged the minister at Paris to banish Voltaire from France. In order to avert the blow, Voltaire tried to make a nominal peace with the church by confessing, and participating in the solemnity of an Easter communion (1768). The bishop wrote him a long letter of unctuous impertinences, to which Voltaire replied by asking very tartly why the discharge of so ordinary a duty called for this insolent congratulation. The philosophers of Paris were bitterly scandalised, and some of them wrote to the patriarch of the sect to remonstrate. Even D'Alembert, his own familiar friend, could not refrain from protest.[1] Voltaire could give no better reasons for his strange lapse than we may hear given every day in our own country, by men who practise hypocritical compliances for the sake of a little ignoble ease, and thus perpetuate the yoke. He owed an example to his parish, as if the example of feigning a belief which he repudiates could be a good example for one to set in any parish. It was very well to shirk these observances in Paris, because there in the tide of business one finds an excuse or is not missed, but in the country no such excuse offers itself. One must stand well with the curé, be he knave or dunce. One must respect the two hundred and fifty

[1] Corr. 1768. *Œuvres*, lxxv. p. 426.

timorous consciences around one. And so forth, down that well-worn list of pleas by which men make anxiety about the consciences of others a substantial reason for treachery to their own. Voltaire, besides all these, honestly added the one true reason, that he did not mean to be burnt alive, and that the only way of making sure against such a fate was to close the lips of spies and informers.[1]

The bishop knew perfectly well that the squire, who had made his Easter communion in so remarkable a manner in 1768, was the author of the Philosophical Dictionary, of which a bran-new edition, amended and revised, made its appearance in 1769; and he appears to have forbidden the priest of Ferney to confess or administer the eucharist to the chief of the flock. Voltaire was at once seized with a fever, and summoned the priest to administer ghostly comfort. The priest pleaded the horrible rumours of the world as to the damnable books of which the sick man was alleged to be the author. Voltaire replied by warning him very peremptorily that in refusing to administer the viaticum he was infringing the law, and the consequence was that he did duly receive the viaticum, after which he signed a solemn act in the presence of a notary, declaring that he pardons his various calumniators; that 'if any indiscretion prejudicial to the religion of the State should have escaped him,' he seeks forgiveness from God and the State; and finally he forgave the bishop of Annecy, who had calumniated him to

[1] Corr. 1768. *Œuvres*, lxx. pp. 198-199.

the king, and whose malicious designs had come to nought. The priest and notary afterwards falsified this amazing declaration so as to appease the bishop, and came to Voltaire praying him not to betray them. 'I prove to them,' he says, 'that they will be damned, I give them something to drink, and they go away delighted.'[1] A younger philosopher of his school remarks with his accustomed gravity on this most singular transaction, that the satisfaction of forcing his priest to administer by fear of the secular judges, and of insulting the bishop of Annecy in a juridical manner, cannot excuse such a proceeding in the eyes of the free and firm man, who weighs calmly the claims of truth and the requirements of prudence, when laws contrary to natural justice render truth dangerous and prudence indispensable.[2] To which reflection we may perhaps add another, suggested by the cruel experience of the church in France within five and twenty years from Voltaire's impious communion, that if any order, secular or spiritual, constrains its adversaries under penalties to the commission of base acts, then if the chances of time should ever transfer the power to the other side, that order has only itself to blame for whatever wrong may mark the retaliation. There is no more dangerous policy in affairs of state than to strip your opponent of self-respect, and this the descendants of the persecutors found out to their extreme cost,

[1] Corr. 1769. *Œuvres*, lxx. pp. 434, 435; lxxv. p. 452. Grimm's *Corr. Lit.* vi. p. 231.

[2] Condorcet, *Vie de Voltaire*, p. 126.

when in 1793 they had to deal with the descendants of the persecuted.

One other curious piece of sportiveness in his dealings with the church deserves to be noticed. In the year 1770 the post of temporal father of the order of Capucins for the district of Gex became vacant. Voltaire applied for it, and the general at Rome, perhaps listening to a word from Ganganelli, or else from the Duchess of Choiseul, sent to Ferney the letters patent conferring upon its patriarch this strange dignity, and also affiliating him to the order. What were Voltaire's motives in so odd a transaction, it is not very hard to divine. Probably, he thought even this humble office would be some protection against persecution. Then it gave him an opportunity of harassing his enemy, the bishop of Annecy. Thirdly, it amused that whimsical element of farce and mischief which was always so irrepressible in him, from the early days when he is said to have nearly damned his own play by appearing on the stage as the high-priest's train-bearer, and burlesquing that august person's solemn gait. Voltaire filled his letters with infinite pleasantries about the new Capucin, and seemed as much pleased at the idea of wearing the cord of Saint Francis, as he had been with the gold key of a Prussian chamberlain.[1] One of his first enjoyments was to write letters to his episcopal foe, signed with a cross and his name : '✠ *Voltaire, Capucin indigne.*'[2] A

[1] Corr. *Œuvres,* lxxi. pp. 25, 27, 30, etc.
[2] Grimm, *Corr. Lit.* vi. p. 358.

story is told by Grimm of a visitor arriving at Ferney, and being greeted by the patriarch with the news that he would find his host a changed man.   'One grows a bigot in one's old age; I have a habit of having some pious work read to me when I sit down at table.' And in fact, some one began to read a sermon of Massillon, Voltaire throwing in exclamations on the beauty, eloquence, imagination of the preacher. Suddenly after three or four pages, he called out ' Off with Massillon !' and launched forth during the rest of the meal with his usual verve and fanciful extravagance of imagination.[1] It is profoundly unedifying, but not the less characteristic.

Voltaire, there can be little doubt, never designed a social revolution, being in this the representative of the method of Hobbes. · His single object was to reinstate the understanding in its full rights, to emancipate thought, to extend knowledge, to erect the standard of critical common sense.   He either could not see, or else, as one sometimes thinks, he closes his eyes and refuses for his part to see, that it was impossible to revolutionise the spiritual basis of belief without touching the social forms, which were inseparably connected with the old basis by the strong bonds of time and a thousand fibres of ancient association and common interest.   Rousseau began where Voltaire left off.   He informs us that in the days when his character was forming, nothing which Voltaire wrote escaped him, and that the Philosophical Letters, that

[1] Grimm, *Corr. Lit.* vi. p. 358.

is the Letters on the English, though assuredly not
the writer's best work, were what first attracted him
to study, and implanted a taste which never afterwards became extinct. The correspondence between
Voltaire and the prince of Prussia, afterwards the great
Frederick, inspired Rousseau with a passionate desire
to learn how to compose with elegance, and to imitate
the colouring of so fine an author.[1] Thus Voltaire,
who was eighteen years his elder, gave this extraordinary genius his first productive impulse. But a
sensibility of temperament, to which perhaps there is
no parallel in the list of prominent men, impelled Rousseau to think, or rather to feel, about the concrete
wrongs and miseries of men and women, and not the
abstract rights of their intelligence. Hence the two
great revolutionary schools, the school which appealed
to sentiment, and the school which appealed to intelligence. The Voltarian principles of the strictest
political moderation and of literary common sense,
negative, merely emancipatory, found their political
outcome, as French historians early pointed out, in
the Constituent Assembly, which was the creation of
the upper and middle class, while the spirit of Rousseau, ardent, generous, passionate for the relief of
the suffering, overwhelmed by the crowding forms of
manhood chronically degraded and womanhood
systematically polluted, came to life and power in the
Convention and the sections of the Commune of
Paris which overawed the Convention.

[1] *Confessions*, pt. i. liv. v.   Date of 1736.

'It will not do,' wrote D'Alembert to Voltaire as early as 1762, 'to speak too loudly against Jean Jacques or his book, for he is rather a king in the Halles.'[1] This must have been a new word in the ears of the old man, who had grown up in the habit of thinking of public opinion as the opinion, not of markets where the common people bought and sold, but of the galleries of Versailles. Except for its theology, the age of Lewis XIV. always remained the great age to Voltaire, the age of pomp and literary glory, and it was too difficult a feat to cling on one side to the Grand Monarch, and to stretch out a hand on the other to the Social Contract. It was too difficult for the man who had been embraced by Ninon de l'Enclos, who was the correspondent of the greatest sovereigns in Europe, and the intimate of some of the greatest nobles in France, to feel much sympathy with writings that made their author king of the Halles. Frederick offered Rousseau shelter, and so did Voltaire; but each of them disliked his work as warmly as the other. They did not understand one who, if he wrote with an eloquence that touched all hearts, repulsed friends and provoked enemies like a madman or a savage. The very language of Rousseau was to Voltaire as an unknown tongue, for it was the language of reason clothing the births of passionate sensation. Emile only wearied him, though there were perhaps fifty pages of it which he would have had bound in morocco.[2] It is a stale

[1] *Œuvres*, lxxv. p. 182.   [2] Corr. 1762. *Œuvres*, lxxv. p. 188.

romance, he cries, while the Social Contract is only remarkable for some insults rudely thrown at kings by a citizen of Geneva, and for four insipid pages against the Christian religion, which are simply plagiarised from Bayle's centos.[1] The author is a monster of ingratitude and insolence, the arch-scoundrel and chief of charlatans, the lineal descendant of the dog of Diogenes the cynic, and other evil things not readily to be named in a polite age. Partly no doubt this extreme irritation was due to the insults with which Jean Jacques had repulsed his offers of shelter and assistance, had repudiated Voltaire's attempts to defend him, and had held up Voltaire himself as a proper object for the persecutions of Geneva. But there was a still deeper root of discrepancy, which we have already pointed out. Rousseau's exaggerated tone was an offence to Voltaire's more just and reasonable spirit, and the feigned austerity of a man whose life and manners he knew, assumed in his eyes a disagreeable shade of hypocrisy.[2] Besides these things, he was clearly apprehensive of the storms which Rousseau's extraordinary hardihood had the very natural effect of raising in the circles of authority, though it is true that the most acute observers of the time thought that they noticed a very perceptible increase of Voltaire's own hardihood, as a consequence of the example which the other set him.

The rivalry between the schools of Rousseau and Voltaire represents the dead-lock to which social

---

[1] *Œuvres*, lxvii. p. 432.   [2] Condorcet, p. 170.

thought had come; a dead-lock of which the catastrophe of the Revolution was both expression and
result. At the time of Voltaire's death there was not
a single institution in France with force enough to
be worth a month's purchase. The monarchy was
decrepit; the aristocracy was as feeble and impotent
as it was arrogant; the bourgeoisie was not without
aspiration, but it lacked courage and it possessed no
tradition; and the church was demoralised, first by
the direct attack of Voltaire and the not less powerful indirect attack of the Encyclopædia, and second
by the memory of its own cruelty and selfishness in
the generation just closing. But Voltaire's theory,
so far as he ever put it into its most general form,
was that the temporal order was safe and firm, and
that it would endure until criticism had transformed
thought and prepared the way for a régime of enlightenment and humanity. Rousseau, on the contrary, directed all the engines of passion against the
whole temporal fabric, and was so little careful of
freedom of thought, so little confident in the plenary
efficacy of rational persuasion, as to insist upon the
extermination of atheists by law. The position of
each was at once irrefragable and impossible. It
was impossible to effect a stable reconstitution of the
social order until men had been accustomed to use
their minds freely, and had gradually thrown off the
demoralising burden of superstition. But then the
existing social order had become intolerable, and its
forces were practically extinct, and consequently such

an attack as Rousseau's was inevitable, and was at the same time and for the same reasons irresistible. To overthrow the power of the church only was to do nothing in a society perishing from material decay and political emasculation. Yet to regenerate such a society without the aid of moral and spiritual forces, with whose activity the existence of a dominant ecclesiastical power was absolutely incompatible, was one of the wildest feats that ever passionate sophist attempted.

If, however, it must be admitted that each of these two famous destroyers was attempting an equally desperate task, it is the contention of these pages that Voltaire was the more right and far-sighted of the two in his perception of the conditions of the problem. We have now for various adequate reasons acquired the habit of looking upon the church and speaking of it, as an organisation outside of society, or at least as a separate organisation and independent integer within it. The truth is that in a Catholic country like France before the Revolution, the church more than the secular order actually was the society, as it had been, though to a far wider degree, throughout Europe in the days of Hildebrand and Innocent. That is to say, it furnished the strongest of the ideas, sentiments, hopes, and associations which bound men together in a single community. The monarchy, the nobles, the old historic French tradition, the various bodies and processes of law, were swept away by the Revolution, virtually never to return, in spite of the transient appearances to the contrary. The church was swept away also, but only for a year or two; and so little effectual was the Revolution, which was in fact Rousseau's Revolution, in permanently modifying its position, that those Frenchmen at the present day who most soberly judge the future of their country and look deepest into its state, clearly perceive that the battle to be fought in the order of ideas is a battle between the new moral and social ideas of the workmen, and the old moral and social ideas which Catholicism has implanted in the breasts of the peasants, and on which the middle class privately and unconsciously lean for the support of their own consciences, though they may have put away Catholic dogma. We may see here, once more, the help which Protestantism gave to the dissolution of the old society, by the increased room it gave, apart from the specific influence of a more democratic dogma, for that gradual intellectual expansion throughout a community, which for those who have faith in the reasoning faculty is the one sure secret of social advance. The subjection of the spiritual power to the temporal, which has commonly followed the establishment of the Protestant communion, has very likely retarded the final disappearance of many ideas which foster anti-social tendencies; but the subjection of the spiritual power in such a set of circumstances has the effect of softening shocks. Protestantism in the sixteenth century, if it could have been accepted in France, would have been a more edifying dissolvent than Voltairism was in the eighteenth; but it is certain that the loosening of theological ideas and the organisation connected with them and upholding them, was the first process towards making truly social ideas possible, and their future realisation a thing which good men might hope for. Napoleon, the great organ of political reaction, knew what he was about in paying writers for years to denigrate the memory of Voltaire, whose very name he abhorred.[1]

In saying, however, that Rousseau's attack was inevitable, we have perhaps said that it was indispensable; for where a society is not able to resist an assault upon its fundamental conditions, we may be tolerably sure that the time has arrived when either these conditions must be dispersed, or else the society must fall into rapid dissolution. We may refute Rousseau's sophisms as often and as conclusively as we please, and may dwell as forcibly as we know how upon the untold penalties which France has paid, and is still doomed to pay, for whatever benefits he may have bestowed on her. But, after all this, the benefits remain, and they may be briefly set down as two in number. In the first place he spoke words that can never be unspoken, and kindled a hope that can never be extinguished; he first inflamed men with a righteous conviction that the evils of the existing order of things reduced civilisation to a nullity for the great majority of mankind, and that it cannot for ever be tolerable that the mass should wear away

[1] Lamartine's *Girondins*, iv. v.

their lives in unbroken toil without hope or aim, in order that the few may live selfish and vacuous days. Rousseau presented this sentiment in a shape which made it the 'negation of society;' but it was much to induce thinkers to ask themselves, and the bondsmen of society to ask their masters, whether the last word of social philosophy had been uttered, and the last experiment in the relations of men to one another decisively tried and irrevocably accepted. Second, by his fervid eloquence and the burning conviction which he kindled in the breasts of great numbers of men, he inspired energy enough in France to awaken her from the torpor as of death which was stealing so rapidly over her. Nobody was more keenly aware of the presence of this breath of decay in the air than Voltaire was. It had seized such hold of the vital parts of the old order, that, but for the fiery spirit and unquenchable ardour of the men who read Rousseau as men of old had read the gospel, but for the spirit and ardour which animated the Convention, and made it alike in the tasks of peace and the tasks of war one of the most effective and formidable assemblies that the world has ever beheld, we do not see what there was to stop France from sinking lower and lower into impotence, until at last the powers who vainly threatened the republic with partition, might in the course of time actually have consummated the threat against the monarchy. This may seem impossible to us who live after the Revolution and after Napoleon; but we must remember the designs of partitioning Prussia in the middle of the century, the accomplishment of a partition of the Italian possessions of the house of Austria in 1735, and the partition of Poland; and why was France to be eternal, any more than the Byzantine empire, or the power of the house of Austria, or the power of Spain, had been eternal? It was the fire kindled by Rousseau's passion that saved her; for even of the Constituent, which was Voltairean, the very soul was Mirabeau, who was Rousseauite.

It will be seen that in one sense Rousseau was a far more original personage than his first chief and inspirer. He contributed new ideas, of extremely equivocal and perilous character, but still new, to the multitudinous discussions which were throwing all the social elements into confusion. These ideas might indeed have been found substantially in the writings of previous thinkers like Montaigne and Locke; but Rousseau's passion invested them with a quality which was virtually to constitute them a fresh and original force. Voltaire contributed initiative and a temperament, which made his propagation of ideas that were not new, as important a fact in social if not in intellectual history, as if he had been possessed of superlative gifts in speculation. This has also to be remembered when we think of comparing him with Diderot, who, while his equal in industry, was greatly his superior both in fresh simplicity of imagination, and in grasp and breadth of positive knowledge. Whoever will take the trouble to turn

over some of the thirty-five volumes of the Encyclopædia, may easily see how that gigantic undertaking
(1751—1765), in which Voltaire always took the
most ardent and practical interest,[1] assisted the movement that Voltaire had commenced. It seemed to
gather up into a single great reservoir all that men
knew, and this fact of mere mechanical collocation
was a sort of substitute for a philosophic synthesis.
As Comte says, it furnished a provisional rallying-
point for efforts the most divergent, without requiring
the sacrifice of any points of essential independence,
in such a way as to secure for a body of incoherent
speculation an external look of system.[2] This enterprise, the history of which is a microcosm of the
whole battle between the two sides in France, enabled
the various opponents of theological absolutism, the
Voltaireans, Rousseauites, atheists, and all other sorts
and conditions of protesting men, to confront the
church and its doctrine with a similar semblance of
organic unity and completeness. The Encyclopædia
was not simply negative and critical. It was an
unexampled manual of information, and was the
means of spreading over the country some knowledge
of that active scientific culture, which was producing
such abundant and astonishing discoveries. The two
streams of dissolvent influences, negative criticism on

[1] See his correspondence with D'Alembert (*Œuvres*, lxxv.)
until 1760, the date of D'Alembert's separation from Diderot
and the Encyclopædia.

[2] *Phil. Pos.* v. 520.

the one hand, and positive knowledge and scientific method on the other, were led into a single channel of multiplied volume and force. There was no real nor logical connection between the two elements, and while one of them has daily grown less serviceable, the other has daily grown more absorbingly power-ful, so as now to be itself the effective indirect sub-stitute for that direct negative criticism, with which the Encyclopædic design had once thrown it into alliance.

Diderot, the third chief of the attack, does even fuller justice than Rousseau to Voltaire's share in stimulating thought and opening the mind of France; and in spite of the extravagance of its first clause, there is a glimpse of true discrimination in the char-acteristic sentence—'Were I to call him the greatest man nature has produced, I might find people to agree with me; but if I say that she has never yet produced, and is never likely to produce again, a man so extraordinary, only his enemies will contradict me.'[1] This panegyric was specially disinterested, because Voltaire's last years had been not least remarkable for his bitter antipathy to the dogmatic atheism and dogmatic materialism of that school, with which Diderot was most intimate personally, and with whose doctrines, if he did not at all times seem entirely to share them, he had at any rate a warmer sympathy than with any other system of that nega-

[1] *Essais sur les règnes de Claude et Néron*, vol. vi. pp. 256 290, and 191 (Ed. 1819).

VII.   FERNEY.   357

tive epoch, when every chief thinker was so vague
positively, so weak constructively, and only the subalterns, like D'Holbach and Helvétius, presumed to
push on to conclusions.

The story of Voltaire's many long-sustained and
unflagging endeavours to procure whatever redress
might be possible for the victims of legal injustice,
has been very often told, and mere commemoration
of these justly renowned achievements may suffice here.
'The worst of the worthy sort of people,' he once said,
'is that they are such cowards. A man groans over
wrong, he shuts his lips, he takes his supper, he forgets.'[1] Voltaire was not of that temper. He was not
only an extremely humane man ; extraordinary vivid-
ness of imagination, lack of which is at the root of so
much cruelty, and unparalleled sympathetic quality,
thinness of which explains so much appalling indifference, animated him to a perseverance in protecting the
helpless, which entitles him to a place by the side of
Howard and the noblest philanthropists.   There were
three years in which the chief business of his life was
to procure the rehabilitation of the name of the unfortunate Calas, and the payment of a money recompense
to his family. He agitated the whole world with
indignation and pity by means of narratives, pleas, short
statements and long statements, passionate appeals
and argumentative appeals.   Powerful ministers, fine
ladies, lawyers, men of letters, were all constrained

---

[1] Corr. 1766. *Œuvres*, lxxv. p. 364.

by his importunate solicitations to lend an ear to the
cause of reason and tolerance, and to lift up an arm
in its vindication.   The same tremendous enginery
was again brought into play in the case of Sirven.
In the case of La Barre and his comrade D'Etallonde,
his tenacity was still more amazing and heroic.   For
twelve years he persevered in the attempt to have the
memory of La Barre rehabilitated.   One of the judicial
authorities concerned in that atrocious exploit, struck
with horror at the thought of being held up to the
execration of Europe by that terrible avenger, conveyed some menace to Voltaire of what might befall
him.   Voltaire replied to him by a Chinese anecdote.
'I forbid you,' said a tyrannical emperor to the chief
of the tribunal of history, 'to speak a word more of
me.'   The mandarin began to write.   'What are you
doing now?' asked the emperor.   'I am writing down
the order that your majesty has just given me.'[1]
There was a something inexorable as doom about
Voltaire's unrelenting perseverance in getting wrong
definitely stamped and transfixed.   If he did not succeed in obtaining justice for the memory of La Barre,
and in procuring for D'Etallonde free pardon, at least
he never abandoned the endeavour, and he was just
as ardent and unwearied in the twelfth year, as he had
been while his indignation was freshly kindled.   He
was more successful in the case of Lally.   Count Lally
had failed to save India from the English, had been
taken prisoner, and had then in a magnanimous way

[1] Condorcet, p. 124.

asked his captors to allow him to go to Paris to
clear himself from various charges, which the too
numerous enemies he had made were spreading
against his character and administration. The French
people, infuriated at the loss of their possessions in
India and Canada, were crying for a victim, and Lally,
after a process tainted with every kind of illegality,
was condemned to death by the parliament of Paris
(1766) on the vague charge of abuse of authority,
exactions, and vexations.[1] The murdered man's son,
known in the days of the Revolution as Lally Tollendal,
was joined by Voltaire in the honourable work of procuring revision of the proceedings; and one of the
last crowning triumphs of Voltaire's days was the news
brought to him on his dying bed, that his long effort
had availed.

The death of Lally is the parallel in French history
to the execution of Byng in the history of England,
and, oddly enough, Voltaire was very actively occupied
in trying to avert that crime of our government, as
well as the crimes of his own. He had known Byng
when he was in England.[2] Some one told him that
a letter from Richelieu, who had been Byng's opponent
at Minorca, would be useful, and Voltaire instantly
urged the Duke to allow him to forward a letter he
had, stating Richelieu's conviction of his defeated
enemy's bravery and good judgment. Voltaire insists that this letter turned four votes on the court-

---

[1] Martin's *Hist. de France*, xv. pp. 569-572.
[2] Corr. 1757. *Œuvres*, lxvi. p. 51.

martial.[1] He informs a correspondent, moreover, of the fact that Byng had instructed his executor to express his deep obligation both to Voltaire and Richelieu.[2] Humanity is erroneously counted among commonplace virtues. If it deserved such a place, there would be less urgent need than, alas, there is, for its daily exercise among us. In its pale shape of kindly sentiment and bland pity it is common enough, and is always the portion of the cultivated. But humanity armed, aggressive, and alert, never slumbering and never wearying, moving like ancient hero over the land to slay monsters, is the rarest of virtues, and Voltaire is one of its master-types.

His interest in public transactions in his latest years was keener than ever. That fruit of Polish anarchy, the war between Russia and Turkey which broke out in 1768, excited his imagination to a pitch of great heat, and the despatch in the spring of 1770 of a squadron from Cronstadt, for the so-called liberation of Greece, made him weep for joy. He implored Frederick not to leave to Catherine alone the burden of so glorious a task. Superstition had had seven crusades; was it not a noble thing to undertake one crusade to drive the barbarous Turks from the land of Socrates and Plato, Sophocles and Euripides? Frederick replied very sensibly that Dantzic was more to him than the Piræus, and that he is a little indifferent about the modern Greeks, who, if ever the arts

---

[1] Corr. 1756. *Œuvres*, lxv. p. 568; lxvi. pp. 1, 19, 20, 40.
[2] *Œuvres*, lxvi. p. 51.

should revive among them, would be jealous to find that
a Gaul by his Henriade had surpassed their Homer;
that this same Gaul had beaten Sophocles, equalled
Thucydides, and left far behind him Plato, Aristotle,
and the whole school of the Porch:[1]—which was,
perhaps, not quite so sensibly said.

The successes of Russia against Turkey in 1770
roused the anxiety of Austria and Prussia, and the
solution of what we know as the Eastern question was
indefinitely postponed by the device of partitioning
Poland (Aug. 5, 1772), the alternative to the acquisition of the whole of that country by Russia, the least
civilised of the three powers. Of this memorable
transaction Voltaire heartily approved, and he gave
thanks that he had lived to see 'such glorious events.'[2]
He insisted, decidedly against the king's will, that
Frederick had devised the scheme, for he found it full
of genius, and to all seeming he discerned none of the
execration which the event he had just witnessed was
destined to raise in his own country in years to come.
His friendship with two of the chief actors may have
biassed his judgment; but Voltaire seldom allowed,
indeed by the conditions of his temperament he was
unable to allow, personal considerations of this kind
to obscure his penetrating sight. He may well have
thought the partition of Poland desirable, for the
reasons which a statesman of to-day may find adequate:
the country's hopeless political anarchy, its crushing
material misery, the oppressive power of the church,

---

[1] Corr. 1772. *Œuvres*, lxxiv. p. 36.   [2] *Ib.* p. 93, etc.

the inevitable and standing peril to Europe of the existence of such a centre of conflagration.   It is worth remarking that Rousseau was much more keenly alive to the gravity of the event, that he protested against what had been done, and that his influence has been one of the main causes of the illogical sympathy of democratic Europe for one of the most pestilent of aristocratic governments.

The accession of Turgot to power in 1774 stirred an ardent sympathy in Voltaire.   Like the rest of the school, he looked upon this as the advent of the political messiah,[1] and he shared the extreme hopes of that great and virtuous man's most sanguine lieutenants. He declared that a new heaven and a new earth had opened to him.[2]   His sallies against the economists were forgotten, and he now entered into the famous controversy of the free trade in grain with all his usual fire.   His fervour went too far for the sage minister, who prayed him to be somewhat less eager in alarming uninformed prejudice.   Still he insisted on hoping all things.

> Contemple la brillante aurore
> Qui t'annonce enfin les beaux jours.
> Un nouveau monde est près d'éclore ;
> Até disparaît pour toujours.
> Vois l'auguste philosophie,
> Chez toi si long temps poursuivie,
> Dicter ses triomphantes lois.

*   *   *   *   *

----

[1] See Morellet, i. pp. 147, 159, etc.
[2] *Œuvres*, lxxv. p. 641.

Je lui dis : ' Ange tutélaire,
Quels dieux répandent ces bienfaits ?'
' C'est un seul homme.'[1]

When it proved that one man alone, ' qui ne chercha
le vrai, que pour faire le bien,'[2] was no match for the
mountain torrent of ignorance, prejudice, selfishness,
and usage, and Turgot fell from power (May 1776),
Voltaire sunk into a despair for his country, from
which he never arose. ' I am as one dashed to the
ground. Never can we console ourselves for having
seen the golden age dawn and perish. My eyes see
only death in front of me, now that M. Turgot is
gone. It has fallen like a thunderbolt on my brain
and my heart alike. The rest of my days can never
be other than pure bitterness.'[3]

The visit to Paris was perhaps a falsification of this
prophecy for a moment. In 1778, yielding either to
the solicitations of his niece, or to a momentary desire
to enjoy the triumph of his renown at its centre, he
returned to the great city which he had not seen for
nearly thirty years. His reception has been described
over and over again. It is one of the historic events
of the century. No great captain returning from a
prolonged campaign of difficulty and hazard crowned
by the most glorious victory, ever received a more
splendid and far-resounding greeting. It was the last
great commotion in Paris under the old régime. The

---

[1] Ode sur le Passé et le Présent (1775). *Œuvres*, xvi. p. 415.
[2] Epître à un Homme (1776). *Œuvres*, xvii. p. 327.
[3] Corr. 1776. *Œuvres*, lxxii. pp. 403, 409, 412, etc.

next great commotion which the historian has to chronicle is the ever-memorable fourteenth day of July, eleven years later, when the Bastille fell, and a new order began for France, and new questions began for all Europe.

The agitation of so much loud triumph and incessant acclamation proved more violent than Voltaire's feeble health could resist, and he died, probably from an over-dose of laudanum, on the thirtieth of May 1778. His last writing was a line of rejoicing to the young Lally, that their efforts had been successful in procuring justice for the memory of one who had been put to death unjustly. How far Voltaire realised the nearness of vast changes we cannot tell. There is at least one remarkable prophecy of his, in the well-known letter to Chauvelin :—'Everything that I see appears the throwing broadcast of the seed of a revolution, which must inevitably come one day, but which I shall not have the pleasure of witnessing. The French always come late to things, but they do come at last. Light extends so from neighbour to neighbour, that there will be a splendid outburst on the first occasion, and then there will be a rare commotion. The young are very happy; they will see fine things.'[1] A less sanguine tone marks the close of the apologue in which Reason and Truth, her daughter, take a triumphant journey in France and elsewhere, about the time of the accession of Turgot. 'Ah, well,' says Reason, 'let us enjoy these glorious

[1] April 2, 1764. *Œuvres*, lxviii. p. 220.

days; let us rest here, if they last; and if storms come on, let us go back to our well.'[1] Whether this meant much or little none can know. It would be shallow to believe that such men as Voltaire, with faculty quickened and outlook widened in the high air to which their fame raises them, really discerned no more than we, who have only their uttered words for authority, can perceive that they discerned. Great position often invests men with a second sight whose visions they lock up in silence, content with the work of the day.

[1] Eloge historique de la Raison (*or* Voyage de la Raison) *Œuvres*, lx. p. 478.

THE END.

Printed by R. & R. CLARK, LIMITED, *Edinburgh.*

The Eversley Series.

Globe 8vo. Cloth. 4s. net per volume.

The Works of Matthew Arnold. 8 vols.
ESSAYS IN CRITICISM. First Series.
ESSAYS IN CRITICISM. Second Series.
EARLY AND NARRATIVE POEMS.
LYRIC AND ELEGIAC POEMS.
DRAMATIC AND LATER POEMS.
AMERICAN DISCOURSES.
LETTERS. Edited by G. W. E.
RUSSELL. 2 Vols.

A Memoir of Jane Austen. By her
Nephew, J. E. AUSTEN LEIGH. To
which is added "Lady Susan," and
Fragments of two other Unfinished
Tales by Miss AUSTEN.

The Holy Bible. Arranged in para-
graphs, with an Introduction by J. W.
MACKAIL, M.A. Vol. 2. DEUTERO-
NOMY—2 SAMUEL. Vol. 3. 1 KINGS—
ESTHER. Vol. 4. JOB—SONG OF SOLO-
MON. Vol. 5. ISAIAH—LAMENTATIONS.
Vol. 6. EZEKIEL—MALACHI. Vol. 7.
MATTHEW—JOHN. Vol. 8. ACTS—
REVELATION.

Essays by George Brimley. Third
Edition.

Chaucer's Canterbury Tales. Edited by
A. W. POLLARD. 2 Vols.

**Miscellaneous Writings of Dean
Church.** Collected Edition. 9 Vols.
MISCELLANEOUS ESSAYS.
DANTE: and other Essays.
ST. ANSELM. | SPENSER. | BACON.
THE OXFORD MOVEMENT. Twelve
Years, 1833-1845.
THE BEGINNING OF THE MIDDLE
AGES. (Included in this Series by
permission of Messrs. LONGMANS
& Co.)
OCCASIONAL PAPERS. Selected from
The Guardian, The Times, and *The
Saturday Review,* 1846-1890. 2 Vols.

Life and Letters of Dean Church.
Edited by his Daughter, MARY C.
CHURCH.

Lectures and Essays by W. K. Clifford,
F.R.S. Edited by Sir LESLIE STEPHEN
and Sir F. POLLOCK. New Edition.
2 Vols.

Letters of William Cowper. Chosen
and Edited, with Memoir and Notes,
by Prof. J. G. FRAZER, Litt.D. 2 vols.

Collected Works of Emerson. 6 Vols.
With Introduction by JOHN MORLEY.
MISCELLANIES. | ESSAYS. | POEMS.
ENGLISH TRAITS AND REPRESENTA-
TIVE MEN.
THE CONDUCT OF LIFE, AND SOCIETY
AND SOLITUDE.
LETTERS AND SOCIAL AIMS.

Letters of Edward FitzGerald. Edited
by W. A. WRIGHT. 2 Vols.

More Letters of Edward FitzGerald.

Eight Dramas of Calderon. Translated
by EDWARD FITZGERALD.

**Letters of Edward FitzGerald to
Fanny Kemble, 1871-1883.** Edited by
W. A. WRIGHT.

Pausanias and other Greek Sketches.
By J. G. FRAZER, M.A.

Goethe's Maxims and Reflections.
Translated, with Introduction, by T. B.
SAUNDERS.
*** The Scientific and Artistic
Maxims were selected by Professor
Huxley and Lord Leighton respectively.*

**Collected Works of Thomas Gray in
Prose and Verse.** 4 Vols. Edited by
EDMUND GOSSE. Vol. 1. Poems, Jour-
nals, and Essays. Vols. 2 and 3. Letters.
Vol. 4. Notes on Aristophanes and Plato.

Works by John Richard Green. 16 Vols.
HISTORY OF THE ENGLISH PEOPLE.
8 Vols.
THE MAKING OF ENGLAND. With
Maps. In 2 Vols.
THE CONQUEST OF ENGLAND. With
Maps. In 2 Vols.
STRAY STUDIES FROM ENGLAND AND
ITALY.
STRAY STUDIES. Second Series.
OXFORD STUDIES.
HISTORICAL STUDIES.

Guesses at Truth. By Two BROTHERS.

**The Choice of Books, and other Liter-
ary Pieces.** By FREDERIC HARRISON.

**The Meaning of History, and other
Historical Pieces.** By FREDERIC
HARRISON.

Earthwork out of Tuscany. Third
Edition. By MAURICE HEWLETT.

Poems of Thomas Hood. Edited, with
Prefatory Memoir, by Canon AINGER.
In 2 Vols. Vol. 1. SERIOUS POEMS.
Vol. 2. POEMS OF WIT AND HUMOUR.
With Vignettes and Portraits.

Collected Essays of R. H. Hutton. 7 Vols.
LITERARY ESSAYS.
ESSAYS ON SOME OF THE MODERN
GUIDES OF ENGLISH THOUGHT IN
MATTERS OF FAITH.
THEOLOGICAL ESSAYS.
CRITICISMS ON CONTEMPORARY
THOUGHT AND THINKERS. 2 Vols.
ASPECTS OF RELIGIOUS AND SCIEN-
TIFIC THOUGHT. Selected from *The
Spectator,* and Edited by his Niece,
E. M. ROSCOE. With Portrait.
BRIEF LITERARY CRITICISMS. Selected
from *The Spectator,* and Edited by
his Niece, ELIZABETH M. ROSCOE.

MACMILLAN AND CO., Ltd., LONDON.

The Eversley Series—*Continued.*

Globe 8vo. Cloth. 4s. net per volume.

Life and Works of Thomas Henry Huxley. 12 Vols. Vol. 1. METHOD AND RESULTS. Vol. 2. DARWINIANA. Vol. 3. SCIENCE AND EDUCATION. Vol. 4. SCIENCE AND HEBREW TRADITION. Vol. 5. SCIENCE AND CHRISTIAN TRADITION. Vol. 6. HUME. With Helps to the Study of Berkeley. Vol. 7. MAN'S PLACE IN NATURE: and other Anthropological Essays. Vol. 8. DISCOURSES, BIOLOGICAL AND GEOLOGICAL. Vol. 9. EVOLUTION AND ETHICS, AND OTHER ESSAYS. Vols. 10, 11, and 12. LIFE AND LETTERS OF T. H. HUXLEY. By LEONARD HUXLEY.

French Poets and Novelists. By HENRY JAMES.

Partial Portraits. By HENRY JAMES.

Modern Greece. Two Lectures. By Sir RICHARD JEBB.

Letters of John Keats to his Family and Friends. Edited by SIDNEY COLVIN.

Epic and Romance. By Prof. W. P. KER.

The Works of Charles Kingsley. 11 Vols. WESTWARD HO! 2 Vols. HYPATIA. 2 Vols. YEAST. 1 Vol. ALTON LOCKE. 2 Vols. TWO YEARS AGO. 2 Vols. POEMS. 2 Vols.

The Works of Charles Lamb. Edited, with Introduction and Notes, by Canon AINGER. 6 Vols. THE ESSAYS OF ELIA. POEMS, PLAYS, AND MISCELLANEOUS ESSAYS. MRS. LEICESTER'S SCHOOL, and other Writings. TALES FROM SHAKESPEARE. By CHARLES and MARY LAMB. THE LETTERS OF CHARLES LAMB. Newly arranged, with additions (1904). 2 Vols.

Life of Charles Lamb. By Canon AINGER.

Historical Essays. By J. B. LIGHTFOOT, D.D.

The Poetical Works of John Milton. Edited, with Memoir, Introduction, and Notes, by DAVID MASSON, M.A. 3 Vols. Vol. 1. THE MINOR POEMS. Vol. 2. PARADISE LOST. Vol. 3. PARADISE REGAINED, and SAMSON AGONISTES.

Collected Works of John Morley. 14 Vols. VOLTAIRE. 1 Vol. ROUSSEAU. 2 Vols. DIDEROT AND THE ENCYCLOPÆDISTS. 2 Vols. ON COMPROMISE. 1 Vol. MISCELLANIES. 3 Vols. | BURKE. 1 Vol. STUDIES IN LITERATURE. 1 Vol. OLIVER CROMWELL. 1 Vol. THE LIFE OF RICHARD COBDEN. 2 Vols.

Essays by F. W. H. Myers. 3 Vols. SCIENCE AND A FUTURE LIFE, AND OTHER ESSAYS. CLASSICAL ESSAYS. | MODERN ESSAYS.

Shakespeare. By Sir WALTER RALEIGH.

Records of Tennyson, Ruskin, and Browning. By ANNE THACKERAY RITCHIE.

The Works of Sir John R. Seeley. K.C.M.G., Litt.D. 5 Vols. THE EXPANSION OF ENGLAND. Two Courses of Lectures. LECTURES AND ESSAYS. ECCE HOMO. A Survey of the Life and Work of Jesus Christ. NATURAL RELIGION. LECTURES ON POLITICAL SCIENCE.

The Works of Shakespeare. 10 Vols. With short Introductions and Footnotes by Professor C. H. HERFORD. Vol. 1. LOVE'S LABOUR'S LOST—COMEDY OF ERRORS—TWO GENTLEMEN OF VERONA—MIDSUMMER-NIGHT'S DREAM. Vol. 2. TAMING OF THE SHREW—MERCHANT OF VENICE — MERRY WIVES OF WINDSOR—TWELFTH NIGHT—AS YOU LIKE IT. Vol. 3. MUCH ADO ABOUT NOTHING—ALL'S WELL THAT ENDS WELL—MEASURE FOR MEASURE—TROILUS AND CRESSIDA. Vol. 4. PERICLES—CYMBELINE—THE WINTER'S TALE—THE TEMPEST. Vol. 5. HENRY VI.: First Part—HENRY VI.: Second Part—HENRY VI.: Third Part—RICHARD III. Vol. 6. KING JOHN—RICHARD II.—HENRY IV.: First Part—HENRY IV.: Second Part. Vol. 7. HENRY V.—HENRY VIII.—TITUS ANDRONICUS—ROMEO AND JULIET. Vol. 8. JULIUS CÆSAR—HAMLET—OTHELLO. Vol. 9. KING LEAR — MACBETH — ANTONY AND CLEOPATRA. Vol. 10. CORIOLANUS—TIMON OF ATHENS—POEMS.

The Works of James Smetham. LETTERS. With an Introductory Memoir. Edited by SARAH SMETHAM and WILLIAM DAVIES. With a Portrait. LITERARY WORKS. Edited by WILLIAM DAVIES.

The Works of Alfred, Lord Tennyson. Annotated by the Author. Edited by HALLAM, Lord TENNYSON. In 9 vols. (*sold separately*). Vol. 1. POEMS. 2. POEMS. 3. ENOCH ARDEN and IN MEMORIAM. 4. THE PRINCESS and MAUD. 5. IDYLLS OF THE KING. 6. BALLADS AND OTHER POEMS. 7. DEMETER AND OTHER POEMS. 8. QUEEN MARY and HAROLD. 9. BECKET AND OTHER PLAYS.

Selections from the Writings of Thoreau. Edited by H. S. SALT.

Essays in the History of Religious Thought in the West. By Bishop WESTCOTT, D.D.

The Poetical Works of William Wordsworth. Edited by Professor KNIGHT. 8 Vols.

The Journals of Dorothy Wordsworth. 2 Vols.

MACMILLAN AND CO., LTD., LONDON.